Residential Design Studio

fb

Residential Design Studio

Robert Philip Gordon

ARCHITECT/PLANNER/DESIGNER

Columbia College Chicago
Chicago, Illinois

FAIRCHILD BOOKS   NEW YORK

VICE PRESIDENT & GENERAL MANAGER, FAIRCHILD EDUCATION & CONFERENCE DIVISION	Elizabeth Tighe
EXECUTIVE EDITOR	Olga T. Kontzias
ASSISTANT ACQUISITIONS EDITOR	Amanda Breccia
EDITORIAL DEVELOPMENT DIRECTOR	Jennifer Crane
DEVELOPMENT EDITOR	Joseph Miranda
MANUSCRIPT DEVELOPMENT	Molly Morrison, Newgen North America
CREATIVE DIRECTOR	Carolyn Eckert
PRODUCTION DIRECTOR	Ginger Hillman
PRODUCTION EDITOR	Jessica Rozler
ANCILLARIES EDITOR	Noah Schwartzberg
COVER DESIGN	Carolyn Eckert
COVER ART	Front cover, apartment interior: Iclaves/ Jean-Paul Viguier, SA d'Architecture. Back cover illustration: Robert Philip Gordon. Back cover photo: John Faier; architect: SMNG-A.
INTERIOR ILLUSTRATIONS	Robert Philip Gordon (except for case studies or otherwise noted)
TEXT DESIGN AND PAGE COMPOSITION	Dutton & Sherman
DIRECTOR, SALES & MARKETING	Brian Normoyle

Library of Congress Catalog Card Number: 2009937748

ISBN: 978-1-56367-841-7

GST R 133004424

Printed in the United States of America

TP08

CONTENTS

EXTENDED CONTENTS

PART IV
Multiples: Walk-ups, Midrises, and Towers 205

CHAPTER 8: **Apartment Buildings 207**

ACKNOWLEDGMENTS

A book like this, seeking to find a broad range of solutions to residential design, can only be written with participation from the professional residential design community. It was important to select the best architects and designers to set examples for students who wish to learn about this subject. Those selected for this book are not only well respected in the design community, but also have contributed to improving the social consequences of their work. This includes the creation of a sustainable environment, reduction of greenhouse gases during construction and use, making residential spaces universally accessible, and providing a community for a diverse range of clients, or end-users of the residential spaces. They represent different regions and different countries so that we can learn from each other. The participation of these architects and designers (credited along with their projects) was essential to this book, and I am grateful to them all for their assistance.

Additionally, no writer can hope to accomplish a finished book without the help of a very experienced team of editors, such as the one assembled by Fairchild Books. Ever since Executive Editor Olga Kontzias proposed a studio residential design book to me, Joseph Miranda has guided the editorial process. I am grateful to both of them for their encouragement and guidance. Molly Morrison skillfully performed the line and copy edits of the text, and forced me to account for every diagram, plan, photograph, and reference, not to mention finishing my thoughts so the reader could understand them better. Thank you Molly for the long hours and patient dialogue.

My wife Nancy Turpin read every word of the first draft, and helped me define the purpose of each chapter. Her interviewing skill helped me deliver a better draft to the editors.

My son, Alex Gordon, an artisan and designer, has been a long time collaborator in our design dialogue. Since the time he grabbed a chisel and helped me scrape the floors in our apartment (about age 7) he has always reached for the right tools for the job. We have discussed many interior remodeling projects and custom furniture designs, which has given me great pleasure and inspiration.

After the manuscript is complete, any book on design must itself be well-designed. The design team at Fairchild Books, including Erin Fitzsimmons, have done a magnificent job, first in receiving, then scanning and keeping track of the artwork. It was always a pleasure to work with Erin. Thank you to Carolyn Eckert, creative director. Also, thanks to Jessica Rozler, production editor. Her resourcefulness and careful attention to detail will be appreciated by all who read this book.

The various residential designs we explore in this book, which range from single-family dwellings to townhouses, apartments, and towers, have several things in common. They are set in the context of their communities, they seek to add variety and choice for clients, and most importantly they seek ways to sustain the environment in which we live. The housing choices we make, as residential designers and users, can lead to the creation of lively and walkable communities in which the car is less important and human social activities can grow. It is the intention of this book to give students a "studio experience" to enter into the residential design profession. They will be shown how to interact with other students, in a collaborative way, and how to respond to outside criticism from faculty, guest critics, and even potential clients.

The Studio Experience

This book incorporates many of the ideas presented in residential design literature, but its main goal is to be a partner in the creation of a comprehensive design studio learning experience. The classroom will become a design studio. The instructor may help to create the kind of furniture and work layout found in many studios. Students may be asked to come up with a name and logo for their studio. Professionals may be invited to discuss their experiences in setting up their own studios, and their first contacts with clients. This can be a lot of fun.

The book contains many examples of simulated projects on actual sites, with realistic, and sometimes funny, client profiles. The instructor, as well as outside critics, can play the role of the client. Students should develop an interview technique, and make use of a client interview checklist (included at the end of Chapter 1) to attempt to ascertain the client's needs and budget. Whenever possible, technical consultants will sit in on studio sessions and offer advice on topics from air conditioning to finish selection.

Instructors and students should use the projects in this book to simulate the actual conditions of a professional design studio, even arguing about money for fees. For example, one student could play the role of a frugal and fussy client, while another attempts to satisfy him or her. The book explores many different housing types, with a wide range of client profiles in specific communities. This process will help create the spirit and approach of actually working with different clients in the profession. Finally, the project can be presented and exhibited in the school or community.

The Environment as Partner in Design

The environment has always played a major role in residential design. Climate, wind, sunlight, and access to water and transportation have been key factors. What is different today is that due to rapid growth we are obliged to shrink our carbon footprint in all things we build, to lower our energy dependency to the greatest extent possible. How we do this ranges from passive solar design to advanced generations of solar panels and windmills.

This book argues that the choice of location and type of residence within a community impact the environment. How green can a home be if one must drive 60 miles each day to commute? A large house on a large lot requires additional roadway infrastructure and increased driving distances. According to the Urban Land Institute, "Rising home prices and increasing energy costs are straining consumers' finances, leading to a decrease in the size of new residences."[1] Furthermore, the Housing/ Transportation Affordability Index takes into account transportation costs as part of the cost of housing, arguing that if there is more money spent on transportation, there is less to spend on housing.[2] We must reduce dependence on the automobile for commuting and convenience shopping. In order to minimize the use of energy while maximizing the amount of light and air, the client and designer must carefully choose the site and place the residence advantageously within the site. Even in the case of apartment planning, layout and materials can make a big difference to energy efficiency. The search for passive solar energy affects window location, and the placement of windows can produce natural cross ventilation. The more use we make of these natural advantages, the less energy we consume and the more we can enjoy our residential spaces. This book argues that the location of the site, whether rural, urban, or suburban, and its immediate context have a great effect on the interior as well as the exterior. This relationship is illustrated for all housing types, with prototypes from many different communities provided in varying contexts.

Since a major theme throughout this book is to use systems and materials that are sustainable and local, we will focus on site-built housing rather than prefabricated units. There is a great environmental cost related to shipping materials to a factory, sometimes at a great distance, and then trucking the final product to the home site on a highway, which could also be a great distance from the factory. This book makes a case for the benefits of using local construction with local materials to the greatest extent possible. Fixtures, windows, doors, and other manufactured products are considered, some of which may also be available locally.

Consideration of residential design in context of the environment includes population and demographic trends. This leads directly to the principles of *universal design*. Federal law now requires accessibility to be a key element of residential design. Design professionals are discovering that universal design appeals to people of all ages and physical abilities, and has become an integral part of our design approach. Varied counter heights, wider doors and corridors, walk-in showers, grab bars, and paddle switches are just a few of the things that all people appreciate.

Historic Background of Housing

Many present-day problems of residential design, particularly those related to sustainability, were resolved in the past. Before there was air conditioning there were sunscreens and natural ventilation. Passive solar design was a necessity. Before there were cars, we had walkable communities and the corner store. Building materials were derived from local resources. During the relatively short period of time when it seemed more efficient to transport materials all over the globe, these lessons were forgotten. This book intends to make use of the lessons of the past to solve the problems of the future.

From the earliest archaeological excavations, there is evidence of shelter built or adapted for human habitation. Many of our present-day residential typology is descended from these earlier forms, which came from the particular conditions of their time and region. From the earliest archaeological excavations, there is evidence of shelter built or adapted for human habitation, including caves, nomadic huts, and tents, which were based on their particular time and region. Many of our present-day residential typology descends from these earlier forms. We may talk of our basements as caves, our attics as aeries or nests, and our decks as lookouts. "Closed houses," with few openings to the street or the city, can be found in hot desert climates and in Roman ruins. Ingenious atrium gardens were designed to let light and air into portions of the homes. In the middle ages, walled cities were built for reasons of security. "Open houses" were designed for the tropics, to encourage ventilation; sleeping porches sometimes surrounded them. Japanese pavilions made use of sliding shoji screens.[3]

Each chapter in this book begins with a description of the antecedents to the specific housing type, dating back to the late seventeenth century. This time period spans the great transition from rural to urban migration, including the industrial revolution and the vast changes in transportation. The historical changes during this period greatly affected housing design. The château at Versailles, France, was built as a point of departure from rural to suburban typology. The château and its grounds had a great influence on domestic residential architecture. It was originally built as a royal hunting lodge for Louis XIII, and then became the official residence of the court of France in 1682 under Louis XIV. Because of the carriage and delivery requirements of the château, both the visitors' entrance and the service entrance were paved in cobblestones and located in the front yard. The backyard, the celebrated garden of Versailles, was private and for the enjoyment of the court only.[4] It could be said that this was a foreshadowing of the automobile age, with street parking and backyard gardens.

Frank Lloyd Wright and the Modern Age

Frank Lloyd Wright's suburban model for the twentieth century followed the same site-planning trend, though Wright would probably vehemently deny the connection to royalist architecture. Wright's houses often included driveways in the front, and, since there were usually no alleys, garbage collection as well. This served as the visitors' entrance and the family entrance on the rare occasions when they approached on foot. For Wright, the backyard was private and used for recreational purposes only.

The ultimate expression of a street-oriented residential site plan is the so-called snout house, a derogatory name given to the suburban plan that places the garage in a prominent location at the front of the site. Again, Wright would probably deny any connection to this typology, but it certainly is related and in direct contrast to the urban model of the same time period.

Urban townhouses built in nineteenth- and twentieth-century London, Paris, New York City, Philadelphia, Boston, and Chicago all had front pedestrian entrances, and, often, service alleys for delivery, parking, and trash collection. By this time, industrialization and the advent of the automobile had literally changed the face of the American home.

Evolution of Modern Urban and Suburban Residential Design

Rapid industrialization in the nineteenth century led to massive change in most American cities. Great numbers of people migrated from farms to the cities. In 1850, 15.4 percent of the population lived in urban areas and 84.6 percent in rural. In 1900, 39.6 percent lived in urban areas and 60.4 percent in rural. By 1990, 75.2 percent lived in cities with 24.8 percent residing in rural regions.[5]

This migration created a need for new forms of housing. Families rushed to cities looking for work. They lived in rapidly expanding warrens of homes near factories, with rooms and floors rented out, usually to working men. These structures became known by the pejorative term *tenements*. Construction of so-called French flats (the Beaurivage in Chicago in 1878 is a notable example) gave a higher-end choice to people who could afford it. But a large number of people, with the aid of new commuter railroads, began moving to the suburbs. These suburbs were near the city centers and eventually became incorporated into the cities.[6]

The suburban house, or bungalow, became a model for good health and social status. Much of what we take for granted in the design of current housing has its roots in the early twentieth-century social conditions. Architectural style, room layouts, ornamentation, furnishings, ideas of public and private zones in homes, and many other elements were the result of magazines that appealed to women. It was women who were charged with the responsibility of creating the household while the men worked. They perused the magazines and builders' pattern books for ideas. Stock-building products were manufactured and their catalogs were read with great interest by all. Pastoral posters were published showing the good life in a leafy suburb. Great promotions such as picnics and carnivals brought families to the suburbs on the weekends via train and streetcar. Brochures and magazine features proliferated, and the Great American Dream of a house in the country was launched.[7]

After the Second World War, the Interstate Highway Commission and the GI Bill made an offer many Americans could not refuse. As a result, highways and railroads extended so far into the countryside that the forests and glens were bulldozed and turned into places given names like Forest Glen. Farmland was destroyed, driving became the national nightmare, and the mall replaced the corner store.

Today, New Urbanists and others look to compact, walkable solutions for suburbs and towns. They strive for a return to the central city in an effort to battle the problems of sprawl—gasoline cost, time lost to commuting, and what some believe to be a generally degraded lifestyle.[8]

Each chapter of this book presents the history of its specific housing type so that the reader may understand, and use, what is still relevant in current times.

Note: The current real estate crisis emphasizes the importance of sustainable urban design as a key component of residential design.

Literature

A career in design requires continuing education and awareness of changes in the field. It requires the architect or designer to investigate new ways of thinking about how people live. Residential design literature is abundant and diverse. In order to aid the student and professional in navigating the material, this book offers chapter endnotes and an annotated bibliography.

Books in the field of residential design may be placed in the following categories:

- Space planning and accessibility standards
- Technical and reference books
- Real estate and market demand
- Photographic essays of specific housing types
- Work of a specific architect or designer
- Social, cultural, and political aspects of housing
- History of residential architecture, regional or global
- Urban design
- Regional planning

- Sustainable housing and energy efficiency
- Universal design, for people with disabilities and the general population
- Style analysis; reviews of various architectural styles, sometimes including details

These categories are rarely combined, so a designer should develop a broad personal library.

Methodology, Our Friend

Chapters in this book are organized as follows: A **Chapter Purpose** outlines the chapter objectives. This is generally followed by the **historical background** of the specific housing type. Students may also be encouraged to do additional historic research. **Client profiles** based on the type of client envisioned for each specific project are included. In exercises, instructors and students may be asked to make up their own clients. Students may also be encouraged to do independent research to determine the characteristics of specific client types or market trends. Review of these profiles should result in a clear vision of the client for whom the residence is being designed. **Client checklists** are provided in some chapters, which may be used to help develop a program and budget. **Prototype designs** and projects based on these designs illustrate the various housing styles and allow the student to become intimately involved in the design process. Site plan, base plans, possible furniture layouts are included. **Exercises** are given for each prototype to help students get started. Students can work on these projects informally in a studio environment with their colleagues. Furniture templates are included in the book for reference in space-planning work. **Case studies in each chapter give examples of** what design professionals have created, including exterior and interior photographs, interior floor plans, and furniture layouts. These will help to influence the student's design approach. Once students have completed projects and exercises, they should be critiqued by instructors, outside professionals, and other students. All of these individuals are part of the studio learning approach to residential design. When possible, the instructor should include potential clients as well. At the end of the semester a student exhibition of finished project renderings can take student designs public. Relax and enjoy the accolades!

The Big Picture

This studio textbook considers the many broad influences that affect the design of housing, while paying close attention to the small practical details that are so important to the client who will actually be living in the home. The process should help the student to understand what to expect in the real world of professional design. They can gain insights into the special relationship that can develop between a designer and client, and how this affects the actual design. So get to work. The coffee is made and your colleagues are eagerly waiting to see your sketches and discuss the project.

ENDNOTES

1. John McIlwain and Melissa Floca, *Multifamily Trends* (Washington, DC: Urban Land Institute, 2007), available at www.uli.org/ResearchandPublications/.
2. Brookings Institution's Urban Markets Initiative and the Center for Neighborhood Technology, *The Affordability Index: A New Tool for Measuring the True Affordability of a Housing Choice* (Washington DC: Brookings Institution, 2006), available at http://www.brookings.edu/reports/2006/01_affordability_index.aspx.
3. Sir Bannister Fletcher, *A History of Architecture,* 16th ed. (New York: Charles Scribner's Sons, 1958), 2.
4. *The Green Guide, Paris,* (Michelin Travel Publications, 2003), 372–379.
5. U.S. Census Bureau, *American Factfinder, Housing/Physical Characteristics,* available at http://factfinder.census.gov/servlet/ACSSAFFHousing?_sse=on&_submenuId=housing_1.
6. Perry R. Duis, *Challenging Chicago* (Chicago: University of Illinois Press, 1998), 60–85.
7. Gwendolyn Wright, *Moralism and the Model Home* (Chicago: The University of Chicago Press, 1980).
8. Andres Duany, Elizabeth Plater-Zyberk, and Jeff Speck, *Suburban Nation: The Rise of Sprawl and the Decline of the American Dream* (New York: North Point Press, 2000).

Residential Design Studio

PART I

Getting Started

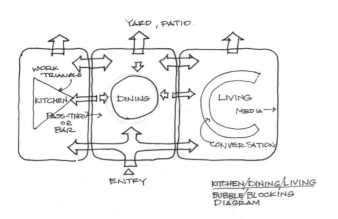

YARD, PATIO.

WORK TRIANGLE

KITCHEN · DINING · LIVING MEDIA

PASS-THRU OR BAR

CONVERSATION

ENTRY

KITCHEN/DINING/LIVING
BUBBLE/BLOCKING
DIAGRAM

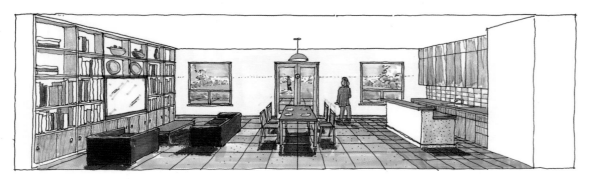

CHAPTER 1

Preliminary Design

Chapter Purpose

The purpose of this chapter is to familiarize the student with the preliminary work that must be done prior to starting a residential design. The student will learn the following:

- How to determine the needs of a client and develop a **program**
- How the housing market affects design
- How to make quick approximations of space layouts through the use of **bubble diagrams**
- The distinction between **base plans** and **space plans**
- How to lay out furniture in a floor plan
- The purpose of zoning laws
- How to estimate the cost of the home

This chapter is an overview of initial client interview, programming, budgeting, site investigation, space planning, and **furniture layout** for individual dwellings, spaces, or rooms within a residence. These preliminaries are all required prior to beginning the actual design for any type of residence.

Introduction

Before drawing the first line on a piece of paper, a designer must confront a series of questions, assumptions, and physical realities that will have a dramatic affect on the final design. The designer must become familiar with how to approach a client, ascertain the client's needs, develop a program, and determine a budget. This approach is applied to a variety of sites and housing types (**Figure 1.1**).

The general principles involved in space planning are illustrated in **Figures 1.2a–d.** These principles can be applied to all home types, though they may be modified for different clients. The individual spaces can be drawn as bubble diagrams. Which spaces adjoin each other, or **adjacencies**, are another consideration. **Figures 1.2a and b** illustrate the circulation through a home in which spaces are connected by corridors or halls. A decision made on dining space will affect the kitchen and living areas. Designers use bubble diagrams and flow diagrams to quickly achieve a layout before committing to hard line drawings.

Once the bubble diagrams and circulation patterns are developed it is possible to draw a **base plan**, which is the exterior **footprint** of the dwelling (**Figure 1.2c**). In the case of remodeling an existing building, the base

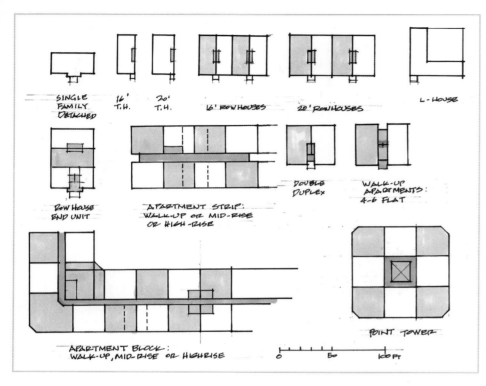

FIGURE 1.1 Comparative Housing Plans. *Left to right:* Single detached, single attached (rowhouse), apartment blocks, and high-rise towers.

plan may be provided in advance of the bubble diagrams. Points of entry and location of windows may be given at this point, or may be developed along with the interior planning. Once the base plan is established, a **space plan** is created that shows the locations of interior walls and stairways and defines window and door locations. When the space plan is agreed upon, a **furniture plan** is drawn to locate the important pieces of furniture (**Figure 1.2d**). Even before the actual furniture is selected, it's important to ensure that standard sizes will fit the space plan.

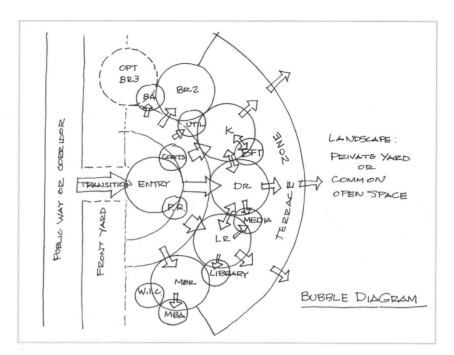

FIGURE 1.2A Bubble Diagram. This type of diagram shows relationships of different spaces in a simplified sketch.

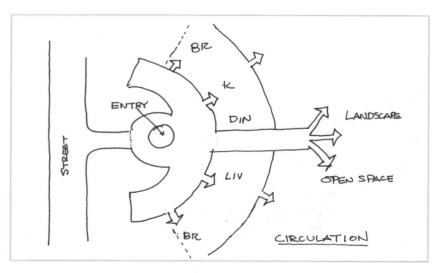

FIGURE 1.2B Circulation Diagram. This type of diagram emphasizes the circulation paths in a dwelling unit and shows where corridors should be planned.

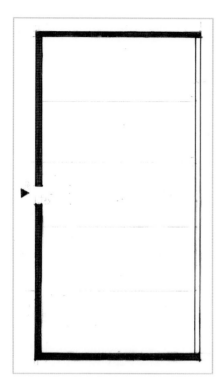

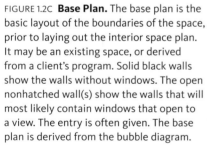

FIGURE 1.2C **Base Plan.** The base plan is the basic layout of the boundaries of the space, prior to laying out the interior space plan. It may be an existing space, or derived from a client's program. Solid black walls show the walls without windows. The open nonhatched wall(s) show the walls that will most likely contain windows that open to a view. The entry is often given. The base plan is derived from the bubble diagram.

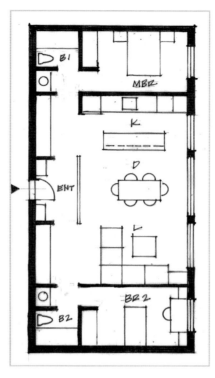

FIGURE 1.2D **Floor Plan/Furniture Plan.** The interior **floor plan** and the corresponding **furniture plan** are derived from the base plan. There is a glass wall for living room, dining room, kitchen, and bedrooms that opens to a view. The bathrooms and closets are placed on the walls that require less light, though a window in a bathroom is very desirable if possible. The furniture is placed in a logical arrangement in the space, according to the client program and designer. In this plan, the entry at the left is shielded from the dining area by an optional glass wall. There is also space for a table and a bench in the entry. There are long closets for coats, utility, pantry and additional storage along the entire back wall.

Context: How and Where Do Americans Live?

According to the recent U.S. Census for the country as a whole, approximately 60 percent of the total dwelling units were single-family detached and 40 percent multifamily attached. (This varies greatly for the large cities. New York City registers only 9 percent of its units as single-family detached. Seven percent of these are rowhouses and most of the others are apartments in multifamily buildings. The majority of these apartments are in buildings of ten units or more. In the city of Chicago, Illinois, 26 percent of the units are single-family detached.[1]

Neighborhood and City

The issues of location, neighborhood context, local zoning, appropriate housing typology, and costs should be well researched. Local zoning and building codes and existing infrastructure are important factors. **Zoning and building authorities** are generally happy to make time for students, concerned taxpayers, and other interested parties. Designers should investigate the water service, sewers, electricity, gas, and planned roads. If the client's preferences are not yet determined, the job of a professional designer is to help them refine their choices and bring a sense of realism to the project. This is important to do early in the process, so the designer and client don't waste time unnecessarily.

Whether planning for an individual owner who will be the occupant or for a developer who will be building for a specific market segment, the neighborhood context and preliminary planning steps are surprisingly similar and extremely important.

The Client

Professional designers work for somebody else, not for themselves. Whether it is a single-family detached home, an attached rowhouse, or an apartment building, the physical needs and attitudes of the future resident must be taken into account as much as possible. The designer must get to know the client. Talking about subjects that may not even be related to the planned residence can give the designer an idea of personal tastes and interests as well as the budget for the job.

The profiles chosen for this book are based on models of actual clients with greatly varying personalities and needs. The makeup of the group of people living together in a household is rapidly changing. It is no longer possible to refer to a "single-family house" because the occupants may not be a "typical" family. Single individuals may form partnerships, divorced people who remarry often bring along multiple sets of children who may occupy the home at different times. Sometimes these situations overlap.

Working at home is much more common today than it used to be. Sometimes all the adults in a household have jobs and there is no designated homemaker. Creating work/life spaces provides a challenge to the designer.

Rising gas prices are forcing the construction of smaller, more compact housing developments and in some neighborhoods, there is little need for a garage. For example, in cities such as Chicago, New York, and Boston, the cost of maintaining a parking space is prohibitive. In Chicago, a parking space recently sold for more than $100,000, and a parking space in the Back Bay section of Boston went for an astonishing $300,000. High-density urban communities are rich with cultural, social, and educational activities within walking distance of the home. Daily commutes in these areas are generally made on buses, trains, and on foot.

The purpose of the client profiles in this book is to acquaint students with the diversity of clientele they may face, the importance of the relationship between designer and client, and to what degree this relationship affects the final design. Designers should develop a client checklist to guide the designer and client through the project and as a tool for recording progress. A sample client checklist is located at the end of this chapter. This sample can be modified for each project.

Construction Costs

The first task for any residential design project is to verify the cost of construction per square foot in the anticipated site area. There are a number of good sources for construction costs by region, but the best place to start is with local builders, realtors, and bankers. A word of caution: The client may be surprised by the costs, which are often escalating. Prepare for this with specific information, such as an increase in the cost of plywood by 30 percent, a city requirement for a certain energy package, or an increase in labor costs of 10 percent in the past year. This will give more credibility to cost estimates (see **Figure 1.3**).

Program

Based on the construction costs in a given locale, the designer and client must develop, refine, and finalize a program. This begins with the client checklist that can start off as a wish list of all items that the client might want in their residence, regardless of price. The designer must help the client to understand the costs of the different parts of the program, such as square-foot costs or details like electrical and plumbing fixtures, cabinets, and flooring. This can be a painstaking process, unless, of course, money is no object for the client.

Contextual Planning

Before starting the floor plan, the designer must consider the neighborhood and the site. The dimensions of the site, adjoining structures, local zoning, and setback restrictions should be noted on a **site plan**. Another major consideration is access by automobiles, pedestrians, fire and safety vehicles, delivery vans, and trash removal providers. The site plan will also show where natural light and ventilation occurs. To create **cross-ventilation** a site must allow windows on at least two sides.

As discussed earlier, whether designing an apartment or a single dwelling, attached or detached, the program can require designing for a variety of clients, such as an individual, a family, or a group of unrelated residents. There might be ground-floor commercial space, even in a single-family detached dwelling as found in multiple-use live/work spaces. The dwelling might be a remodeling of an existing structure in a neighborhood with its own specific characteristics, such as the availability of shopping, parking, and access roads. Whatever the programmatic requirements, the preliminary approach is the same.

In the interest of **sustainability**, this book concentrates on small- to medium-sized dwellings. The designer must determine the overall area of the dwelling, break down each space, and then estimate the final budget.

#	ROOM/SPACE	AREA/s.f.	COST	NOTES
	RESIDENTIAL PROGRAM / BUDGET		DATE	
	Fig 1-3		CLIENT	
	Interior Space		x$125/SF	
1	ENTRY	40	5,000	
2	COAT CLOSET (Guests and Residents)	20	2,500	
3	POWDER ROOM	30	3,750	
4	KITCHEN	120	15,000	
5	PANTRY	25	3,125	
6	BREAKFAST ROOM	100	12,500	
7	DINING ROOM	150	18,750	
8	LIVING ROOM	250	31,250	
9	MEDIA SPACE (Maybe included in LR)	100	12,500	
10	LIBRARY	120	15,000	
11	MASTER BEDROOM	160	20,000	
12	MASTER BATH	100	12,500	
13	WALK-IN CLOSET 1	50	6,250	
14	WALK-IN CLOSET 2	50	6,250	
15	UTILITY ROOM/LAUNDRY	40	5,000	
16	LINEN CLOSET	5	625	
17	BEDROOM 2	120	15,000	
18	BATHROOM 2	75	9,375	
19	CLOSET	20	2,500	
20	BEDROOM 3	120	15,000	
21	BATHROOM3	75	9,375	
22	CLOSET	20	2,500	
23	CORRIDORS AND CIRCULATION (One Story)	180	22,500	
24	HOME OFFICE	300	37,500	
	Interior Square Feet	2,270	$283,750	Interior Cost
	Exterior Built Space		x$50/SF	
25	BASEMENT	2,350	117,500	
26	FRONT PORCH	100	5,000	
27	BACK PORCH	100	5,000	
28	DECK (No roof)	200	10,000	
29	GARAGE	600	30,000	
30	SHOP	600	30,000	
	Exterior Built Square Feet	3,950	$197,500	Exterior Cost
	Yard / Landscaping		x$10/SF	
31	FRONT YARD LANDSCAPING	250	2,500	
32	BACK YARD LANDSCAPING	1,250	12,500	
33	SIDE YARD LANDSCAPING	500	5,000	
	Square Feet	2,000	$20,000	Landscaping
	Total Square Feet	**8,220**	**$501,250**	**Total Cost**

FIGURE 1.3 **Program/Budget.** The client program and area breakdown are multiplied by the construction cost per square foot to estimate the project budget.

Consulting with real estate professionals, mortgage bankers, and home-builders helps to determine a realistic price the client can afford.

Space-Planning Principles

The layout of the residence and its relationship to the site is planned using a series of bubble diagrams and **circulation diagrams**, as shown in **Figures 1.2a,b.**

While brainstorming with the client, a series of loosely formed circles, or bubbles, are drawn. The name of each space is written on the corresponding bubble. Different schemes and adjacencies should be drawn without investing a lot of time in each one. Diagrams, notes, arrows, colored pens, and other devices can help in plotting where the sun or street noise will come in, or which space will have the best view. Sometimes, designers use Post-it notes so that spaces can be moved around. This helps to determine the final room configuration before proceeding with more detailed or hard-edged planning.

The following are some general principles to consider when approaching the design of key residential spaces in all types of projects.

Site and Landscaping

All space planning begins with the site and the landscape. For instance, if there is heavy traffic on an adjoining street, an interior courtyard may be appropriate. Orientation of the plan is based on sunlight and other natural considerations, such as wind and view. A view toward a forest preserve can be a compelling interior design factor (**see Figure 1.4**).

Space-planning decisions are also based on the programmed floor area, available land, and zoning and setback constraints. A smaller lot may require that the home be planned with multiple levels. Space planning can also depend on the location of adjoining buildings. If there is a building on both sides, there can be no side windows. Wall thickness and window area are dependent on the climate and wind direction. Designers should start their planning with the site (**Figure 1.5**).

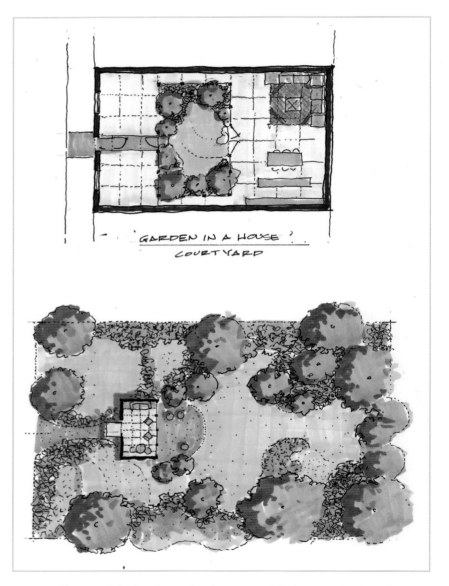

FIGURE 1.4 **House and Garden.** Determine the context of the house on the site. Is it primarily a house placed in a landscape, or is it a dense site with small garden, possibly enclosed?

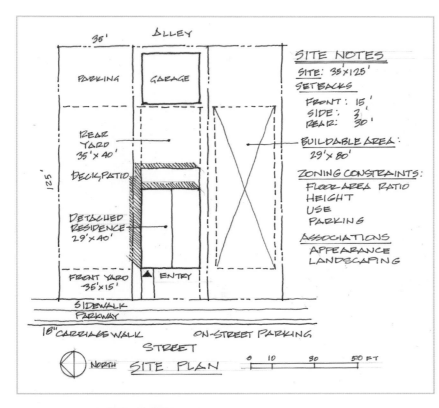

FIGURE 1.5 **Site Considerations.** Site influences on home design include location of entry, parking, yard, sunlight, and ventilation. Zoning constraints should also be considered, such as required setbacks and buildable area.

Getting In: The Transition from Public Way to Private Residence

Consider the approach to the residential building. In an apartment building, one may enter a lobby, an elevator, or a corridor. In the case of a single-family dwelling—attached or detached—the entrance will probably be at or near the ground level. There is currently a debate in the urban residential design field as to whether people should enter directly from grade or climb a stairway to a front porch. The issue of accessibility, however, dictates that we provide a substantial number of ground-level entrances and living spaces.

If one enters directly from the sidewalk, there may be a small front yard. If there is a yard, there should be provision for a small storage area for garden tools and an exterior hose bibb for connecting a garden hose.

Now let's look specifically at the entrance to the building. A ramp should be provided even if the front door is only 6 inches above grade (a 6-foot-long ramp would be required for accessibility). Also, provide a canopy or inset entry for protection from the elements. This is also a good place for newspaper and mail drop-off.

Focus on Essential Residential Spaces

This is an introduction to the essential residential spaces. More detail is provided in other chapters.

Entries

The most important single element in a residence is the interior entry (**see Figures 1.6a–f for entry possibilities**). It is also frequently overlooked. First impressions are strong, and many personal judgments are made in the first few minutes after entering a space. The exact configuration for the foyer is determined by interviews with clients. The budget is a factor, as well as the degree of formality desired in a foyer and the amount of activity anticipated in the space. There are many considerations that occur and must be considered for all entries in all building types.

Sometimes there is just enough room allowed to enter the unit, often directly into the living area. An area of 3 feet by 3 feet is allotted and deemed sufficient by some developers. But consider what must take place in this small space:

- A visitor waits until the host opens the door. (There should be an awning above the door to protect against the weather.)
- The visitor opens the door and enters. The weather can be very cold or hot on the exterior so there should be an **air lock** or **vestibule** to keep the interior comfortable and to conserve energy.
- People are observed and greeted, so there should be a mirror for guests.

FIGURE 1.6A **French Grand Foyer.**

FIGURE 1.6B **Simple Coat Pegs.**

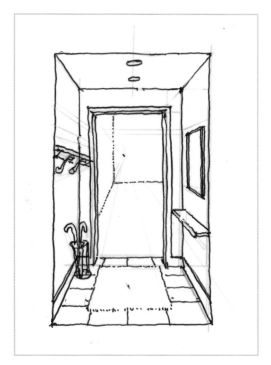

FIGURE 1.6A **Small Entry.** A small entry can accommodate space for coat hanging, a mirror, a picture wall with lighting, and a door to the vestibule.

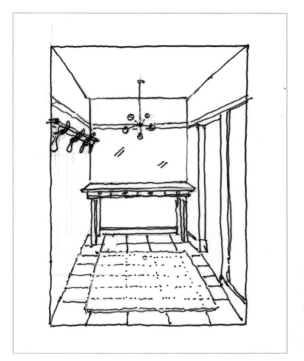

FIGURE 1.6C **Medium Entry.** This entry accommodates an entry table with drawers for keys and mail, hanging space for coats, a mirror, and a pocket door for air lock.

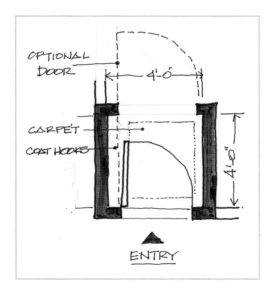

FIGURE 1.6B **Small Entry.**

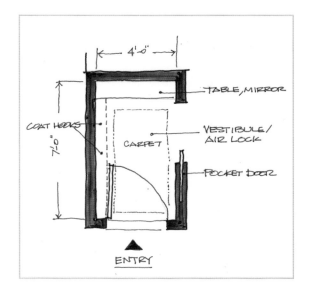

FIGURE 1.6D **Medium Entry.**

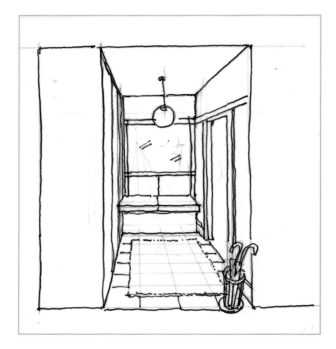

FIGURE 1.6E **Large Entry.** This entry allows for a closet with doors and separate areas for guest and household coats.

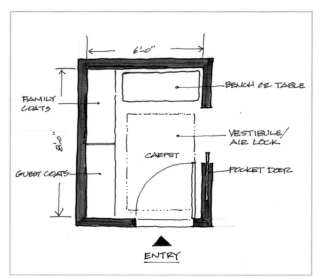

FIGURES 1.6F **Large Entry.**

- There should be a place to remove coats, hats, and even boots in many climates. A place to sit down and remove wet boots is useful.
- There should be an umbrella rack.
- The floor should be a hard surface that is easy to clean.
- In most climates, there is often a need to hang coats. If they are wet, they should be hung on pegs. There is a distinction between where "family" coats are stored and where guest coats are hung. The client may prefer to have a coat rack just for guests, two closets, a closet and pegs or coat rack, or just pegs. This is a convenient place to leave keys. There can be a private drawer or just a hook.
- A person may enter with a load of groceries or other packages. There should be a place to set them down while removing a coat. A table 28 to 36 inches high is convenient for this. Guests also may want to leave packages or purses in the foyer.
- If the home is in a wet climate, there may be a need to store indoor shoes here, perhaps in a drawer or on shelves or at least on a mat.

Now the visitor or resident is ready to proceed into the dwelling. But look at what has occurred in the few minutes during the entry sequence. Instead of allotting only 10 square feet, the client may want to program 35 to 50 square feet for the foyer. That's only 25 to 35 square feet more for the entire dwelling unit, but a lot more functionality for the entry space.

Powder Rooms

Adjoining the foyer, it is important to have a so-called powder room (**see Figures 1.7a,b**). If the budget allows it, this is the obvious location for one of the great luxuries in a home. Guests can use it when they enter and are not required to go into private areas of the home to use a toilet. This keeps a clear division between the public and private spaces of the home. If the program includes visitor sleeping accommodations in the living room, the powder room might have a shower. This is well worth the 10 square feet and the extra fixture. (For more details, particularly on accessibility, see Chapters 6 and 7).

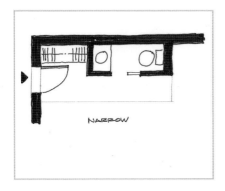

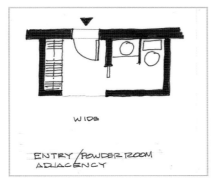

FIGURE 1.7A **Narrow Entry Plan/Powder Room.** Even in a narrow entry, space can be provided for a powder room.

FIGURE 1.7B **Wide Entry Plan/Powder Room.** This wide entry includes a closet and powder room.

Living Rooms

People live everywhere, but the term *living room* persists. Perhaps it should be called the sitting area, lounge, or entertainment area. The first decision is to determine what the room will be used for. Then, where will people enter this room (**see Figures 1.2a,b**). A small hallway or foyer can serve to organize the circulation. It can provide the option to enter a room without passing through another. This provides more peace and quiet for the kitchen, dining, or living room. In older homes, if money was no object, there was often an anteroom or a reception area where guests could wait until they were ready to be received. Look again to the client preferences, program, bubble diagrams, and adjacency requirements.

A hallway or corridor is not wasted space. Besides separating and connecting different rooms and concealing storage, it can also serve as a gallery. Good lighting should be provided for family photos or artwork.

What goes on in the living room these days doesn't stay in the living room. This of course varies from person to person and family to family. But most people sit around in comfortable chairs or sofas. They might talk to friends and family members, snack from low coffee tables, watch TV, or listen to music. Some people sit around and read. Furniture and lighting should be planned according to the shape and function of the room (**Figures 1.8a–d**).

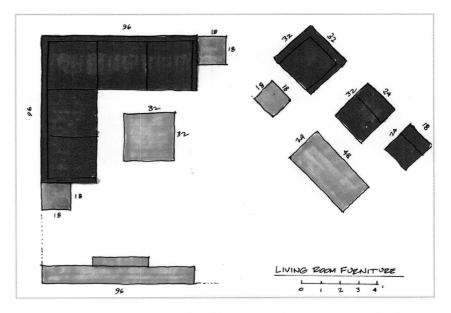

FIGURE 1.8A **Living Room Furniture Plans.** These simple diagrams of common furniture arrangements can help plan the layout for a living room. Actual furniture sizes should be used.

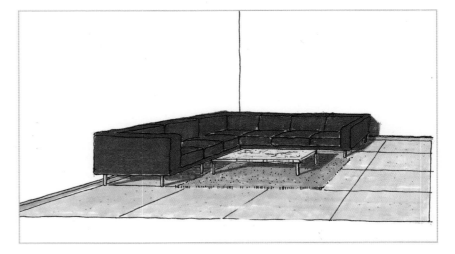

FIGURE 1.8B **Living Room Furniture Sectional Seating.** This diagram illustrates different styles of living room seating arrangements.

FIGURE 1.8C **Modern Living Room Furniture.**

FIGURE 1.8D **Traditional Living Room Furniture.**

Also, see where the best view is and where natural light falls into the space. Decide where the focus of the room should be. Should it be the exterior view or a coffee table or media wall?

The hearth was an important Victorian-era phenomenon. It defined the purpose of the home and family. Author Perry Duis described a typical scene in a Victorian-era Chicago home: "When the Glessner family moved to their new house at Eighteenth Street and Prairie Avenue in 1887 (it's now an architectural landmark) they built one final fire on the hearth of their old home, then transported the glowing coals across town and used them to light the first fire in their new home."[2] This was just sixteen years after the Chicago Fire! Today, if there is a hearth, it may take the form of a flat-screen television. With air quality a growing concern, as well as for purposes of sustainability and cost, fireplace hearths are disappearing as the organizing principal of the living room. This affects the layout of the room. A current trend is to place a flat-screen television in its own frame above a fireplace. Or the TV might have a video of logs burning. To each his own.

The living room should be adjacent to the kitchen for food access, which makes the usefulness of that powder room evident, especially if the main bathroom is on the second floor. The living room should also be adjacent to the dining room for informal entertaining using both spaces.

Kitchens and Dining Rooms

Kitchens and dining rooms should be near each other for convenience. (Kitchen and bathroom layouts will be discussed in detail in Chapters 5 and 6). It may be best to enter the dining room directly from the entry because it is a social gathering space, centrally located between living and kitchen spaces. But it should also be possible to enter the kitchen without passing through the dining room for service and groceries.

The shape and proportion of the dining room is directly related to the shape of the dining table and the number of people anticipated at a typical seating. Though the client may like the idea of being able to entertain large crowds, it might be preferable to design for typical family seating and allow for expansion for occasional guests. Seating between six and eight people is reasonable. This will result in one of the plans shown in

Figure 1.9. In addition to the dining table and chairs, the client may want a storage cabinet for dishes and flatware, especially if the kitchen is small.

In some of the large apartments the author has remodeled, the servants' call button remained under the table, though it connected to nothing. This was usually a beautiful brass button. The kitchen was remote, so that guests wouldn't smell or hear anything emanating from it. But in this age, when servants are rare, the dining room should be adjacent to the kitchen and the living area.

Great Rooms

The living room, dining room, and kitchen are often considered as individual spaces, but there is a growing trend toward what are known as great rooms. This term describes a single space that combines the functions of the living room, dining room, and kitchen. In American residential

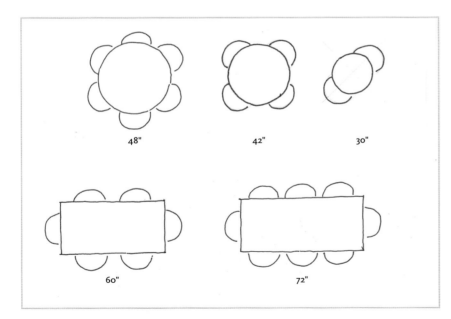

FIGURE 1.9 **Dining Room Tables.** Seating arrangements determine the size of the dining room.

design, the changing roles of family members and informal lifestyles have created a demand for these multiuse spaces. While the kitchen is still kept separate in most European dwellings, this is also beginning to change. Frank Lloyd Wright started this trend in his Usonian houses of the 1920s and 1930s, and it continues today.[3]

Often, multiple family members prepare and serve meals. Sometimes everyone sits around the dining table, and at other times they eat at a counter or bar between the kitchen and dining room. To the dismay of some, there is also a tendency to watch television during dinnertime, or at least in the same space. A bubble diagram, space plan, and perspective for a great room are shown in **Figures 1.10a–c.** It is often desirable, especially in moderate climates, to have an outdoor dining space, such as a yard or terrace, adjoining the great room.

Bedrooms

Bedrooms perform a multitude of functions. Sleeping is one of them, of course, but bedrooms are also used as a separate private area, especially in small dwellings. It is not unusual to place a reading chair and lamp in the bedroom if space allows, or a small desk, a bookshelf, and even a TV set. But the designer should be careful not to crowd too many functions into a bedroom. Some clients don't want the home office in the bedroom, for example, because they need to be away from work when resting and sleeping.

A bedroom is also a room for romance and lovemaking. Don't let the other functions interfere with this. There should be a generous window with a nice view, preferably private, even though window coverings will be necessary for light and privacy.

The bed should have a bedside table with a light (one on each side if there are two people). A shelf or drawer for books or small bottles below the tabletop is important so that a clean surface can be maintained. Most people keep a clock here too. A bedroom does not have to be large. It should be adequate for its functions and should feel cozy. Client preference for a full-, queen-, or king-sized bed is critical to the space plan (**see Figure 1.11**).

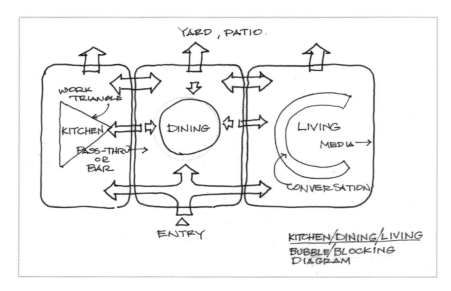

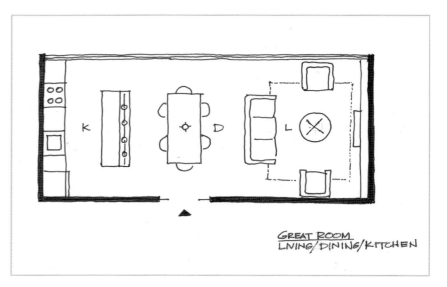

FIGURE 1.10A **Great Room Bubble Diagram.** Great rooms combine the kitchen, dining, and living rooms for a larger and more flexible space. Bubble diagrams help to plan how the space will be used.

FIGURE 1. 10B **Great Room Floor Plan.**

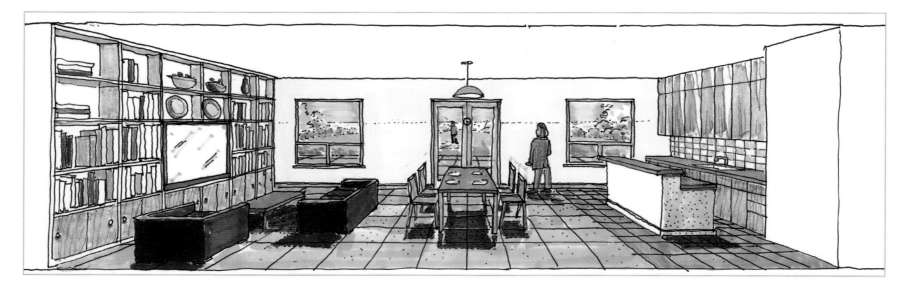

FIGURE 1.10C **Great Room Perspective.** This is a perspective drawing of a great room is derived from the bubble diagram.

Walk-in closets (**Figure 1.12**) are conducive to a peaceful bedroom. Some clients prefer not to have closets open into sleeping areas because they have a tendency to remain open and spill into the room. Separate walk-in closets for each person are ideal and should be placed between the bedroom and the bathroom.

A bathroom should be placed adjacent to the bedroom. In a master bedroom suite, the bathroom should have a private entry from the bedroom.

All of these rooms or spaces—foyer, living/dining/kitchen, bathroom, and bedroom—are fundamental to the modern dwelling. Their functions are part of our daily lives. They provide adequate living spaces and can be accommodated in small areas. However, many of us need rooms for other activities.

Special-Purpose Rooms

Many people now work in their homes and require space for a home office, storage, and a space for meeting with clients. According to a recent *New York Times* article, the Democratic pollster Mark Penn noted that "4.2 million Americans now work exclusively from home (a nearly 100% increase from 1990), while some 20 million do it part time."[4] Clients may also require a **workshop** for making furniture, repairing equipment, packing and shipping, and so on. It's very important to keep these functions separate from the living space, as anyone who has ever worked at home will tell you. Unused space in a garage, storage room, or basement can be turned into a workshop and the same standards for light, fresh air, and ventilation apply. Frank Lloyd Wright described the basement as an "unwholesome" place.[5] "From it comes damp atmosphere and unhealthy conditions. The tendency is to throw things into it . . . and forget them." He also considered it dangerous and a place where people fell down stairs. He adds that it is also an expensive space, as it can cost almost as much as above-ground space. Nevertheless, there are times when a basement can be made habitable.

In the days of computers and electronic files, home offices can be relatively compact. They can be accommodated by adjoining corridors or remodeled closets, as shown in **Figure 1.13**.

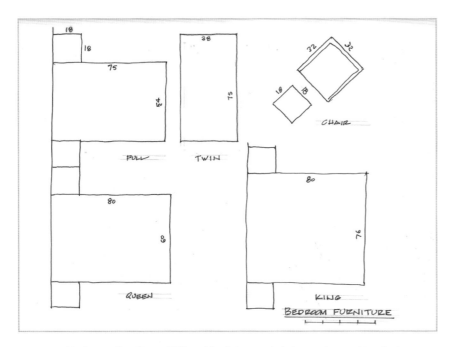

FIGURE 1.11 **Bedroom Furniture.** Different bed sizes and chairs can be used in a bedroom. Space for wardrobes, media (if required), tables, and desk must also be estimated.

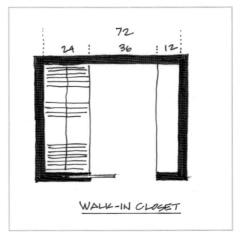

FIGURE 1.12 **Walk-in Closet.** A fully accessible walk-in closet, with a 36-inch-wide corridor between shelves and hanging space.

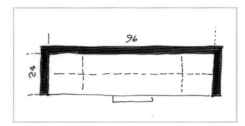

FIGURE 1.13 **Mini Home Office.** Home offices come in all shapes and sizes. A mini can be efficiently squeezed into a closet or hallway. Doors can be added to screen the clutter of the workplace from view.

As in all of the rooms in a home, the planning of electrical outlets, cable outlets, and telephone jacks have become critical in furniture layout and space planning for home offices. The layout must be "nailed down" before locating the outlets.

Another special purpose room is a **library**. People who enjoy reading require a great amount of book storage; perhaps floor-to-ceiling shelving. Books should be protected from intense natural light, which can harm the bindings and covers. A separate library with a reading chair and table is a good idea for these clients.

Recent surveys indicate that **media rooms** are becoming more of a part of daily life. Large, flat-screen televisions and sophisticated sound systems dominate many homes. A modest version can be incorporated into the great room or living room. Some prefer to keep that function away from daily life and require a separate room.

A **guest room** can be a double-edged sword. When does an adult child become a guest? At what point can their bedroom(s) be converted to other uses? Do we really want a space where an uninvited guest can outstay their welcome? If one uses a guest room as a media room also, what about when guests stay for an extended period of time? These program and budget questions are of great importance in determining whether or not to have a separate room solely devoted to guests.

If a client lives in an apartment, there may be a community laundry in the building. However, a **laundry room**, or even a small (30 inches square) laundry closet is a great convenience. It should be located near the dressing area and clothing storage. There is usually a plumbing stack available in the nearby bathroom, but make sure there is special provision for a washer/dryer hookup. In a single family home, laundry plumbing is usually a given.

Whether the client is an art collector or simply prefers family photographs, be sure to provide enough space for hanging and exhibiting these works. Good lighting is essential. Track spotlights from the ceiling or separate picture lamps are well suited to this purpose. Corridors and foyers can be very successful **gallery** areas, as can other rooms in a home, even bathrooms.

Furniture

Furniture layout is the starting point for interior planning. Frank Lloyd Wright often said that home planning starts from the "inside out," that is, the exterior shell is derived from understanding the way people use their interiors, and particularly how furniture is located. Sample furniture sizes for space planning purposes are shown in **Figures 1.8 through 1.11**.

FIGURE 1.14A **Views of Special Rooms.** Pantry.

FIGURE 1.14B **Views of Special Rooms.** Laundry room.

FIGURE 1.14C **Views of Special Rooms.** Home office.

The key to designing a living room is to lay out the seating. First, determine the purpose of the room and how people will use it. Is it for social purposes, conversation, or private reading and contemplation? Is there a compelling view? Is viewing media an important function of this room? Will people lounge or sit straight up? In a comprehensive book about chairs,[6] Galen Cranz makes the point that there is no one good seating position. Ms. Cranz argues for changing posture frequently for better health and comfort.

Figures 1.8a–d illustrate plans and sketches of typical living room furniture. Dining room tables and chairs are shown in **Figure 1.9**. A combination of living and dining room furniture is shown in the great-room plan (**Figure 1.10b**) and bedroom furniture is shown in **Figure 1.11**. Clients or designers may select specific custom furniture or family keepsakes for the interior, but the sample sizes given here help to start the space-planning process. (*Tip:* The student can trace these furniture plans. Then they can be cut out and moved around while space planning.)

Client Checklist

The client checklist that follows may be used as a preliminary guide for ascertaining a client's needs and budget. It can then be developed into a program and budget matrix. It is assumed that accessibility and sustainability will continue to be addressed throughout the interview and design process. This checklist should be filled out prior to or during the first client meeting. Then the real design fun can start.

Chapter Summary

You now have a sense of the extensive preliminary work that is required before starting to design for an individual client. From site investigation to client interview, the designer must ascertain a definitive program and cost estimate prior to beginning the design. The designer must also research the relevant zoning and building codes for the community and consider issues of accessibility and sustainability.

This chapter has also provided ideas and tips for planning individual rooms and spaces and how they relate to each other (adjacencies). Aids for quickly laying out a space—bubble diagrams and blocking diagrams—were introduced, and the importance of the base diagram, which is the plan for a building's exterior walls, was explained. These diagrams are useful for all housing types and will be used throughout this book.

EXERCISES

1. Explore your city and find an area or neighborhood where you would like to live or plan a residence. Take photos and make sketches of existing residences. What type of residence is appropriate for this neighborhood? What are the housing prices? Check with local realtors. Discuss this with your instructor if this is a class project. This will help determine the context for new residential design.

2. Based on the given budget, and local construction costs, determine a program starting with the gross affordable area. Then break it down into sub-areas, also based on the program. Do this on a spreadsheet, and adapt it for your future projects.

3. Draw at least five bubble diagrams for different layout options. Based on a selected bubble diagram, draw some freehand concept sketches of the planned dwelling. If this is a single-family residence, include the site boundaries and any zoning setbacks required. Locate street, alley access, and on-site parking. Take the adjoining structures into account as well. If this is an existing apartment, start with the given base floor plan, or, if necessary, measure it on site. For an apartment building, be sure to show the corridors and entry points.

There are additional exercises in the Instructors Guide that will help students understand what is necessary in the preliminary phase of the design.

KEY TERMS

Adjacencies: Spaces that should adjoin, such as kitchen and dining room or bedroom and bathroom.

Air lock, or vestibule: A space at the entry that can be closed to the interior when a person enters. Particularly important in cold climates. Helps conserve energy and comfort.

Base plan: Plan of the exterior walls of the dwelling. In the case of remodeling an existing building, the base plan may be given in advance of the bubble diagrams.

Bubble diagrams: The use of simple sketched circles, or bubbles, to generally lay out spaces in a residence. Many bubble diagrams can be produced in a short period of time so that client and designer may come to a conclusion as to the plan layout.

Circulation/flow diagrams: Diagrams showing the likely circulation in a residence; for example, from entry to kitchen to dining room to living

CLIENT CHECKLIST

1. Client Profile

☐ Family makeup; children (gender), adults

☐ Family members who may be handicapped

☐ Some spaces for temporary or flexible use?

☐ Will people work from the home? See clients?

☐ Other special requirements:

_____

_____

2. Program

☐ Location or region

☐ Room requirements

☐ Square footage

☐ Budget or construction cost (client's budget)

IMPORTANT: Obtain current construction cost estimates for new construction and remodeling in the region from the local National Association of Homebuilders chapter or from individual builders. Check references and interview other recent home buyers.

☐ Visit new home sites.

☐ Color or style preferences

_____

_____

3. Foyer

☐ Means of entry to unit (e.g., direct from exterior or through a corridor?)

☐ Are stairs required to gain entry? (This would be a problem for accessible units.)

☐ What are requirements for guest coats and family coats (linear feet of hanging space, pegs).

☐ Chair or bench for sitting while removing boots. Place or surface for drainage. Umbrella rack.

☐ Shelf for gloves and hats, hooks for keys

☐ Is the mailbox at the door or in a mail room elsewhere? This affects the use of the room and the hardware, as well as a staging place for distribution of mail to residents.

☐ Staging surface for next outing? (To hold books, briefcases, etc.)

☐ Floor finishing. Are "walk-off" carpets required for inclement weather?

☐ Mirror

☐ Will foyer be a place to exhibit family photos or artwork? (Wall space)

☐ Lighting. Overhead or spot lighting for artwork? Three-way switch?

_____

_____

4. Living Room

☐ What are the uses anticipated for this room?

  ☐ Conversation

  ☐ Media

  ☐ Reading

  ☐ Entertaining

  ☐ Informal eating

☐ Open to a dining area?

☐ If a single-family home, does it open to a yard?

☐ If an apartment, is there an adjoining balcony or terrace?

☐ Are there any particular furniture pieces that are already owned that should be incorporated?

☐ New furnishings (e.g., lounge seating, chairs, coffee table or ottoman, end tables)? Include floor finish, such as wood or tile.

☐ Home office (specify how big, what type of furniture, and should it be hidden from view with screens or sliding doors?)?

☐ Lighting type? (e.g., general overhead lighting, task lighting, reading lamps, wall sconces)?

_____

_____

5. Dining Room

☐ Is this a separate formal space, or is it open to kitchen, living room?

☐ How many people will normally be served, and what is the maximum number anticipated to sit at a table.

☐ When entertaining large groups, is there provision for buffet-style serving and seating?

☐ A buffet or storage area for dinnerware in the dining room or a pantry? Or storage in kitchen cabinets only?

☐ New furnishings (e.g., dining table, chairs, benches, buffet, end tables)? Include floor finish, such as wood or tile.

☐ Lighting preferences (e.g., over dining room table, wall sconces, general lighting)

_____

_____

6. Kitchen

☐ Open counter or bar, pass-through only or closed with doors?

☐ Workspace arrangement: L-shaped, U-shaped, or galley?

☐ Is it a gourmet type of kitchen, or casual light cooking only?

☐ Does client cook frequently?

continued on the next page

☐ How many people normally participate in cooking, dishwashing? Will children or handicapped people be working in kitchen?

☐ Will people eat in the kitchen? Small table or counter seating?

☐ Linear feet of base and wall cabinetry. This may require a detailed survey of kitchen utensils and dinnerware.

☐ Countertops: Different work surfaces for different activities. Length of surfaces and materials should be thoroughly considered (stainless steel, stone or marble, wood, plastic laminate; slide-under, desk-type counters for universal access?)

☐ Wall cabinets: Length and height? What is ceiling height of kitchen? How much storage is required? What area is budgeted in overall space planning for kitchen? Glass panels or doors? Open shelving?

☐ Base cabinets: Provision for accessible workspace (lower countertops with open space underneath for wheelchair seating)

Appliances:

☐ Oven: One or two? Stainless steel or porcelain?

☐ Range: Electric or gas? Accessibility requirements

☐ Refrigerator: Size and type

☐ Sink: Single bowl or double?

☐ Trash disposal: Where will trash be disposed? Is recycling provided for? Will it be in the kitchen or at a remote location?

☐ Home office space adjoining kitchen for personal activities, calendar, recipes, telephone, computer?

☐ Pantry or all storage in cabinets? Sizes?

7. Bedrooms

☐ How many bedrooms will be needed, and what is the hierarchy? Master bedroom for parents, separate bedroom for each child, separate bedrooms by gender, or even dormitory style for large families or unconventional living arrangements. This may be accompanied by study areas for homework and social areas. Much of this can be determined in the Client Profile, but size and furnishing requirements must be clarified programmatically.

☐ Type of bedroom: Consideration should be given to whether or not at least one bedroom should be set aside for elderly or handicapped people. A ground-floor bedroom, which can be opened up for visitors, is desirable here.[7]

☐ In a small unit, the bedroom can be opened up to the living room with a pair of French doors to emphasize space.

☐ Will closets be within the bedroom or separate walk-in type?

☐ Will there be other activities/furnishing in the bedroom, such as desk, chair, shelves, media, bedding storage?

☐ View: Is the view private or will opaque window covering be required? In most municipalities, windows are required by code for natural ventilation in all rooms classified as bedrooms.

☐ Size(s) of bed(s).

8. Bathrooms

(*Note:* The number and types of bathrooms will vary, depending on client needs and budget. This will be discussed and illustrated in more detail in the chapter on bathrooms. The following are some common questions to ask a client.

☐ How many bathrooms will you need?

☐ Who will be using them?

☐ At least one bathroom should be accessible. Will it be the master bathroom? This means. at minimum, a shower with no threshold, grab bars, a wide door opening, a wheelchair-accessible sink, and a high toilet.

☐ Will the master bathroom contain a shower and a tub?

☐ Will there be two sinks in the master bathroom?

☐ Develop a fixture list with catalog cut sheets to serve as a specification.

☐ A hardware list with catalog cuts should also be developed.

☐ Towel bars: extent and location

☐ Pocket doors or swinging?

☐ Choose tile for floors and walls. Nonskid tiles are desirable for floors.

☐ Is there a need for an operable window or will there be a vent fan?

☐ What type of lighting is required for the vanity?

☐ Electrical outlets and switches: locations and types

9. Home Office

(*Note:* Whether for personal or business use, the home office is becoming an obligatory part of new home planning. Location and size will be determined by the client's needs and budget. The following are common considerations for all home offices.

☐ Size of desk space required?

☐ How many people will use the office?

☐ Required storage space, specifically file space, bookshelves, closet or storage room for bulky equipment, or guest coats

☐ Type of furniture (desk chair, etc.). Will there be a conference table or a coffee table with lounge seating?

☐ Specify general and task lighting types

☐ Location of outlets: This is particularly important for computers and other office equipment, as well as lighting.

Sources: See Notes 8 and 9.

room. This helps to determine where corridors should be located and partitions built.

Cross-ventilation: Means of opening windows on two faces of a dwelling unit to allow the warm air to exit and cool air to enter. This type of ventilation, common before air conditioners, helps keep occupants comfortable and cuts down on electrical costs.

Footprint: Outline of the building on the site.

Furniture layout: After determining the client's furniture requirements, the designer should arrange the furniture in plan. Sometimes this occurs before the walls are decided, because furniture placement can affect where walls should go. An open plan (few walls) is generally more flexible for different furniture arrangements.

Program: The rooms, spaces, and requirements a client has for the planned residence. This program should be developed considering local construction costs and the client's budget.

Site plan: A plan, usually at a smaller scale, that shows the entire site for the residence. It should clearly show adjoining streets, sidewalks, landscaping, alleys, and other external features that could affect the residential design. It may also include notations for setbacks.

Space plan: Shows the locations of interior walls, stairways, and defines window and door locations.

Sustainability: Method of building that requires that all materials used can be replaced. Also refers to the reduction of energy use and air pollution. Location of a residence near public transportation and within walking distance of work and daily needs and auto-dependency are now considered key factors in a sustainable environment.

Walk-in closet: An extra large closet, usually with a door. Keeps the wardrobe function separate from the bedroom.

Zoning and building authorities: Agencies in a locality that are responsible for drafting and enforcing zoning ordinances and building codes. In small communities, the National Building Code is sometimes adopted, but zoning ordinances can exist in even the smallest townships.

ENDNOTES

1. U.S. Census Bureau, American FactFinder, B25024 Units in Structure – Universe: Housing Units. 2006 American Community Survey. Basic information on the makeup of the American Housing Inventory. Includes single-family detached dwellings and the various types of multi-family dwellings. Updated frequently.
2. Perry R. Duis, *Challenging Chicago* (Chicago: University of Illinois Press, 1998), 85.
3. Frank Lloyd Wright, *The Natural House* (New York: Bramhall House, 1954).
4. Mark Penn, *New York Times Magazine*, November 4, 2007, 17.
5. Wright, *The Natural House*, 158.
6. Galen Cranz, *The Chair: Rethinking Culture, Body, and* Design (New York: W.W. Norton, 1998).
7. Wid Rosenfeld and Jeffrey P. Chapman, *Home Design in an Aging World* (New York: Fairchild, 2008), 20.
8. National Kitchen and Bath Association. "Planning Guidelines with Access Standards." Available at www.nkba.org/guidelines/default.aspx. Hard copies of this essential source for kitchen planning are available at www.nkba.org/guidelines/order.aspx.
9. Christine McFadden, *The Essential Kitchen* (New York: Rizzoli). This is a comprehensive guide to the tools and utensils available for modern kitchens.

PART II

Low-Rise Dwellings

1-STORY RANCH

CHAPTER 2

Single-Family Detached Houses

The American Dream, A New Model

Chapter Purpose

The purpose of this chapter is to give students background in the considerations involved in a wide variety of single-family home designs. Students will learn about the history and recent background of the home-building industry, market considerations for residential designers, and current zoning and environmental conditions for new homes. Floor plans are discussed in detail, from how the site affects the interior floor plan to how to determine necessary separation between public and private zones within a house for adults and children. A variety of client profiles are included along with discussions about how residential designers can accommodate changes in family makeup. Students are reminded of the importance of accessibility and sustainability and successful designs of single-family homes are explored through case studies.

Background

The single-family detached home has been the preference of most Americans since World War II. In 2006, 60 percent of the homes in the United States were single-family detached dwellings.[1] Single-family lots with side-yard setbacks are larger, have wider fronts, and provide greater green space than the smaller lots required for attached houses. Larger houses can be built on these lots. Buyers of these homes undoubtedly feel that there are many other advantages, both social and financial.

This pattern may be about to undergo a significant change. According to a report by the Urban Land Institute, the median size of a new single-family residence, which was about 750 square feet in the 1940s, increased to 2,200 square feet in 2006. As described by McIlwain and Floca, "this inexorable rise is coming to an end; . . . the median size of the new American home is going to begin to decrease."[2] The authors cite rising energy costs and economic difficulties as key contributing factors to this decrease. With increasing fuel costs, crowded highways, changing job locations, and evolving family structures, the goal of a large single-family dwelling may no longer be feasible for many people.

New factors must be taken into account in the design of new single detached residences. The sites and homes will probably be smaller. They will be located in denser neighborhoods, within reasonable walking and cycling distances to work, shopping, schools, and other daily activities. This chapter seeks to examine these new elements and incorporate them into client preferences, site locations, and programming of new single detached homes.

Founding Myths

One of the founding myths of American shelter is that most people would prefer to live in a single-family detached home, and that through hard work and thrift they could afford it. Though there may be some "typical" families out there, the reality for most people is somewhat different.

First of all, the definition of family continues to evolve. Family composition includes a growing number of elderly people and single people. According to the U.S. Census Bureau, 42 percent of all Americans aged 18 and older are unmarried. Family units may be made up of parents and children from various households, multiple generations living under one roof, or unrelated individuals sharing a household. A "typical" household with a working father, stay-at-home mother, and their schoolaged children, now represents just over 10 percent of the population.[3] Affordability is also a growing issue. Recent economic distress, including mortgage foreclosures, inflation, deteriorating employment, and the high cost of gasoline, has made it difficult to ascertain how many people can afford to live in single-family detached homes.

As mentioned earlier, in 2006 about 60 percent of the U.S. population lived in single-unit detached housing and the remaining 40 percent lived in rowhouses and apartments. However, the market for single-family homes may be decreasing. For example, in cities, where approximately 75 percent of the population lives, the proportion of people living in single-family residences is relatively small. In New York City, for example, only 9 percent of the population lives in single-family detached units. In Chicago the figure is approximately 26 percent.[4] The lots for these urban single-family homes are much smaller and narrower than their suburban counterparts. Side-yard setbacks are also smaller. Though it is difficult to project far into the future, it is clear that the trend is toward smaller single-family units, even in the suburbs.

It is incumbent upon designers of new residences to consider that everyone is going to have to do more with less. Design professionals will be charged with designing more home in less space. They will have to learn to be lean and mean, efficient and clever. European designers have already solved many of these problems. This book includes case studies of European townhouses and apartment plans in Chapters 3 and 8.

The Story of Single-Family Detached Homes

The four most important historic periods affecting the current definition of a single-family home are

- Nineteenth century (Victorian period): American and European models
- Early twentieth century: industrial and urban housing
- Post World War II: housing boom and the suburbanization of cities
- Late twentieth and early twenty-first century: the American nightmare?

The Nineteenth-Century Ideal

The idea of the American Dream is deeply rooted in the American consciousness.[5] Our historical sense of this dream stems from nineteenth-century Victorian morality and the marketing efforts of the early homebuilders. Health, family structure, nature, hygiene, upward class mobility, and in general a higher standard of living were the rewards for being good citizens. Despite many opinions to the contrary, this dream remains a strong part of how we think about and design homes.[6]

Early Twentieth Century: Moving Around in the City

Development of the single-family home coincided with the development of new means of transportation, which included suburban train lines and, eventually, the automobile. This made suburban living very convenient and affordable at first. Most of the early suburbs were close to the central city.

Few architects sought to design affordable single-family homes for the middle class (and this is still the case today), Frank Lloyd Wright was a notable exception. He agreed to design a house for Herbert and Katherine Jacobs near Madison, Wisconsin, for the modest construction cost of $5,000, which translates to about $150,000 in 2009 dollars. This house became a model for a new generation of home designers. It was perhaps the most influential home design in the history of American residential architecture.[7]

Other factors were also at work in determining residential design. President Herbert Hoover's model code and the subsequent single-use zoning ordinances enacted by many cities and counties encouraged the construction of single-family homes in separate residential zones. It effectively eliminated the corner store with living space overhead, virtually outlawing Main Street U.S.A. (until it was reinterpreted by Disneyland).[8] Originally, the Federal Housing Authority (also known as Fannie Mae) would only finance single-family detached houses. Today, Fannie Mae buys mortgages on mixed-use buildings but only 25 percent of projected rent can be nonresidential. So Main Street remains illegal.[9]

Post World War II

After World War II, ever-increasing commuting distances created demands for highway expansion. This required vast highway construction and demolitions in the core of many cities.[10]

The Dream was advanced and made possible by generous mortgage allowances and subsidies from the federal government. Programs established by the Fannie Mae and the Department of Veterans Affairs ensured that all returning servicemen could afford a home. These subsidies favored single-family detached suburban homes rather than attached rowhouses, remodeling, or mixed-use developments. The move to suburbia was also subsidized by the Interstate Highway Act of 1956. This legislation allowed for cheap gas, making it relatively inexpensive to build and sell homes in suburban single-family developments, such as Levittown, New York, and Park Forest, Illinois. In fact, it was usually cheaper to buy than to rent.[11]

Codes for the design of single-family detached homes, following the Hoover model, were enacted by local authorities across the country. Along with separate-use zoning, these new ordinances required generous minimum lot sizes, side-yard setbacks, and parking requirements, all of which contributed to the phenomenon of **sprawl**. Furthermore, parking requirements for shopping were instrumental in creating the shopping mall, effectively eliminating most local businesses.[12]

Where Are We Now and How Did We Get Here?

The American Dream has turned extremely dark for some. Flight to the suburbs led to a dearth of maintenance in the central cities, which quickly deteriorated. By then the Dream had become a nightmare for many.

Most central cities in the United States were densely built, with apartment buildings, rowhouses, and small single-family houses mixed together. They had been deteriorating and were neglected during a fifteen-year period that encompassed the Great Depression and World War II. The plight of the cities became a crisis in the 1960s. While land was available in the central city, it was more expensive and was deemed less desirable. This combination of factors was responsible for creating the environment—some would say the illusion—that single-family detached homes in the suburbs provided the most desirable way of life.

Government policies, including gasoline and highway subsidies and large-scale urban renewal projects, were major factors in creating our current situation. Changes in family structure have affected the programs of our homes. Social changes, particularly race and economic issues, have also played a large part in defining how we want to live today and in the future.

Today, architects design only one-quarter of all new single-family homes built each year.[13] The remaining three-quarters of the market presents a golden opportunity for the design profession to step up and improve the quality of the residential environment. Architects and residential designers of the future will have to take into account emerging social and environmental factors in order to develop a new model for the single, detached home. Following are some prototype projects for detached homes. Each project includes narrative, a client profile, plans, renderings, and analysis.

Single-Family Detached Home Prototypes
A Small Home for One Person: One-Story Cottage (Figures 2.1a–h)

Historically, workers' cottages were built quickly and in large numbers to accommodate rapid industrialization and population expansion. They were often very small, about 400 square feet, and consisted of just two rooms. Some of these homes still exist in older cities, but have been modernized and expanded. The main benefit of these homes is that they are small and cheap.

A modern version of this home, slightly larger at 600 square feet, and built of brick with up-to-date interior conveniences, could serve as a starter house for a first-time buyer.

It could also work for a single or retired person of any age who wishes to maintain an independent life and seeks the benefit of home ownership without the high costs of a larger home.

- Site: 25 feet wide by 60 feet deep
- Footprint/area: 20 feet wide by 30 feet deep (600 square feet)
- Single story at or near grade
- Living/dining/kitchen, one bedroom or sleeping space

Client Profile

The client would enjoy a small garden and doesn't own a car. The site is within a five-minute walk to shopping and public transportation. Guest parking is on the street. Homeowner's association rules provide for one designated on-street parking space in front of each house. An additional parking space could be provided either in an off-site lot or on a permeable pad at the rear of the site, off the alley. No garage is permitted. Entry to the house should be direct and provide easy accommodation for different physical abilities. (See site plan, **Figure 2.1b**.) The client wishes to have an efficient and flexible interior space. The kitchen should open to the living/dining area, and the sleeping space should double up as a study. (See plans in **Figures 2.1c, f.**)

Tips

For all elevations, consider sill heights in relation to the interior plan, i.e., different heights for windows near tables and desks. Living room lounge chairs may require lower sills. Living, kitchen, and dining area can accommodate French doors for a balcony or terrace. The bedroom may have a balcony. For bathroom and kitchen windows, note fixture locations and privacy considerations.

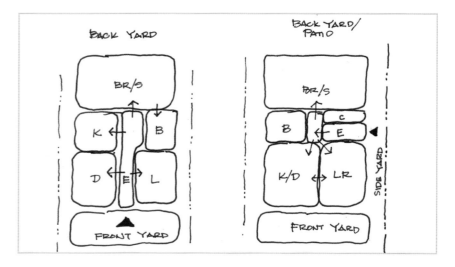

FIGURE 2.1A **Bubble Diagrams for One-Story Cottage.** Two options: front and side entry.

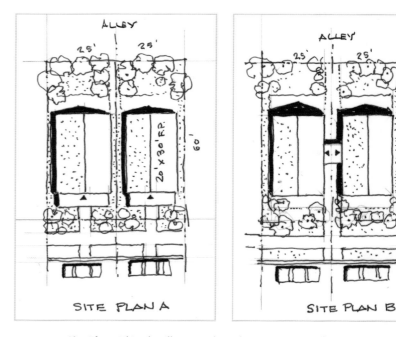

FIGURE 2.1B **Site Plans.** This plan illustrates how the entry concept from Figure 2.1a applies to the site.

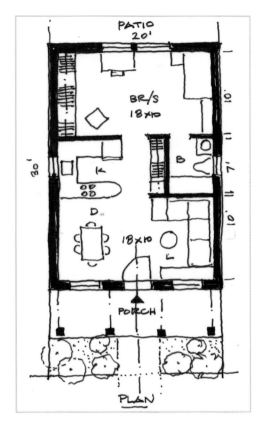

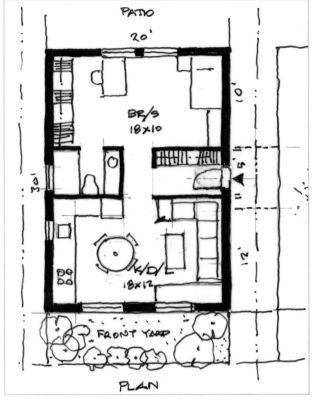

FIGURE 2.1C **Floor Plan, Front Entry.** Kitchen, bathroom, living, dining, and sleeping spaces with furniture layout.

FIGURE 2.1F **Floor Plan, Side Entry.** Kitchen, bathroom, living, dining, and sleeping spaces with furniture layout.

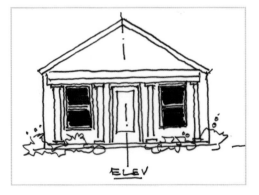

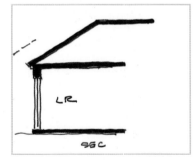

FIGURE 2.1D **Front Elevation, Front Entry.** Showing porch and windows.

FIGURE 2.1E **Section of Front Porch.**

FIGURE 2.1G **Front Elevation, Side Entry.** Showing appearance of the front with entry to the right.

FIGURE 2.1H **House with Side Entry, Section of Front Yard.** Without a front door, the front yard has more space for landscaping.

CASE STUDY 2.1

City Homes of Humbolt Park

Humbolt Park, Chicago, IL
Pappageorge/Haymes, Ltd., Architects

A winning entry to the New Homes for Chicago program sponsored by the city of Chicago, the project's eighteen single-family homes on scattered sites were developed for sale to moderate-income households. The plan provides 1,400 square feet of living space on two levels, with a planned expansion option. Drawing from the character of the surrounding community, four facades were created, offering buyers a choice of appearance and materials.

street view

backyard view

In a small house, efficiency and storage are very important. There should be a generous bedroom closet and adequate space for hanging coats at or near the entry. If possible, guest coats should be separate from those of the residents, possibly on pegs.

Exercises
1. From the base plan, try different bubble diagrams for layouts.
2. Based on a selected diagram, provide a space plan that differs from the prototype.

A Small Home for Two to Four People: Bungalow or Ranch House, One Story (Figures 2.2a–f)

In the early 1900s, brick houses of one to one and a half stories, called **bungalows**, were built in many cities throughout the country. The name *bungalow* comes from *bangla,* or *bangala,* which describes the type of houses in the Indian province of Bengal. The main characteristic of the bungalow is that all the living space is on one level. Sometimes attics and basements were added and later converted to workshops or sleeping spaces. Many bungalows were built in the craftsman style, with stained glass and built-in oak cabinets. Borrowing from the popular Prairie style, they provided a high-quality living space for the middle class for relatively little money. There were thousands of bungalows built in most major cities in the period following World War I, and they are still very popular.

After World War II, another housing boom took place. In the 1950s, houses were trimmed down from the Victorian models. These were sometimes built without basements or attics and became known as **ranch** houses. Perhaps the name was meant to evoke a Western-style single-floor ranch, with wide open spaces around it. In the mass production of post–World War II housing, the quality diminished from that of the earlier bungalows.

Though smaller than the suburban Victorian models, the 800- to 1,000-square-foot footprint was an upgrade from the smaller homes designed for working people in the nineteenth century. After the Depression and World War II, when smaller houses had been built, and the immediate postwar period, there was a second housing boom and

expansion of existing houses. Veterans returned from the war, families were growing at a rapid pace, and extra bedrooms and yard space were needed. Automobiles were also being purchased in record numbers. The two-car garage became a necessity.

There remains to this day a certain utility to this type of house. For one thing, it's all on one level, which makes it comfortable and accessible. It is small enough to remain affordable but large enough to accommodate a family of four, providing two children can sleep in one bedroom, probably in a bunk bed. It is the right size for two adults and one child or an adult parent in the second bedroom.

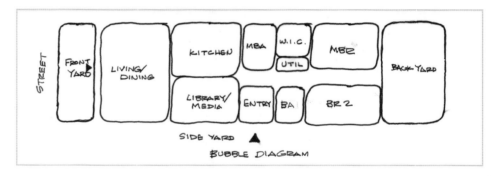

FIGURE 2.2A **Bubble Diagram for Bungalow or Ranch House.** Layout of major spaces, showing alternate entries at front or side (or both).

FIGURE 2.2B **Space/Furniture Plan.**

- Site: 25 feet wide by 125 feet deep
- Footprint/area: 20 feet wide by 50 feet deep; 1,000 square feet
- Single story at or near grade

Client Profile

A young couple, recently married, anticipates having a family. They are currently both working. The husband works as a schoolteacher and the wife is a librarian. They have steady earnings but limited savings, so they need an economical house. At 1,000 square feet, this house can be purchased for between $150,000 and $175,000 in many locations. The couple has saved $25,000 so they can afford a down payment of $15,000 to $20,000 plus moving expenses and furniture. The relatively low mortgage payment will allow them to build equity for a larger house in the future if they wish.

They both like gardening, so the front yard and backyard are important. They only need one car, but a second off-street space for guests would be helpful. Until their first child is born, they will use the second bedroom as a TV room or guest room. They have need for one bathroom, but want to provide space for the addition of a second bathroom later on.

Program

The layout is surprisingly generous for such a small footprint (**Figure 2c–e**). A large living/dining space can be open to the kitchen, creating a great room. There is adequate space for a TV/media room or library adjoining the great room. The entrance can be open or enclosed. There is enough space for a bathroom adjoining the foyer as well as a laundry room in the corridor off the hallway.

The client may enter directly from the front or from a side entry. Parking is from the rear off the alley. Guest parking is on the street in the front. All in all, this house can accommodate a family for a long time. It can be comfortable, though tight, with small children, but could become just the right size for a retired couple when children leave home. And it would be accessible for older people. No new mortgage required!

FIGURE 2.2C **Front Elevation of House at Grade.** Terrace garden at front, patio and yard at rear.

FIGURE 2.2D **Front Elevation of Raised House with Side Entry.** Raised ranch on basement foundation. Alternatively, this could be built on pilotis.

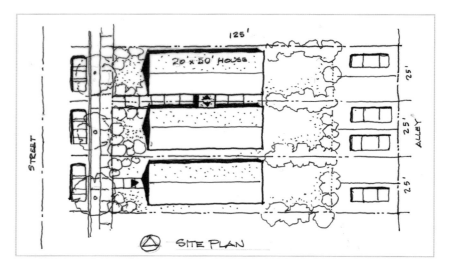

FIGURE 2.2E **Site Plan.** Two entries, small front yard and a large backyard. Two-car parking is at the rear of site and guest parking is at the front.

FIGURE 2.2F **Corner Bungalow On Top of Garage.**

Tips

As an alternate, a raised bungalow can be set on top of a lower or ground-level basement, which could provide increased living space or a shop or home office. Building on **pilotis** instead of a basement foundation would protect the house from flooding. Other advantages might be security and better views.

Exercises

1. Decide on a programmatic use for the basement. Draw a space plan for a possible basement. Show the required stairway.
2. Make a detailed cost estimate for the basement interior improvements. Show linear and square footage of walls, fixtures, finishes.

CASE STUDY 2.2

Lakeside Village Green

Lakeside, Michigan
SMNG-A, Architects

The design of six homes in three duplex structures in Lakeside, Michigan, complements the village character of this small community. The site plan allows for the existing triangular green and 100-year-old trees to be preserved as part of an easement dedicated to perpetual community access area use. The exteriors of the structures emulate late nineteenth- and early twentieth-century houses along Pier Road. Low-scale massing with dormers, front porches, and overhanging eaves contribute to the aesthetic. The interiors are designed as open plan spaces with cathedral ceilings in all bedrooms. Basement levels and garages are out of view at the rear of the structures.

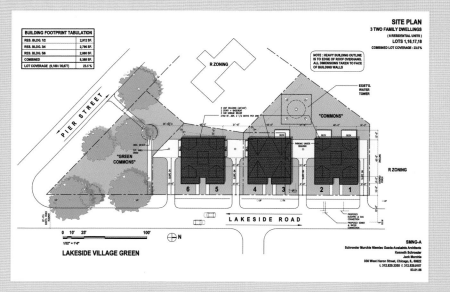

floor plan

facade

site plan

Compact Home for Two to Four People: Two Stories with Garage at Grade (Figures 2.3a–h)

Many communities have a high demand for land. As a result, the sites are smaller, only 80 feet deep, and there are no alleys. Small, two-story homes with attached garages are common in such areas.

In order to accommodate parking without taking up a lot of yard space, the garage can be built at grade level to maintain a compact footprint. One disadvantage of this type of neighborhood is that the curb cuts for the garages take up a large proportion of on-street parking spaces. They also disrupt pedestrian paths. This can be alleviated with pedestrian walkways on the opposite side of the street from the garages.

- Site: 35 feet wide by 80 feet deep. Access is from the street, which is considered the front.
- Footprint: 25 feet by 40 feet (1,000 square feet)
- Two stories
- Total area: 2,000 square feet, including garage

Client Profile

The clients are two people who want to live in a single-family home, but do not have a great need for space. One works at a distance and commutes by car, while the other works in the neighborhood. They are able and willing to use the stairway inside the house.

The clients wish to have the convenience and security of an enclosed garage at grade level, which also could be used as a workshop. There should also be flex space with a bathroom at grade level, which could be used as a home office, guest room, garden room, or an extra bedroom for a returning parent or young adult. The clients fit the profile of what is sometimes known as the sandwich generation, because they are caught between their parents and their children.

Exercises

- Design a corridor on the ground floor that would allow people to pass through the flex space without disturbing the downstairs resident.

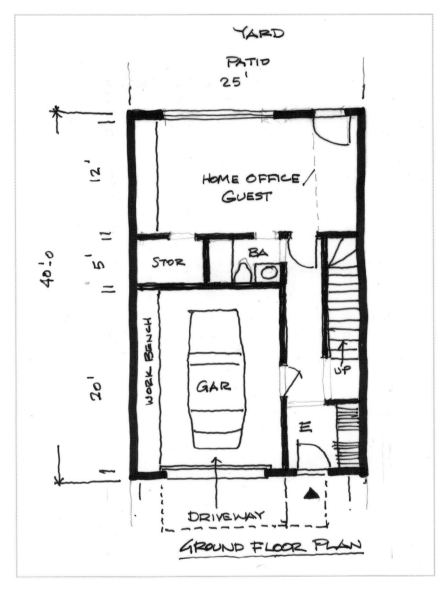

FIGURE 2.3A **Ground Floor Plan for Compact Home.** Ground-floor garage and entry. The garage may double as a shop and there is enough space for a home office in the rear, with an optional bathroom.

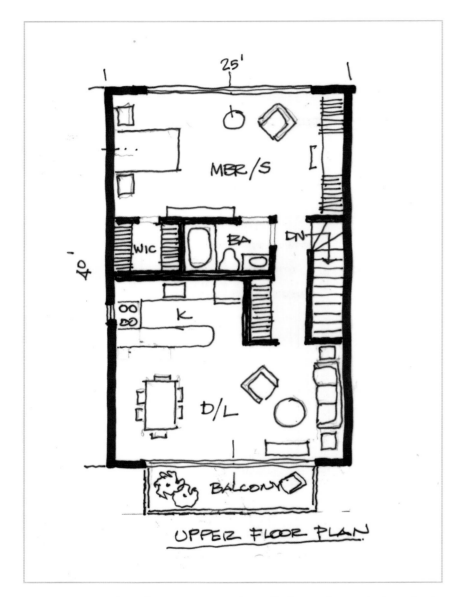

FIGURE 2.3B **Upper Floor Plan.** A great room is located in front and master bedroom/study at rear. At 24 by 12 feet, the bedroom can double as a study or entertainment room. The living/dining space opens to a balcony. An optional third floor can be added, creating a total area of 1,800 square feet.

FIGURE 2.3C **Elevation: Two Stories.** In a two-story house, a balcony can be built adjacent to the living room.

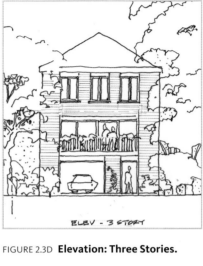

FIGURE 2.3D **Elevation: Three Stories.**

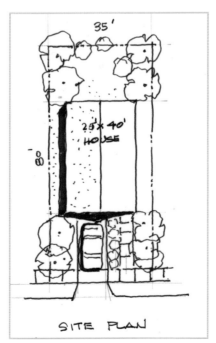

FIGURE 2.3E **Site Plan.** A 5-foot side-yard setback on each side allows 10 feet between houses. There is a 20-foot front yard and a 20-foot backyard.

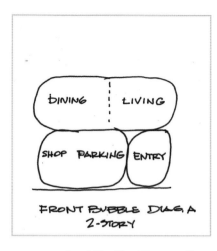

FIGURE 2.3F **Front Stacking Diagram: Two Stories.**

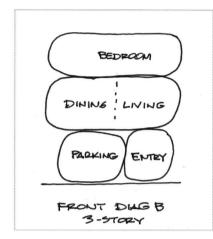

FIGURE 2.3G **Front Stacking Diagram: Three Stories.**

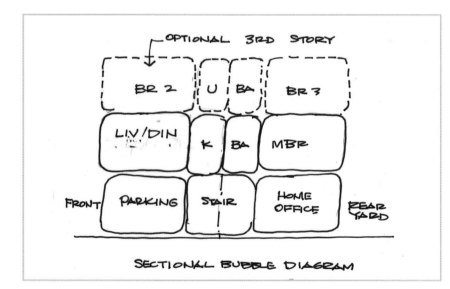

FIGURE 2.3H **Sectional Stacking Diagram.** Sectional cut from front to back shows how the different spaces fit together.

- Place a third story on this house, with two bedrooms and a bath on the third floor.
- Draw alternate elevations, taking the plan and furniture into account.

A Typical Home for a Typical Family (Figures 2.4a–d)

If typical families existed, they would live in typical homes. These homes would be of median size (estimated at 2,200 square feet in 2006). This prototype demonstrates the spaces that can be accommodated within this area and how they can be arranged.

- Site: 75 feet wide by 100 feet deep. Access from the street, considered the front; no alley
- Footprint: 1,100 square feet or 2,200 square feet
- House may be one or two stories
- One story: 60 feet wide by 37 feet deep
- Alternate: two stories (see **Figure 2.4a** for a comparison of alternate footprints)
- Total area: 2,200 square feet, plus garage

Client Profile and Program

The client family can afford a house of median size. In this "typical" family, there are two parents (a man and a woman) and two children (one boy and one girl). The father works as an insurance executive. His wife needs a home office for family activities. The areas of the individual rooms are flexible, as long as the total does not exceed 2,200 square feet. The family wants to create public zones for entertaining away from children and private zones for children's activities. The private zones may also be useful for libraries or small media rooms, which are not accessible to larger crowds.

The program is as follows:

- Living/dining/kitchen: great room
- Small home office adjoining kitchen
- Recreation room, media, or library
- Bedrooms: master bedroom and two smaller bedrooms

CASE STUDY 2.3

Lake Front House

New Buffalo, Michigan
Michael B. Rosen, Architect

The site is long, narrow, and heavily wooded; it is on a bluff overlooking Lake Michigan. The dense thicket of trees on the side towards the road has been retained to provide privacy. Selective tree removal and pruning on the other side allow views of the lake. All rooms are oriented to receive winter sunlight, and all, except for the children's bedrooms, have lake views.

   An entry foyer links a bedroom wing and living wing. The living wing is two stories high with a study on the second floor. The house is built with a combination of conventional and heavy-timber framing. The exterior is sheathed in vertical tongue and groove siding.

corner view

front exterior

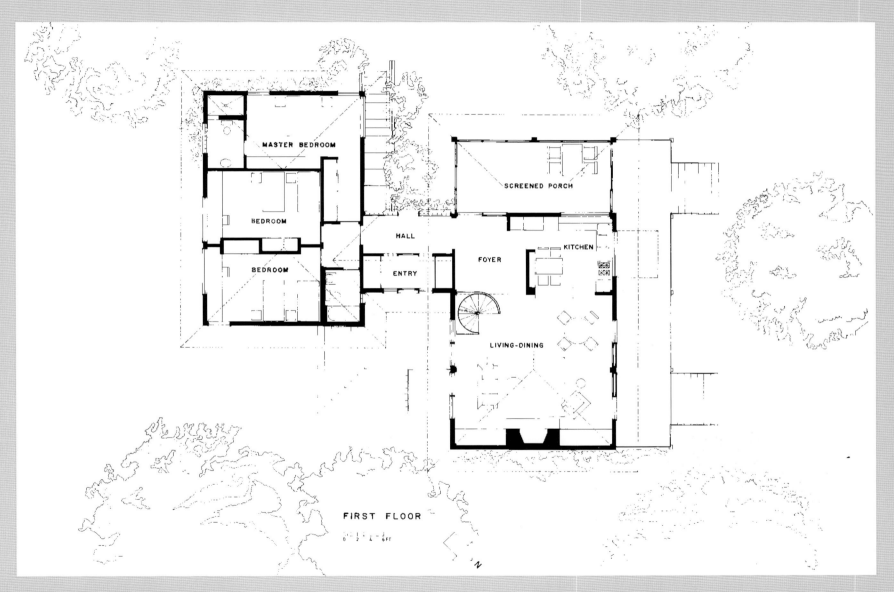

MASTER BEDROOM

BEDROOM

BEDROOM

SCREENED PORCH

HALL

FOYER

KITCHEN

ENTRY

LIVING-DINING

FIRST FLOOR

0 2 4 6FT

floor plan, first floor

continued on the next page

continued from the previous page

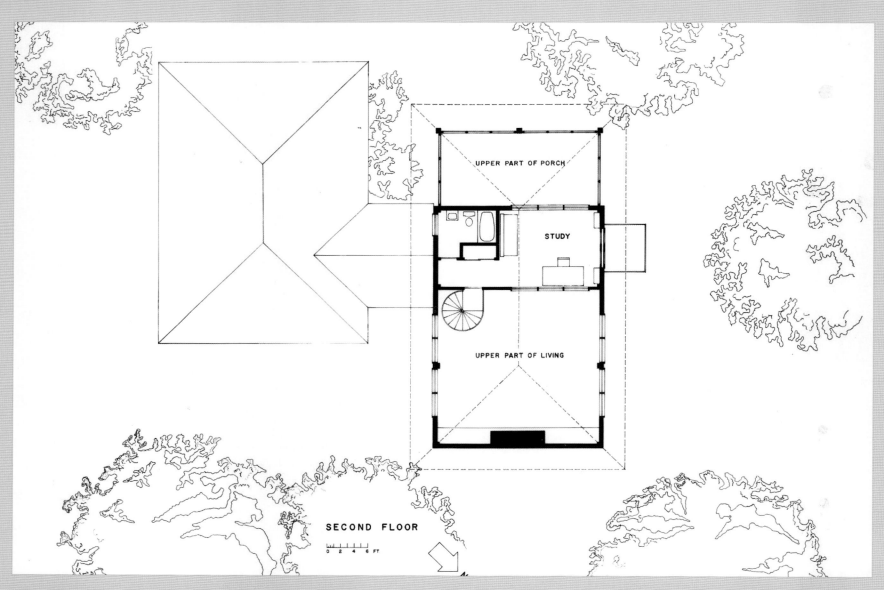

UPPER PART OF PORCH

STUDY

UPPER PART OF LIVING

SECOND FLOOR

0 2 4 6 FT

floor plan, second floor

dining room with deck

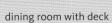

great room

- Bathrooms: master bathroom, bathroom 2, bathroom 3; powder room near the foyer or great room
- Mud room for backyard entry
- Front entry to accommodate guest coats, umbrellas, and wet boots
- Corridors should be efficient and double as display areas for family photos and artwork.
- Two-car garage with workshop space
- Basement optional

Exercises

1. Explore different possibilities for the house footprint. The total area of 2,200 square feet may be on one level or two. The front may be wide or narrow, depending on the site. Try different footprint options to determine the best layout for the program. Choose one.
2. Draw a base plan, showing the exterior outline of the building and the likely entry openings.
3. Draw **zone diagrams** to determine the way public and private spaces can be separated in this house.

A Home for a Blended Family (Figures 2.5a–f)

As pointed out earlier, the definition of a typical family is rapidly changing. Families with a mother, father, and two children now comprise only 10 percent of the U.S. population. More often than not, families who share a home consist of two adults, same sex or not, with two sets of children. These groupings may or may not be compatible. One set of children may be loyal to their own parents and hostile toward the others. New alliances may be formed and gender issues, especially for teenagers, present interesting problems regarding sleeping arrangements. Some families prefer to keep their children apart and visit with each group separately, but there are times when all may be together under one roof.

Even assuming both parents are loving and open to good relationships with all the children, there must be flexibility in residential planning. First, there must be enough space to accommodate all residents comfortably and with a certain amount of privacy. Second, the physical layout of the space should reflect the family history and allow for expres-

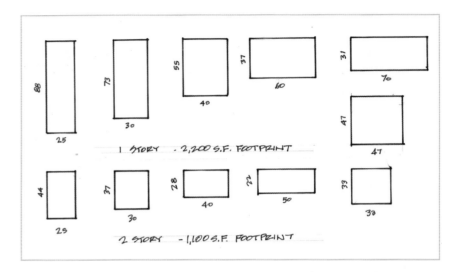

FIGURE 2.4A **Optional Footprints for a 2,200-Square-Foot House.** One- and two-story versions are shown.

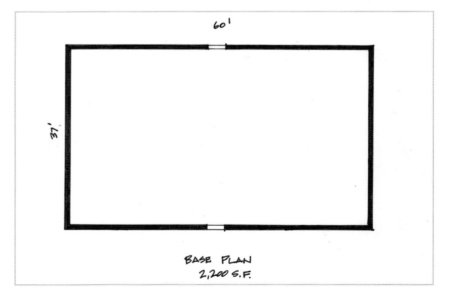

FIGURE 2.4B **Base Plan for a Single-Story House.** Wide-front house, 60 feet wide by 37 feet deep with two entries, one each at center of front and back.

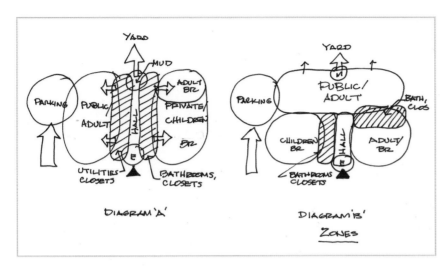

FIGURE 2.4C **Zoning Diagrams.** These diagrams show two different layouts for possible zones in the house.

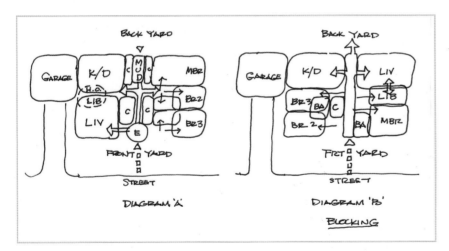

FIGURE 2.4D **Blocking Diagrams.** These two blocking diagrams show how the individual rooms would be located based on the two zoning diagrams.

sions of separation as well as common areas where all may voluntarily come together. There is also the possibility that an elderly parent will join this ménage. Designing this house is a challenge. It will require more space and a larger budget than a conventional house.

Client Profile

The client for this project is a blended family. The parents are both divorced. Each has two children, one boy and one girl, just to make it interesting. They both have shared custody of their children. The child-visit schedules are arranged, but there are many overlapping periods. Each parent is a working professional and earns a substantial income. They each require some private space in the home, whether in a home office, den, library, or recreation area. The objective is to create two separate, private zones for the two sets of children, but with adjoining common areas so that they may come together when they wish. In addition to privacy for the two sets of children, each adult requires a small private space.

It is assumed that each adult needs a car, but they don't want their children to drive on their own, so a two-car garage would be adequate, providing there is some extra space for a shop and garden tools. The children can all walk to school. The local shopping and entertainment district is a short walk as well. There should also be guest parking at the front of the house, with a drop-off point at the door.

The client is open to the idea of either a one-story or two-story home. They have asked the designer to provide two conceptual alternatives so that they can compare the advantages and disadvantages. Sunlight and natural ventilation are very important. The orientation of the house should take this into account. The location is in a northeast climate, so the home should include the benefits of passive solar heating.

- Site: 100 feet wide by 125 feet deep. Alley in back.
- Footprint: one story, 60 feet wide by 80 feet deep
- Footprint: two stories, 50 feet by 50 feet each, approximately 2,500 square feet
- Total area: approximately 5,000 square feet

CASE STUDY 2.4

Kenwood Gateway

Chicago, Illinois
David A. Swan, Architect

This 1990 development grew out of a competition the architectural firm won in 1986, held by the Department of Urban Renewal. The challenge was to design single-family homes or townhouses on a one-acre site in Kenwood, a historic neighborhood in Chicago. The proposal evolved from a rowhouse development to a duplex development and finally a development of fourteen freestanding single-family houses. The original site plan was retained. Adjustments were made to suit the building type. The single-family houses were each 3,000 to 4,000 square feet, with many options offered as upgrades. These options were meant to individualize each unit, using components such as balconies, terraces, bay windows, trellised gables, and masonry banding to create a homogeneous whole while each house was unique. This project shows the importance of maintaining a flexible conceptual design to accommodate a changing housing market.

front landscaping

front facades

rear alley with garages

continued on the next page

continued from the previous page

interior

balcony

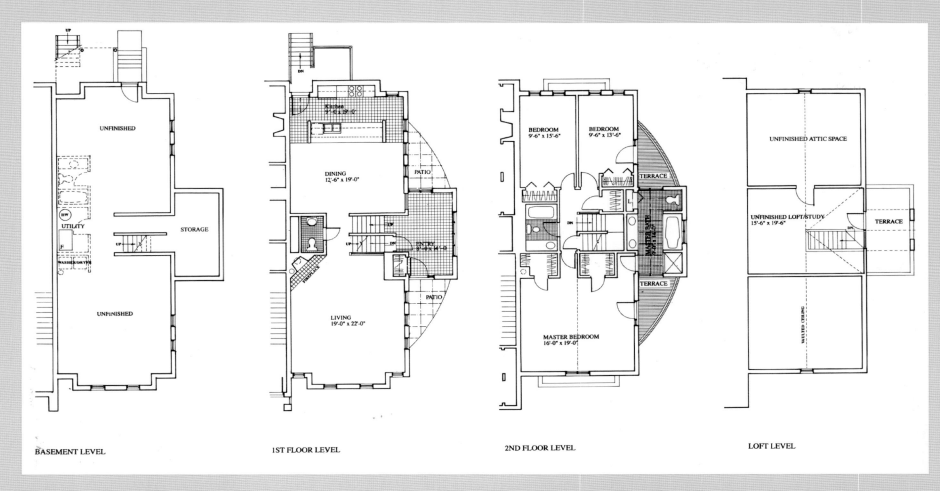

BASEMENT LEVEL

1ST FLOOR LEVEL

2ND FLOOR LEVEL

LOFT LEVEL

floor plan

continued on the next page

continued from the previous page

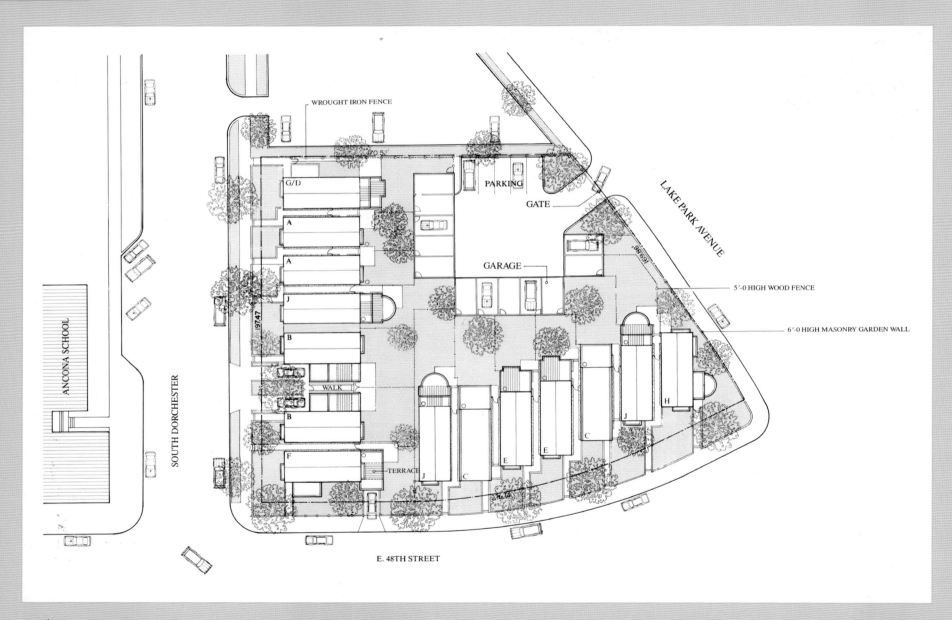

site plan

Program

- Community: suburb, close to the city, or outer area of a city. Medium density, with apartments near the neighborhood center, and single-family houses nearby
- Formal entry hall, with closets and furniture
- Kitchen/dining/living: great room
- Home office
- Media space, set up for projection of movies for four to twenty guests. There should be an equipment room for the media, including controls for stereo speakers placed throughout the house.
- Garden room or screened porch
- Mudroom entry from the backyard
- Bedrooms: master, four children's bedrooms, and one guest room. The guest room may be used for an elderly parent for a period of time and must be accessible.
- Bathrooms: master bath, one full bathroom for each bedroom, and one powder room for the guest room
- Informal entertainment areas for adults and children that could be used for homework as well. These are common areas, meant to promote familial and cooperative projects.
- Three-car garage with shop in one space, at back of site, near alley
- Backyard patio

Exercises

1. Consider various options and sleeping arrangements for this blended family. Should the sleeping rooms be designated by gender rather than original family?
2. Consider shared bathrooms to cut down on the plumbing. Consider a half bath (toilet and sink only). Can bathrooms or showers be shared? Is the latter option possible given the privacy requirements for the two sets of children?
3. Given the base drawings (**Figure 2.5e**), draw a layout of the individual rooms to scale. This is called a **blocking diagram.** An example is given in **Figure 2.5f**.

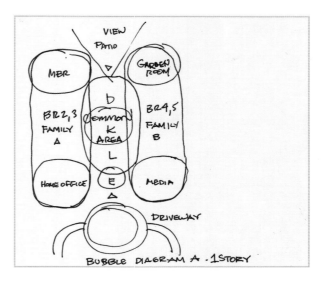

FIGURE 2.5A **Bubble Diagram, Single Story.** Space arrangement with rooms on one level, showing divided zones for two families that live together from time to time.

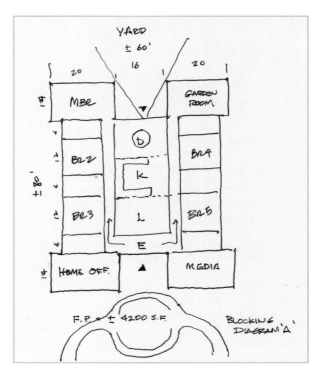

FIGURE 2.5B **Blocking Diagram, Single Story.** This diagram illustrates how different spaces can be arranged within the zones.

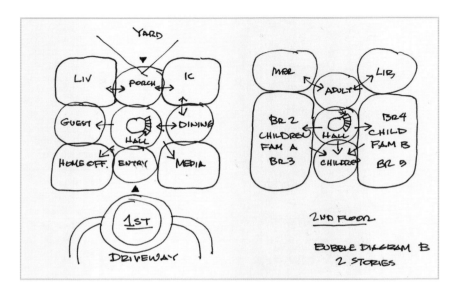

FIGURE 2.5C **Bubble Diagram, Two Stories.** The same program is arranged on two levels. Observe the separation between public and private, adult and child spaces.

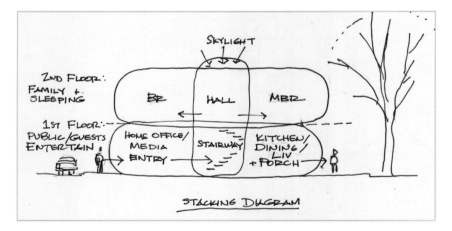

FIGURE 2.5D **Stacking Diagram.** This diagram illustrates vertical arrangement of spaces. Bedrooms and personal family rooms are on the upper level. Public areas, including the kitchen, dining, living, and entertainment spaces are on first, or ground, level. There is also space for a home office, media center, and guest room on the ground level. The vertical stairway presents an opportunity for a grand hallway with spiral stairs, which can be capped with a skylight.

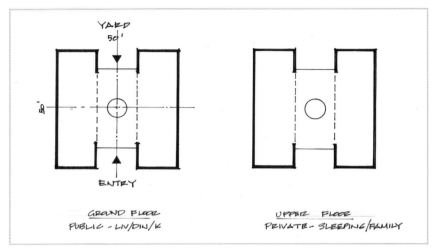

FIGURE 2.5E **Base Plan, Two Stories.** The base plan can be used to determine the best way to achieve a program. Bubble diagrams, blocking diagrams, and floor plans can be traced over base plan.

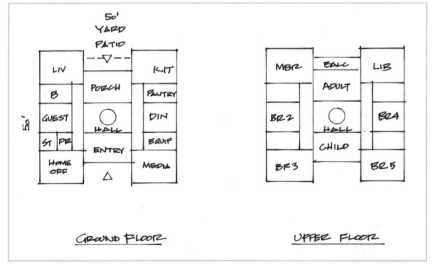

FIGURE 2.5F **Blocking Diagram, Two Stories.** Individual rooms are placed within the zones on each level.

CASE STUDY 2.5

Del Canto House, "A Garden in a House"

Chicago, Illinois
Rodrigo del Canto, Architect

This house was designed to be inhabited by a father of two daughters who live with him part time. They all love to entertain and to cook, but not always at the same time. The building is actually two structures of glass and steel. It was an experiment in simplicity and the challenges that arise when all details are exposed and connections, edges, and corners are open to view. The two buildings are connected by a glass-enclosed stairway and bridges. Together with the house they enclose an open courtyard. A lily pond graces the front entry. In order to avoid birds flying into the glass because of its reflectivity, and to provide softness to the crushed granite courtyard and glass-and-steel entrance, a set of curtains hang 40 feet in the air. The curtains also provide a sense of privacy for the entryway.

front view

entry with stairway

continued on the next page

continued from the previous page

The front building houses a large living room on the first floor, the girls' suites on the second floor, and an entertainment center with its own kitchen and full bathroom on the third floor, as well as a laundry room. A large terrace off the third-floor entertainment area overlooks downtown Chicago and the lakefront. The rear building houses the kitchen and dining room on the first floor, a study at midlevel, and a garage below. The second level has a master suite with a large terrace facing the neighboring garden. It is also accessible from the kitchen/dining area. A guest suite on the third floor has its own terrace.

The metal-grid bridges between the two buildings are a reminder that the connection between father and daughters is like a bridge that overcomes obstacles. But it is also a division between the spaces so that the young women can take their own independent course in life as they mature.

dining room

foyer with interior garden

fireplace detail

closet

bedroom

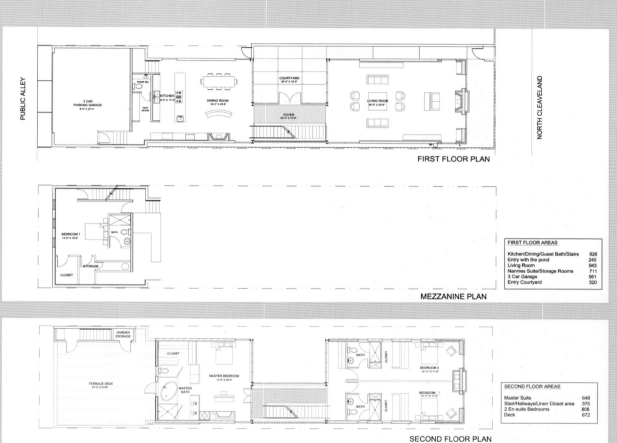

plans

FIRST FLOOR AREAS

Kitchen/Dining/Guest Bath/Stairs	826
Entry with the pond	240
Living Room	943
Nannies Suite/Storage Rooms	711
3 Car Garage	561
Entry Courtyard	320

SECOND FLOOR AREAS

Master Suite	648
Stair/Hallways/Linen Closet area	375
2 En-suite Bedrooms	808
Deck	672

THIRD FLOOR AREAS

Entertainment Room	341
Bar	54
Full Bath	72
Laundry Room	40
Deck	389
Stairs/Hallway	240
Guest Suite	392
Deck	304

continued on the next page

continued from the previous page

roof terrace

atrium

kitchen view

A Wide-Front Expandable One-Bedroom Home (Figures 2.6a–e)

- Site: 100 feet wide by 125 feet deep
- Footprint: 40 feet by 30 feet plus 10-foot terrace expandable to 60 feet wide by 30 feet deep plus terrace. Garage on ground level, living space entirely on upper level.

Client Profile and Program

Two adults would like a detached home on one level, with a single bedroom and a generous bathroom suite. Space should be provided for entertaining and for studies or home offices for both people. It should be a compact house, but with a wide front to take advantage of the wide lot. In the future, the client may want to widen the house for a media room and expanded living space and library, but there are no plans for additional bedrooms. They will occupy the house themselves, with no children and no guests. They simply want the luxury of space. Parking is in a garage below the living space. The remaining basement space will be used as a shop, home office, or garden room, which will also have overhead garage doors for security and a wide opening that may be used for yard parties.

Exercises

1. Draw bubble diagrams to try different space layouts. Consider that the house must be expandable without disruption to the first, basic phase.

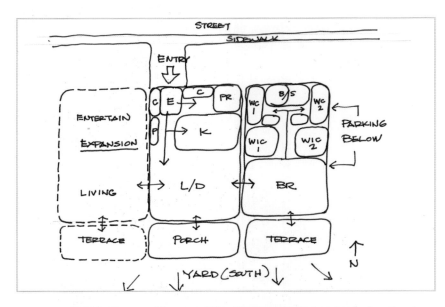

FIGURE 2.6A **Bubble Diagram, House and Site.** This house is designed to be functional as a compact base house, then expanded for a large living/entertainment space in its second phase. The wide front (and rear) afford a panoramic landscape view. Flexible space on the terrace allows open terraces and a screened porch. The overhang to the south prevents sunlight from entering in the summer and allows it to enter in the winter. A garage may be provided in the basement.

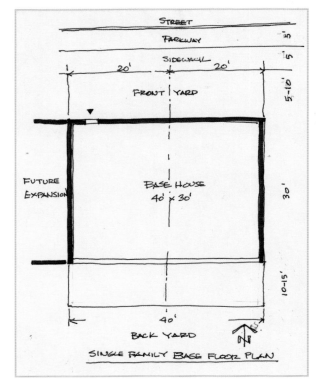

FIGURE 2.6B **Base Compact Floor Plan.** Footprint is 40 feet wide by 30 feet deep and a terrace 10 feet deep.

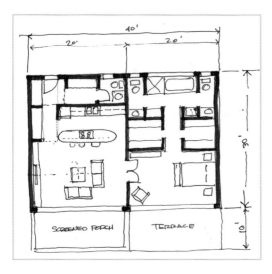

FIGURE 2.6C **Compact Floor Plan, Furniture Layout.** This floor plan includes a wide terrace or porch across the south wall.

2. Draw sections to depict how the garage fits under the house. Consider three possibilities:

  a. There is a sloping site, so the front entry is at grade with the garage in a basement below.

  b. There will be a midlevel stairway, going up half a floor level to enter the house and down a half level to the garage.

  c. The site is flat, with the garage at grade. An enclosed stairway takes you to the front entry of the house at the upper level.

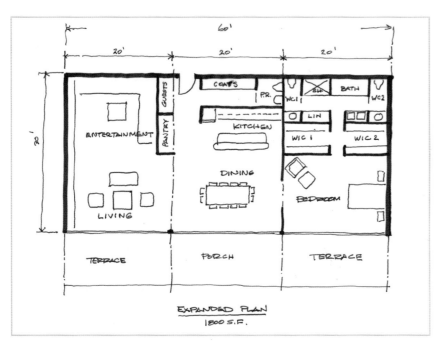

FIGURE 2.6D **Extra-wide Plan.** The footprint for this three-bay version is 60 feet wide by 30 feet deep with a terrace 10 feet deep.

FIGURE 2.6E **Perspective View.** Perspective drawing of the three-bay plan. A screened porch is at the center, with open decks on each side. The house is raised on pilotis.

Collective Housing, or Co-Housing (Figures 2.7a–c)

Collective housing is group housing for independent adults living together. A growing segment of the residential market is choosing collective housing, which is also known as co-housing. A directory of Co-Housing Communities estimates that at least 100,000 people now live this way in the United States. They are called **intentional communities** because people decide to enter into them voluntarily, rather than accidentally.[15] There are indications that people of all ages want the sociability of group living, with a certain amount of privacy. Some of these communities allow children and others do not. They may be composed predominantly of retirees, young and old singles, or a mixture of both.

It is also widely understood that older people don't want to be segregated into old folks' ghettos. They want the stimulation of living among young people. In countries where this type of housing is popular, like Sweden, the older people assist the younger with child care, while the younger population can tackle the physical jobs like gardening or repairs. It is reasonable to expect that this housing choice will gain popularity. The collective housing prototype explores the limitations of public and private space, and the different choices that must be made by the client.

- Site: the building can be situated lengthwise or with the narrow side facing the front on a site if the site is deep enough. Attention should be paid to prevailing breezes and sun direction.
- Footprint: 80 feet by 120 feet

Client Profile

A mixture of clients will occupy this building. They have come together to purchase the land and employ a residential designer. They are single divorced people, widows and widowers, students, young people just starting out, and some married couples. They can choose to buy two units if they wish. They are well-to-do and can afford to hire a cook or have meals brought in from outside. Maintenance is done by a company for the common areas, while individuals are responsible for their own private maintenance. Transportation to the town center is arranged at regular times each day, so there is no need for private automobiles.

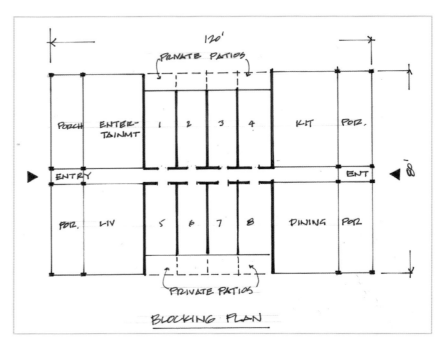

FIGURE 2.7A **Block Plan for a Shared House.** Common rooms are located at the two ends with eight private living/sleeping rooms between them. There is a common kitchen for group meals, but these are usually not mandatory.

Co-housing offers a multitude of ownership possibilities. It can be owned collectively, as in a co-op, or in individual condominium-type units with shared common spaces. There could also be a single owner who rents the units to the others.

Program

This house is designed for a very warm, tropical climate, such as southern Florida. It takes advantage of natural ventilation, using overhangs, sun screens, and solar heating and cooling. Above all, there should be generous screened porches and patios. It is a one-story building and is totally accessible.

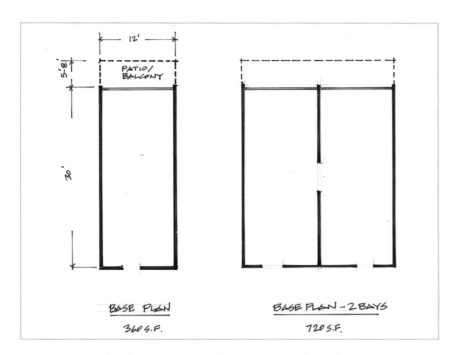

FIGURE 2.7B **Base Plans for Single Living/Sleeping Space and Double Unit.**

- Eight individual private units, each 360 square feet plus private patio. Must provide space for living, sleeping, food preparation, bathroom, and storage closets. There may be individual undercounter washer-dryers in the units.
- Collective kitchen: 960 square feet. Should include some informal sit-down eating space. This room may include a collective laundry. It should be light, airy, and well-ventilated.
- Dining area: 960 square feet. There should be enough room for tables to feed all the residents, but comfortable for a small group of people as well. Light and airy.
- Entertainment room: 960 square feet for media, home theater, and games
- Living/sitting area: 960 square feet for quiet conversations, reading, and guest visitors

Exercises

1. Imagine people of different types and ages living together. What are the advantages? What are the problems and potential conflicts? Design the Client Questionnaire and Interview to determine the best way to anticipate problems of this particular type of client in advance.
2. Sketch different arrangements for the private units. Show the possibility of combining two units for one couple.
3. Draw a furniture layout for the common areas. This can be done by cutting out pieces of colored paper and moving them around. (See Chapter 1 for standard furniture sizes.)

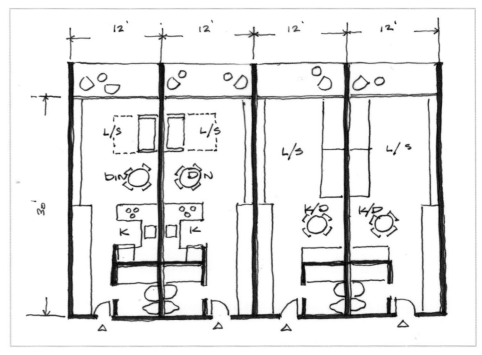

FIGURE 2.7C **Possible Space Plan/Furniture Layout for Living/Sleeping Spaces.** One unit has a larger kitchen for people who like to cook. The other unit has a small built-in kitchen for light cooking, but it has a larger living/sleeping area.

Residence with Business Addition (Figures 2.8a–c)

The term **empty-nester** refers to someone who has raised a family and the children no longer live at home. Many people in this situation choose to modify their existing homes, rather than moving to a new location.

- Site: 250 feet wide by 125 feet deep
- Zoning: mixed residential and business uses are allowed in this zone, providing that the business is screened from the street with landscaping, there is no signage, and off-street parking is provided for the business. Setbacks are the same as for residential requirements: rear yard, 30 feet; side yards, 25 feet; front yard, 20 feet. This leaves a net buildable area of 125 feet by 75 feet for the house and addition.
- Footprint: residence is 60 feet wide by 37 feet deep. Addition will be 30 feet by 60 feet. Two-car garage, 24 feet by 24 feet, is attached and set back on the site so as not to dominate the entry.

Client Profile/Program

This is the same family that lived in the typical three-bedroom house of 2,200 square feet (**see Figures 2.4a–d**), except now they are older and retired. They don't want to leave their home, even though the children have moved away.

They both want to continue working. They have worked for others in the design industry but their dream is to have their own design studio, specializing in residential design and landscaping. This site is ideal for their business.

The challenge of this project is to maintain a residential environment for their living space and a separate environment for their work. The design studio requires 1,800 square feet and a separate driveway and parking. There should be two separate spaces, one for production of drawings and the other for client meetings, and a private office for accounting. There should also be adequate space for document storage and printing capability. A reception area should include a receptionist's desk and the necessary telephone, fax, and intercom capabilities, as well as client seating. An enclosed connection between the two spaces is essential, as this is a northern climate (**see Figure 2.8**).

Planning for the original house is taken into consideration (**see Figure 2.4c,d**). The gallery is connected through the library so that it doesn't interfere with the normal family functions. It is also a nice transition zone from residence to work.

Exercises

1. Consider other footprints and locations for the design studio. The area is still 1,800 square feet, but the length and width may vary. Provide four to five off-street parking spaces.
2. Draw a furniture layout for the new design studio. Provide for computers, drafting tables, document printing, and storage.
3. Reconfigure the interior plan of the residence. Since the children no longer live there, bedrooms may be eliminated or combined. What other uses can be made of these spaces when there are no guests?

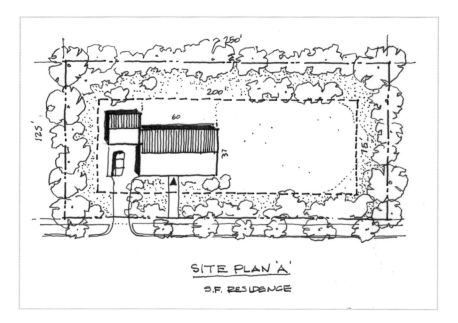

SITE PLAN 'A'

S.F. RESIDENCE

FIGURE 2.8A **Site Plan A.** This 2,200-square-foot single-family residence sits on a large lot, 250 feet wide by 125 feet deep. There is driveway access from a curb cut in front and no alley in the back. There is a large vacant area on the right end of the site.

Tip

Don't forget to negotiate your fees! This goes especially for experimental or unique custom houses. Each student should keep track of the time they spend for each aspect of the project. Ask local designers for rate sheets to get an idea how much professional designers charge for their work. Include costs for overhead, such as rent, utilities, and insurance. Learn to estimate how much each activity will cost. In an exercise, explain your fees to the client and learn to negotiate the amount needed for the project.

Chapter Summary

This chapter provided a background in the design of single detached homes. The history of this type of home, what it means to people, and the

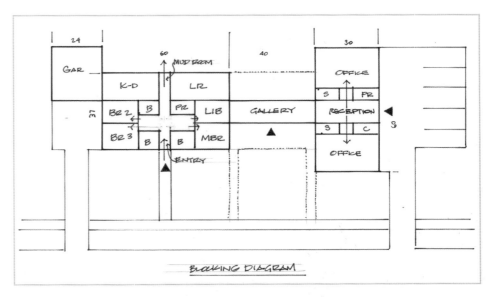

FIGURE 2.8C **Blocking Diagram.** Using the blocking diagram, show how the house layout ties in with the office. There is a library in the house, which serves as an anteroom to the gallery that connects to the office space. This gallery provides separation between the residential and business functions. A new curb cut and driveway is required for the office function to protect the privacy of the residents. Family kitchen, dining, and living spaces are located across the rear of house, oriented toward the private yard.

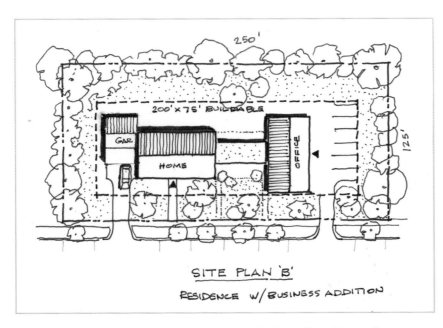

FIGURE 2.8B **Site Plan B.** The home is expanded to include an office addition. There is an enclosed hallway connecting the house to the office. Off-street parking is provided for the office building.

different types of clientele as well as house types was followed by prototypes for student research and design work and actual case studies.

It is projected that after exposure to the single detached home as a type and exploring different prototypes for different client types, students will be better equipped to enter the field of residential design. The principles applied to this type of home design are useful in the other housing types as well. As we will see in the following chapters, the designers of multiunit buildings often attempt to use single detached home iconography to personalize their buildings.

CASE STUDY 2.6

Icosahedron House on the Indiana Dunes

Beverly Shores, Indiana
Robert P. Gordon, Architect
Ron Gordon Photography

This addition leaves the original house undisturbed while guests, or perhaps a business, use the addition. The owners had an old cottage that had been built by hand on the site many decades earlier. The site has a magnificent view of Lake Michigan. The owners needed more space for guests, but did not want to change the site. Due to the steeply sloped lot and lack of an access road, it would have been very expensive to bring equipment up the hill. So the architect designed a system of prefabricated triangles that could be bolted together to form an icosahedron.

This shape allowed for a high ceiling volume and abundant triangular windows for viewing Lake Michigan. The volume of the icosahedron, which was about 20 feet high, made it possible to add sleeping lofts in the upper area. The triangles were erected in a shop and hauled up the side of the hill with a pulley. They were erected by hand on the site. The foundation is on piers, which minimized excavation and hauling of concrete. The remaining materials were similarly pulled up the side of the hill. The exterior finish is natural cedar shakes, which blend with the wooded site.

exterior view with surrounding balcony

exterior view

interior

continued on the next page

continued from the previous page

detail

rendering

KEY TERMS

Area: Total area of the house, including all stories

Blended families: A term that refers to composite families, made up of untraditional elements. For example, two divorced people with children marry, and their house has to accommodate all family members at one time or another.

Blocking diagram: Layout of individual rooms within the given base plan. Not a final detailed plan, but one that helps to estimate the amount of space needed for each room and the circulation patterns.

Bungalow: Single-family low-profile house with all the living space on one level. Sometimes a basement and attic are added. Named for *bangla*, or *bangala*, a type of houses in the Indian province of Bengal.

Co-housing: A housing collective; where independent adults agree to live together because they prefer living in a group rather than in individual homes. They share certain daily activities, such as shopping and cooking. The owners can also play an active part in planning and developing the community.

Empty-nesters: People who have raised a family, their children have moved away, and they now can live more comfortably.

Footprint: The area of the house at grade level on the site

Intentional communities: Groups of people living together who share common values. Sometimes they own property, sometimes they rent.

Net buildable area: Legal area for building after taking required setbacks into account.

Ranch house: Similar to the bungalow, except built later, in the 1950s; generally lacked the quality and craftsmanship of the earlier bungalows.

Sprawl: Excessive homebuilding beyond reasonable commuting distance; requires substantial road building and infrastructure. Long commutes require wasteful use of gasoline and so sprawl is associated with the destruction of the environment and diminishing viable farmland.

CASE STUDY 2.7

"House in a Garden"

Kenwood, Chicago
Robert P. Gordon, Architect
Ron Gordon Photography

This house was designed for an "empty nester" couple who had moved from Texas to Chicago and wanted a garden environment surrounding their house, with a deck on the south face. They also wanted to celebrate their new lifestyle with a large common space for kitchen, dining, and entertaining. However, it was also important to remain independent, so they wanted two separate studies. The architect proposed arranging the studies around a two-story open atrium to take advantage of the south orientation and flood all interior spaces with light. The sounds of birds and trees from the garden fills the house, despite the proximity to the bustling Hyde Park neighborhood.

exterior

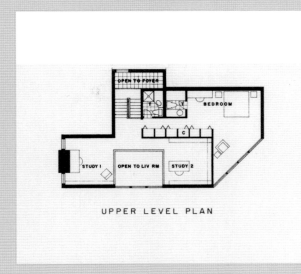

UPPER LEVEL PLAN

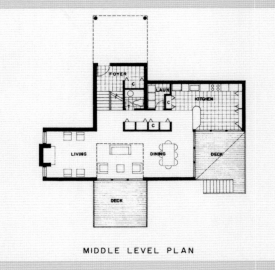

MIDDLE LEVEL PLAN

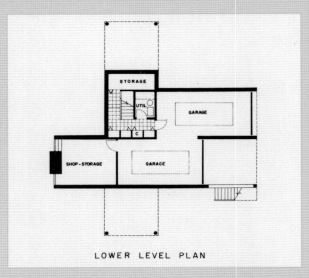

LOWER LEVEL PLAN

floorplan

continued on the next page

continued from the previous page

interior

Zone diagrams: Similar to bubble diagrams, they describe the different zones in a house, such as public/private, adult/child, entertaining/sleeping. These zones are drawn without breaking them down into individual rooms, which permits a quick exploration of layout possibilities.

ENDNOTES

1. U.S. Census Bureau, American FactFinder, *2006 American Community Survey:Units in Structure—Universe: Housing Units.*

2. John McIlwain and Melissa Floca, *Multifamily Trends* (Washington DC: Urban Land Institute, 2006).

3. Gwendolyn Wright, *Building the Dream* (Cambridge: MIT Press, 1981), xviii.

4. U.S. Census Bureau, American FactFinder.

5. Wright, *Building the Dream.*

6. Gwendolyn Wright, *Moralism and the Model Home* (Chicago: The University of Chicago Press, 1980).

7. Frank Lloyd Wright, *The Natural House* (New York: Bramhall House, 1954), 81–91.

8. John Norquist, *The Wealth of Cities* (New York: Basic Books, 1998), 105.

9. Ibid., 107

10. Jane Holtz Kay, *Asphalt Nation* (New York: Random House, 1997).

11. Andres Duany, Elizabeth Plater-Zyberk, and Jeff Speck, *Suburban Nation: The Rise of Sprawl and the Decline of the American Dream* (New York: North Point Press, 2000), 7–8.

12. Ibid.

13. Kermit Baker, "Architecture Firms Design a Quarter of Single-Family Homes," *AIArchitect*, September 2001.

14. The Fellowship for Intentional Community, a Missouri-based non-profit organization. *Directory of Intentional Communities.* As cited in an article by Martha Irvine in the *Chicago Tribune* Home section, August 10, 2008.

15. Wid Chapman and Jeffrey P. Rosenfeld, *Home Design in an Aging World* (New York: Fairchild, 2008), 44.

CHAPTER 3

Attached Townhouses

Chapter Purpose

This chapter discusses the development of the attached townhouse. We begin with the history and background of this type of structure and investigate its advantages and disadvantages. A variety of site plans are provided as well as a discussion of how the site plan affects interior planning. The location of the staircase is key to the entire layout of a townhouse, including the circulation around it. Narrow spaces are characteristic of townhouses, and they provide a number of challenges to the designer, such as how to get the most out of a narrow space that only has windows on the shorter wall. Other concerns include the organization of public versus private spaces within a residence (usually on different levels) and accessibility for individuals of varying ages and physical abilities. A number of different prototypes for townhouses are provided as well as case studies of successful townhouse projects.

History and Background

Townhouses have their antecedents in the crowded, narrow streets that sprung up in the factory towns of England during the Industrial Revolution. In some cities they are called **rowhouses**, specifically indicating that they are attached to each other. They were designed to be practical and economical. They housed workers and their families in dense, often overcrowded conditions near their factory jobs. A vivid description of life in these homes in 1937 England is described in George Orwell's *The Road to Wigan Pier*.[1] The very narrow houses, usually rented to workers, were constructed in long, unbroken sections, several hundred feet long. They were built back to back, with a front house and rear house. All toilet facilities were common and located at the rear of the houses. This meant that residents of the front houses were required to walk 600 feet to the toilet and then wait in queues in the cold, damp mud. It is no surprise that the later variations, with single houses, front and back doors, and private gardens, were greatly appreciated. For some, the prospect of home ownership allowed them a greater economic position in society.

Charles Dickens described early houses in *Hard Times*, weaving them into his tales of life in nineteenth-century Coketown: "There are houses on each side, both of which you can touch with the fingertips of each hand by stretching out your arms to their full extent."[2] They were not intended to impress people, or even to be comfortable, but they were practical and cheap.

Townhouses were built in great numbers in London, Dublin, New York, Boston, Philadelphia, Baltimore, Chicago, and other rapidly industrializing cities. They are urban houses, usually located in or near the center of the city. They were originally small, sharing common **party walls**, and were therefore cheaper to build. With a minimum of exterior walls, townhouses are also more economical to heat, remodel, and maintain.

Despite their humble beginnings, townhouses have survived and evolved to become a highly desirable and valuable dwelling type in the modern city. Many old examples still exist and have been remodeled. New versions have been built in virtually all cities and suburbs. Even the small ones, if well located, command handsome prices, sometimes millions of dollars.

The attached townhouse provides the privacy and independence of a detached house combined with the economy of shared walls and denser sites. For some, it is an ideal urban housing type.

Characteristics and Features of Townhouses

Typically, townhouses are quite narrow. They range from 14 to 22 feet in width and share common walls with their neighbors. A major advantage of townhouses is that they are "through" units, with front and back exposure. This creates ample cross-ventilation and the availability of a private backyard and individual front door for each unit. The unit owners can have private parking spaces located conveniently nearby or even within the home. Most townhouses don't require elevators, although these can be included in the plan for residents who are unable to climb stairs.

Another important characteristic of the townhouse is the inclusion of an internal private staircase. Dickens describes a "mysterious" staircase in *Hard Times*, where life revolved around Mrs. Sparsit's staircase:

> She erected in her mind a mighty Staircase, . . . The figure descended the great stairs, steadily . . . she maintained her catlike observation . . . through everything animate and inanimate that at any time went near her stairs.[3]

In order to have a private house on a narrow lot an owner must accept using a staircase for daily activities. The manner in which the designer solves the staircase issue is a significant factor in the overall design of the house. There are many advantages to private stairways:

• They are for the exclusive use of the owner.

- They can be places to change the level from which you view the surroundings and other people. This can be important if the views from the lower floors are blocked, so an additional floor can be added for view.
- If the walls of the stairway are solid, they can be used to display artwork and family photos. Or they can be open and light, conveying a more informal atmosphere.
- If the public rooms of the house, including kitchen, dining room and living room are on the main floor and the bedrooms are above, the staircase is a natural divider. Guests have access to the main floor while the upper floor is used for more private and intimate activities for the family, such as sleeping, bathing, and quiet activities.
- There is a feeling of security that comes with sleeping above the ground floor. At least intruders would have to work their way up the stairway.

There are also some disadvantages that must be taken into account in the design of townhouses:

- They are inaccessible to people who are unable to climb stairs. A separate space must be maintained on the ground floor for independent living.
- They use a lot of space. A typical, compact stairway takes a minimum of about 40 square feet per floor, plus the hallway. When these dimensions are combined for three floors, the total square footage is enough for another room.
- There is constant "up and down." If you forget your wallet upstairs, or if there is no powder room on the main floor, you can get a workout.
- They can be noisy, especially if they are open.

The mystery and mastery of the staircase must have been considerable to residents in the early days of these multistory private homes.

Levels and Zones in Townhouse Planning

Since different activities may naturally occur on different levels, it is useful to describe these levels in detail. Public areas in a home are used for guests, entertainment, and extended family gatherings. These usually take place in the kitchen, dining, and living spaces on the **main level** of the house. The **upper level** generally contains the private or intimate functions of the house, such as private bedrooms, dressing rooms, and bathroom spaces. All family members need privacy and this is where they find it. The **grade level**, or **basement** if one exists, can be described as a service area. Utility rooms for mechanical equipment, a shop, a home office, a recreation room for children, and even a parking space can occur at this grade level.

The **main level** contains the kitchen, living, and dining areas. It can be located above the basement or garage level or at grade. Children can be upstairs sleeping while a party is going on at the main level. To maintain accessibility, a powder room is necessary on this level. A main level at grade can be especially useful for accessibility or as living space for people who are unable to climb stairs.

The **upper level** contains bedrooms, bathrooms, studies, and the like. There may be more than one upper level in a unit. One bedroom may face the front while another faces the rear. A unit with three stories can accommodate two additional bedrooms. A linen closet and laundry/utility room are very important, and should be placed near the bedrooms and closets. This is to avoid the prospect of carrying laundry throughout the house, or "invading" the public areas. A laundry room can be a little noisy and might interfere with an evening of entertainment on the main floor, so its placement must be confirmed by the client.

The **grade level** is located at or near grade or the sidewalk. This level, often referred to as the basement or English basement, sometimes includes a workshop or a guest room. A garage may also be designed for the grade level, but can be disruptive to the streetscape and pedestrian way. It also may not be allowed in certain zones. Otherwise, as we will see in some of the prototypes, a midlevel entry with a porch can encourage streetscape sociability and allow a basement level below.

The Impact of Site Planning on Interior Architecture

The big picture of the site plan directly affects the smaller picture of the individual townhouse. A look at the site plans (**see Figures 3.1a–d**) clarifies the reasons for the layout of the townhouse. Also, the narrower the unit, the less amount of streetscape is required, including sidewalks, sewers, utilities, landscaping, and road. This contributes to the economy of this type of house. For example, a 20-foot-wide house would require only half as much landscaping, curbwork, sidewalks and streets as a house that is 40 feet wide with the same gross area. Although a ground-level garage at the front is possible, a driveway creates an obstacle for pedestrians and takes up parking spaces on the street. A rear alley for parking and service might be a better option. The choice of site plans directly affects the interior layout.

Site Plans

Historical/Traditional (Site Plan 3.1a)

The earliest attached houses in North America were built in Philadelphia, Boston, New York, and Baltimore in the eighteenth and nineteenth centuries. These narrow lots were also not very deep. The lots were laid out without alleys, so that all services and egress was from the front. Parking was not yet a problem. Figure 3.1a shows a version of a historical block with an internal courtyard. Corner lots allow for wide houses with generous front exposure. Entry is always from the front, with private gardens in the rear.

The site plan is an important determining factor of the interior layout. For example, since the front is the public side of the house, the informal rooms are oriented toward the rear. Breakfast areas, dining rooms, kitchens, and the master bedroom normally face the backyard.

Townhouses with Rear Alleys (Site Plan 3.1b)

As development moved westward, more land was available, so lots became somewhat deeper. They usually included an alley at the back for services and, later on, for parking. This type of site has proven to be very practical in many cities. There are two entries to this type of home. The family probably parks in the rear garage or parking space, so there is a need for a rear entrance, perhaps with a **mudroom**. This is a good place to hang coats and store garden tools. The front entry is more formal. Visitors and pedestrians enter from the front, so it should be neater and less cluttered.

Front porch entries are traditional in some cities. These usually occur in houses with basements, so the main level of the house is about 4 to 5 feet above grade. While porch entries are preferred by many home owners, there are advantages to grade-level entry. You don't have to shovel snow on the sometimes perilous entry stairway, for example.

Chicago loves its alleys and is currently updating them with permeable paving in order to conserve water. The water drains through the joints and into the sand, then the soil, instead of being directed to sewers and eventually flooding basements or being wasted.

Parking Courts (Site Plan 3.1c)

More recently, parking courts have been devised so that people can park near or under their homes. This allows for a pedestrian, landscaped environment in the front where the formal front entry is located. A rear door, alongside the parking court, can also be used by guests who arrive by car and use the owner's guest parking space. A townhouse built on a lot with a parking court often contains a grade-level garage as well. Since this is not the main pedestrian walkway, placement of the garage doesn't interfere with the normal flow of pedestrians.

The Commons (Site Plan 3.1d)

In areas of high density, where private parking is either unnecessary or is provided nearby but off-site, a common yard space can be provided behind the houses, adjoining the private yards. This shared yard is often referred to as a *commons,* which allows for informal socializing as well as supervised play areas for children. The landscaping for this common area can be maintained by an association of homeowners. The advantage is a very lush landscaped area that does not require private maintenance. It also provides a very pleasant back-door entry to the house for yard parties

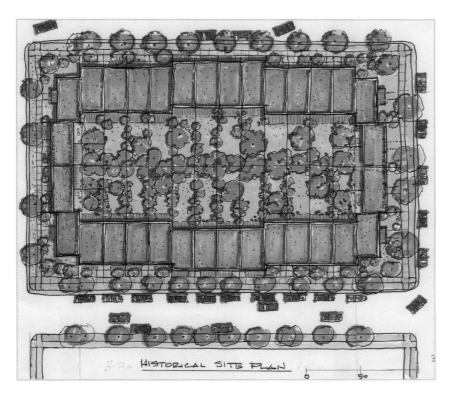

FIGURE 3.1A **Historical Site Plan.** This site plan shows an enclosed block.

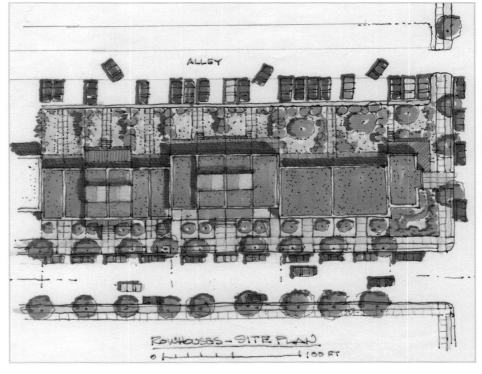

FIGURE 3.1B **Site Plan.** A conventional street with alley, parking behind.

and neighborly visits. Each homeowner still has a private yard, which may be fenced, in case they don't want to partake in the communal activity.

All four types of sites—traditional, rear alley, parking court, and commons—have advantages and disadvantages. Certain clients prefer one type to the others and this will affect the interior layout. It is up to the architect or designer to explain the options to the client.

Townhouse dwellers live closer together than residents of single-family detached homes, but they have more privacy than apartment dwellers (see Chapter 8). Though residents give up a certain amount of privacy and independence due to the narrow lots and having to share common walls

and sometimes common grounds, they do retain some of the benefits of a single-family residence, such as private yards, individual doors, and private stairways. It has been said that townhouses are a perfect balance between the advantages and disadvantages of houses and apartments.

Townhouse Prototypes
Sixteen-Foot-Wide Units

The narrow sixteen foot-wide townhouse (**Figure 3.2a**) has proven very practical for balancing economic construction costs and efficient interior planning.

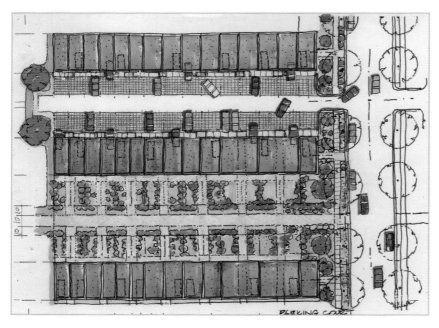

FIGURE 3.1C **Site Plan.** Off-street pedestrian entries with parking court behind

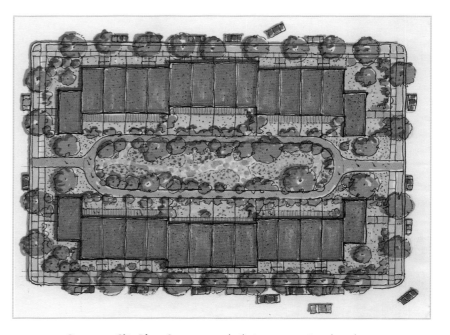

FIGURE 3.1D **Commons Site Plan.** Common yards that are open at each end

FIGURE 3.1E **Elevations for Prototypes.**

*Basic Two-Story, Two-Bedroom Townhouse with Grade-Level
Entry (Figures 3.2a–d)*

Client Profile

A family of four members desires a modest-cost unit with no basement. The structure will have two stories with the main floor at grade level. They like to garden, so easy access to the patio or yard is important. Parking is at the rear of the site.

Exercises

1. Create a space plan on the base plan.
2. Make a furniture layout from the space plan.

*"Raised" Two-Story Townhouse with Basement and
Porch (Figures 3.3a–c)*

Raising the house one story above grade leaves space for a shop or storage at grade level.

Client Profile

Two to four people: a single adult with a single child, or two adults with two children who share one bedroom. A basement is desirable for storage and an additional recreation space or workshop. A front porch is also desired as an entry and sitting area to provide sociability with neighbors. The garage may be at the rear of the site.

Exercises

1. Create a space plan on the base plan.
2. Try several different entry-plan possibilities, showing a closet and seating.
3. Distinguish between front and rear entries.

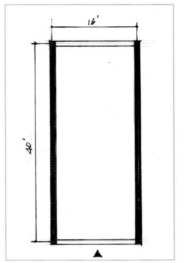

FIGURES 3.2A **Base Plan for Basic 16-foot-wide Two-Bedroom Rowhouse.** This is the simplest and most economical rowhouse form.

FIGURES 3.2B **Elevation for Basic 16-foot-wide Two-Bedroom Rowhouse.**

FIGURES 3.2C **Section of Basic 16-foot-wide Two-Bedroom Rowhouse.**

CASE STUDY 3.1

Fulton Grove Townhouses

San Francisco, California
Solomon E.T.C., Architects

Fulton Grove is a new take on the historic lanes of San Francisco. The townhouses are separate from but connected to the streets. Sixteen small three-story townhouses, each with its own entry, garage, and rear garden, face each other along a tree-lined private drive. Access at both ends is through large openings in new buildings that span the lane. The townhouses are sunlit, modern versions of a traditional San Francisco residential style. Each unit has a projecting bay along the drive.

Specifications

NUMBER OF UNITS: 22

PARCEL SIZE: .50 acres

UNIT CONFIGURATION: two-bedroom townhouses, one-bedroom flats

PARKING RATIO AND TYPE: 1:1 covered, four guest spaces at surface

ACCESS TO UNITS: at grade, stair walkup

SQUARE FOOTAGE: 30,080 gross square feet

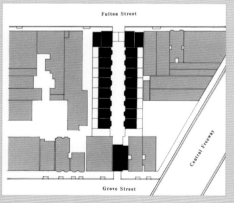

site plan

aerial view

entry

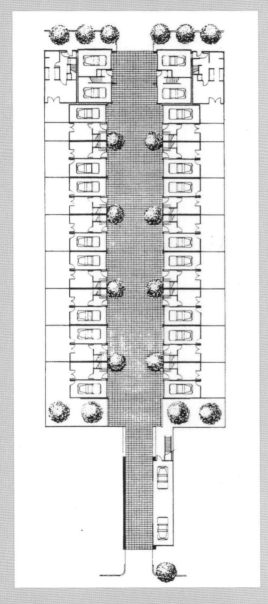

first floor

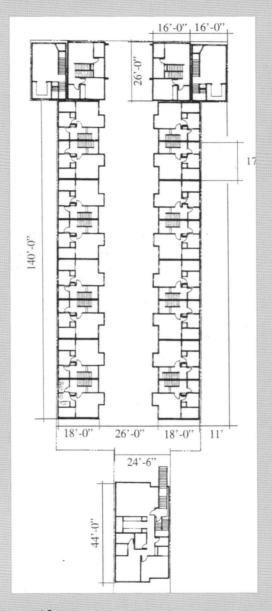

second floor

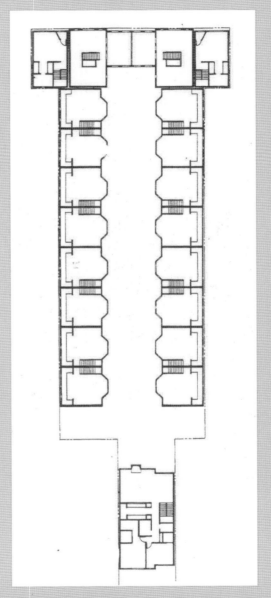

third floor

continued on the next page

continued from the previous page

courtyard

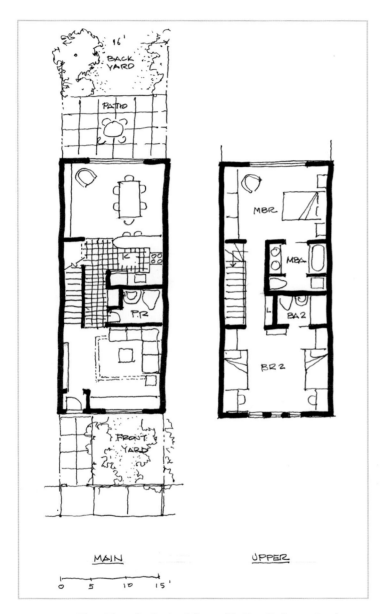

MAIN   UPPER

0   5   10   15'

FIGURES 3.2D **Floor Plans for Basic 16-foot-wide Two-Bedroom Rowhouse.** Space is made for an entry as well as a kitchen and bathroom, and living, dining, and sleeping spaces. The first floor is at grade level.

FIGURES 3.3A **Elevation for Basic Rowhouse with Basement.** The entry is about a half level above grade. Accessibility is an issue for this type of house.

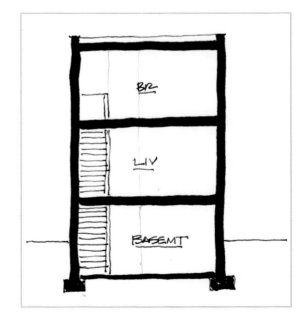

FIGURES 3.3B **Section for Basic Rowhouse with Basement.**

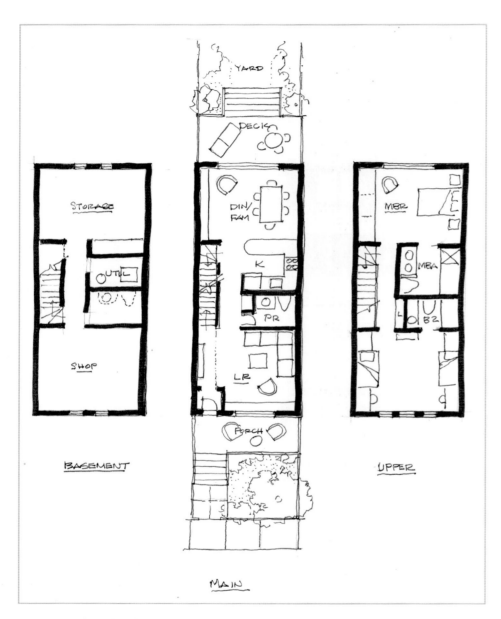

FIGURES 3.3C **Floor Plans for Basic Rowhouse with Basement.** Layouts show entry at the porch, the basement, and the upper floor.

Townhouse with Garage at Grade Level Within Unit (Figures 3.4a–d)
Similar to the unit described above, this raised house allows for grade-level use, in this case a garage.

Client Profile
The client lives in a very cold climate, with lots of snow, and hates the winter. The goal is to minimize discomfort. The client wants to park within the house in a heated garage. The driveway will also be heated to

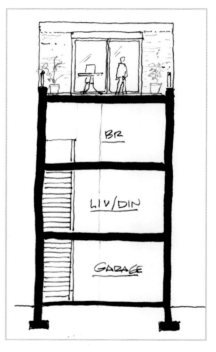

FIGURE 3.4A **Elevation for Rowhouse with Garage at Grade Level Within Unit.** Same as the basic unit in Figure 3.3, but raised above grade to make space for garage and a family room. This provides good security because living levels are above grade. The grade level can be closed and secured.

FIGURE 3.4B **Section for Rowhouse with Garage at Grade Level Within Unit.**

CASE STUDY 3.2

The Willows

Chicago, Illinois
David A. Swan, Architect

This development was sponsored by the City of Chicago Department of Urban Renewal in 1976. At two acres, it was one of the largest vacant sites in the luxurious Lincoln Park neighborhood. The concept was to surround a private park with 32 townhouses. This was achieved through the design of two different floor plans, a corner unit and an inside unit.

AREA: 88,500 square feet

private courtyard

continued on the next page

continued from the previous page

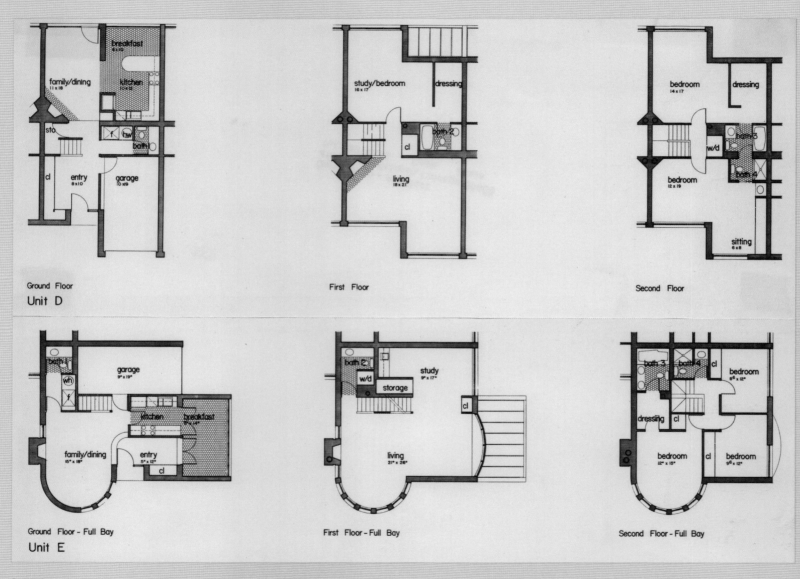

Ground Floor
Unit D

First Floor

Second Floor

Ground Floor – Full Bay
Unit E

First Floor – Full Bay

Second Floor – Full Bay

floor plans

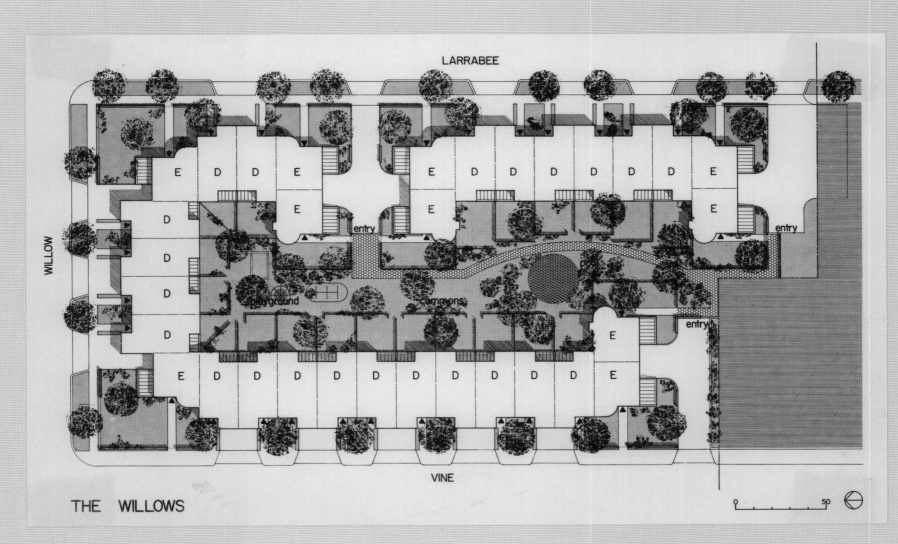

LARRABEE

WILLOW

VINE

THE WILLOWS

0 · · · · · 50

site plan

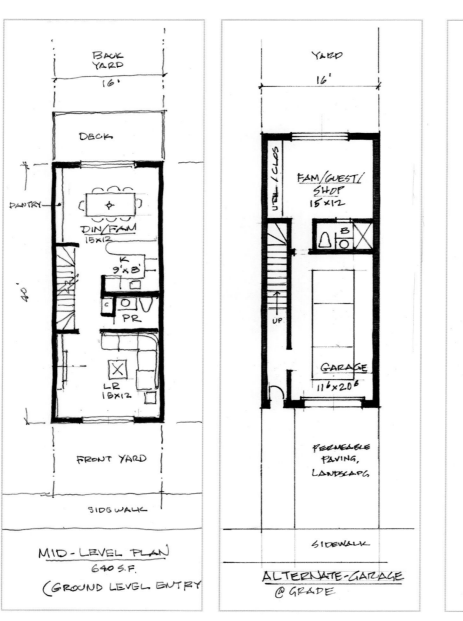

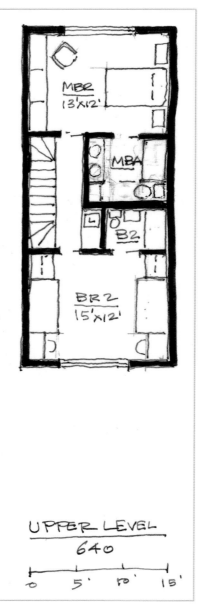

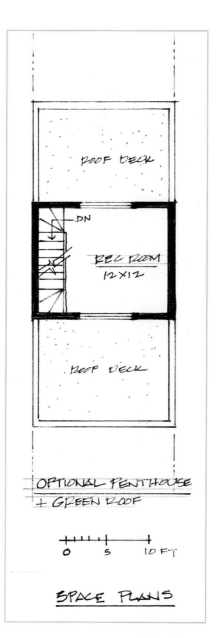

FIGURE 3.4C **Floor Plans for Rowhouse with Garage at Grade Level Within Unit, Mid Level.**

FIGURE 3.4D **Floor Plans for Rowhouse with Garage at Grade Level Within Unit, Upper Level.**

CASE STUDY 3.3

Egandale

Chicago, Illinois
David A. Swan, Architect

Egandale is a lowrise housing development of 50 townhouses situated in the northwest corner of the University of Chicago community of Hyde Park. It is situated on a site of two and one-half acres, previously owned by the Chicago Osteopathic Hospital. It is surrounded by high-density six-unit apartment buildings on all sides but one. The site was long and narrow, a typical Chicago street. The site planning approach was to provide an alley down the middle of the site for servicing, and build housing along the two principal streets. There are ten different unit types for this development. A flexible base plan was developed for the whole building. The final mix was determined by sales. Most of the units were designed with bays to play off the bays of the surrounding six units. This allowed the development to blend in nicely with its neighbors.

street view

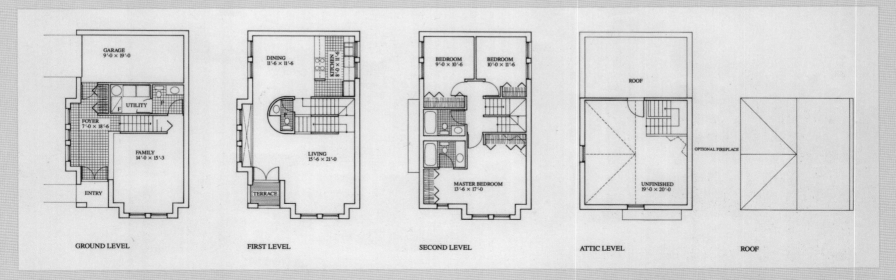

floor plan

Embassy Club

Chicago, Illinois
Pappageorge/Haymes Ltd., Architects

The almost eight-acre site of a former factory was transformed into an exclusive neighborhood of 96 townhouses, 37 single-family residences, and 77 condominiums. Contextual characteristics of adjacent townhouses, single-family homes, and the existing three-story loft building on the site suggested building type locations and the site-planning strategy. Three access points were created to organize the site and each resulting interior street was given a unique character. A tree-lined boulevard, a promenade of rowhouses terminating in a court, and a gateway offer the opportunity for distinctive environments. Twelve different unit configurations, landscaping, and building exteriors are molded to respond to these site-planning concepts and result in a controlled yet uniquely lively series of spaces.

entry with individual garages

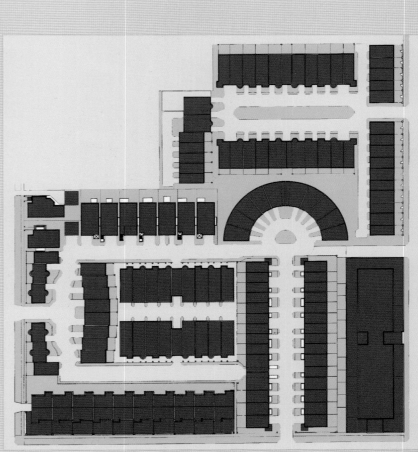

above: site plan

left: front driveway

continued on the next page

continued from the previous page

yard view

curved buildings

terrace entry

front driveway

melt fallen snow. This way, the client could go to a downtown activity that has a parking garage and not even have to take a coat! (Better have one in the trunk for emergencies, though.)

Exercises
1. Create space plan on base plan.
2. Show different uses for grade level space adjacent to the garage. Explore uses of space when car is not parked.

Duplex Townhouse with Independent Unit at Grade (Figures 3.5a–e)
An up-down duplex townhouse allows for an accessible grade unit, with a family unit above.

FIGURE 3.5A **Elevation for Duplex with Independent Unit at Grade.** The independent unit could be used by a family member, or a separate person. Located at grade level, it is 100% accessible.

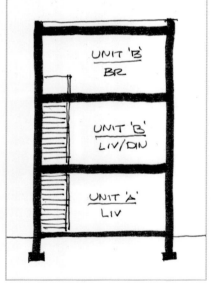

FIGURE 3.5B **Section for Duplex with Independent Unit at Grade.**

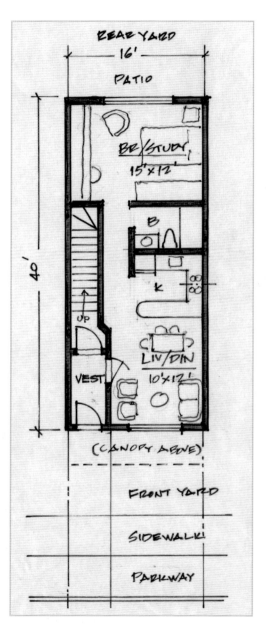

FIGURE 3.5C **Floor Plan for Independent Unit at Grade.**

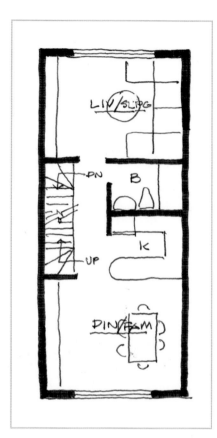

FIGURE 3.5D **Floor Plan, Duplex, Main Floor of Top Unit.** The upper unit is two stories and could accommodate a large family. The corridor/stairway could be used for discreet monitoring of a resident on the lower level.

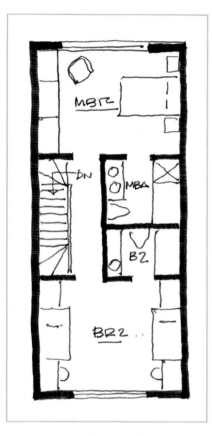

FIGURE 3.5E **Floor Plan, Duplex, Upper Floor of Top Unit.**

Client Profile

A single family member, possibly an older child, adult brother or sister, or a parent, moves back home to live with a family of two to four members. The single member lives at grade level and wants to maintain independence. The grade-level space requires a kitchen and bathroom. This arrangement works for all parties, as the adults in the main part of the house would prefer not to cook or shop—or clean!— for the downstairs resident.

Exercises

1. Create an alternate space plan for the upper level duplex (Figure 3.5e).
2. Make a furniture layout from the space plan.

Twenty-Foot-Wide Units

Basic Two-Story Townhouse with Three Bedrooms (Figures 3.6b–f)

The wider 20-foot townhouse allows greater flexibility for interior space planning.

Client Profile

The clients, two people, have four children, perhaps from two different families. The children require two bedrooms and a bathroom separate from the adults. The three bedrooms must be on the same floor for economy and efficiency, and because the clients like it that way. They also don't want to climb another set of stairs to a third floor. A washer and dryer are required on the bedroom floor.

The 20-foot width permits two bedrooms on one side, at 9 feet by 12 feet each. It also provides a more generous space at grade level for the living and dining rooms. A powder room is required on the main floor, for the clients' convenience as well as for guests.

CASE STUDY 3.5

Willow Court

Chicago, Illinois
Pappageorge/Haymes Ltd., Architects

A railroad switching yard in the heart of Chicago's Bucktown neighborhood was converted into an elegant, modernist townhome complex. The site design staggers the homes, minimizing the impact and creating landscaped courtyards with gateways to the homes behind. Large black steel cantilevered bays provide expansive views and light. Two colors of brick emphasize the design forms and massing. Each of the 56 units is capped with a penthouse terrace featuring spectacular views of the city. The site features a difficult challenge with a 20-foot rise from one end to the other created by the abutment of an infrequently used railroad line. This grade change was retained and the existing retaining wall was used on the front edge of the site with an entry paved in brick and landscaped to soften the environment.

corner view

penthouse view

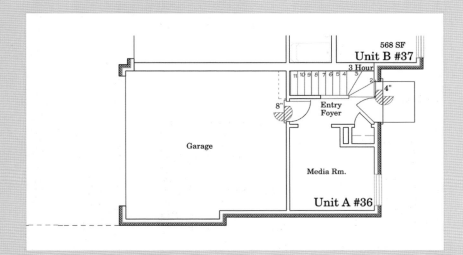

first floor

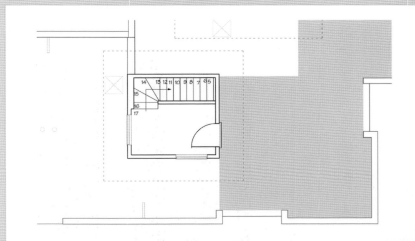

penthouse plan

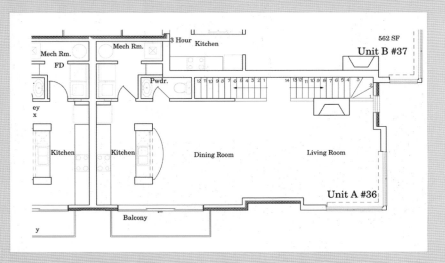

second floor

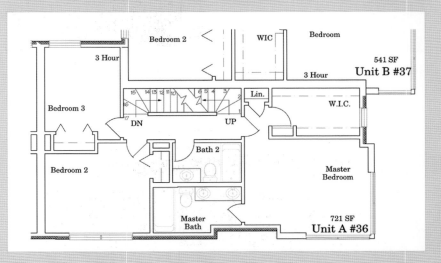

third floor

continued on the next page

continued from the previous page

parking court

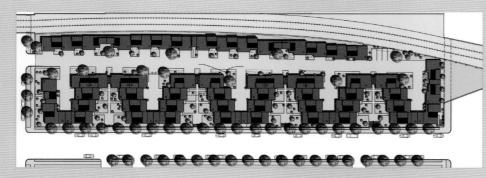

site plan

windows

interior

dining room

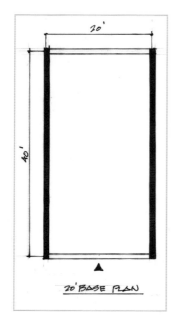

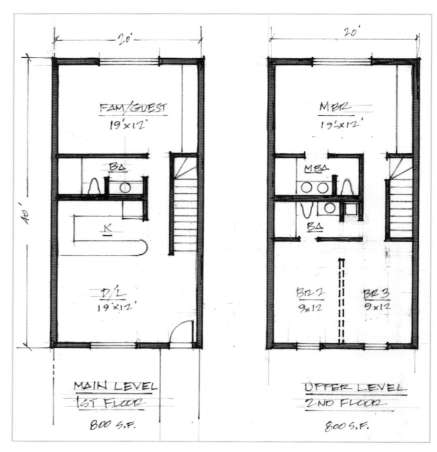

FIGURE 3.6A **Base Plan for Basic 20-foot Townhouse with Three Bedrooms.** This wider unit allows for two small bedrooms across the front or rear. The configuration of three bedrooms at one level is convenient and economical.

FIGURE 3.6B **Elevation for 20-foot Townhouse with Three Bedrooms.**

FIGURE 3.6D **Floor Plans for 20-foot Townhouse with Three Bedrooms.**

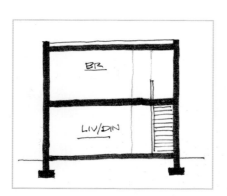

FIGURE 3.6C **Section of 20-foot Townhouse with Three Bedrooms.**

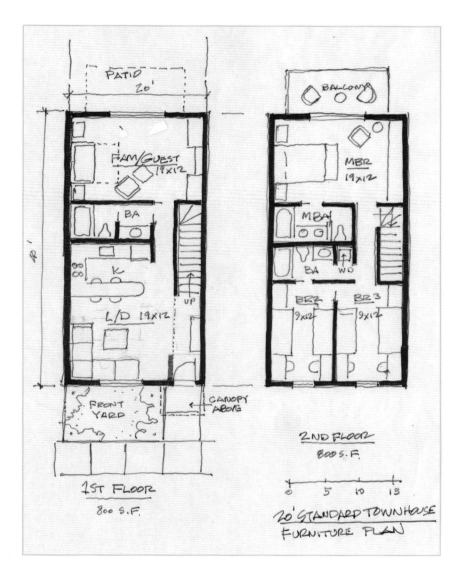

FIGURE 3.6E **Furniture plan.**

Exercises
1. Draw several different bubble diagrams for this 20-foot wide house. How is it different from the previous 16-foot wide house?
2. Create a space plan based on the given base plan.
3. Make a furniture layout for the space plan.

Open Plan (Loft) (Figures 3.7a–c)
A townhouse with an open plan allows complete flexibility for interior space use.

Client Profile
This townhouse is designed for two artists. They use the ground floor as a studio and sometimes as a sales space. Since they work in various media, complete flexibility is needed for walls and space layouts. They also constantly change their living arrangements. The sleeping area can be found in any location in the unit. The living and dining spaces also shift frequently. It is very important to these two artists that there is natural light and ventilation in the kitchen and bathroom.

FIGURES 3.7A **Elevation for Open Plan Unit.**
This unit type allows flexible planning and use. Ideal for clients with changing needs. With few interior partitions, the space appears larger, much like a loft.

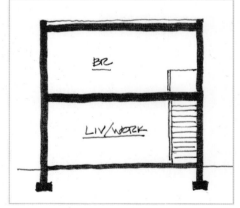

FIGURES 3.7B **Section for Open Plan Unit.**

CASE STUDY 3.6

53rd Street and University Avenue

Chicago, Illinois
David A. Swan, Architect

In the heart of the University of Chicago community, and during a housing recession, the architect, who was also the developer, took the risk of designing luxurious wide-front townhouses. The zoning would have allowed eight units, but the architect chose to build four. Each floor is set back with a terrace and curving trellises facing the south. An abundant landscape is integrated into the residences for a true indoor-outdoor experience. The materials included Endicott brick with curved steel pipes supporting sets of hemlock louvers on the terraced side. A central stairway rises through a two-story space in the living room, filling the house with light and views to the yard at all levels.

deck detail

site plan

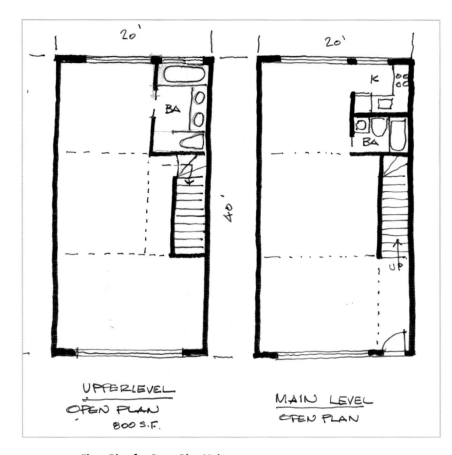

FIGURES 3.7C **Floor Plan for Open Plan Unit.**

The ground floor level must have the appearance of a retail space for their business, both from the inside and out. (For more on mixed-use buildings see Chapter 9.)

Exercises
1. Draw a number of bubble diagrams showing different work arrangements and living spaces.
2. Create several space plans on the given base plan, based on the bubble diagrams.

Double Duplex, Two to Four Independent Units (Figures 3.8a–e)

This is a very flexible prototype. It allows for different combinations of tenancy and ownership. It can be ideal for multigenerational families.

Client Profile

An older family member with disabilities lives with a family of two to four additional members. The generation in the middle must care for their parents as well as their children. The older member(s) cannot climb stairs and must live at grade level and want to maintain their independence. This requires a separate kitchen and bathroom with a walk-in shower. The family living in the main part of the house also wants to maintain a high degree of privacy for all family members. A development made up of this type of unit provides benefits for the so-called caretaking generation.[4] In general, half of the units are accessible, those at grade level and the unit

FIGURE 3.8A **Elevation for Double Duplex.** Essentially, this is a fourplex apartment in the form of a double rowhouse. Each unit can be used privately or shared with a family member who values privacy and wishes to remain independent. Doubling up the units allows for shared use of the entry vestibule and leaves more space for the living/dining space. This housing type might be especially useful for a large extended family.

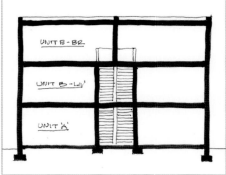

FIGURE 3.8B **Section for Double Duplex.**

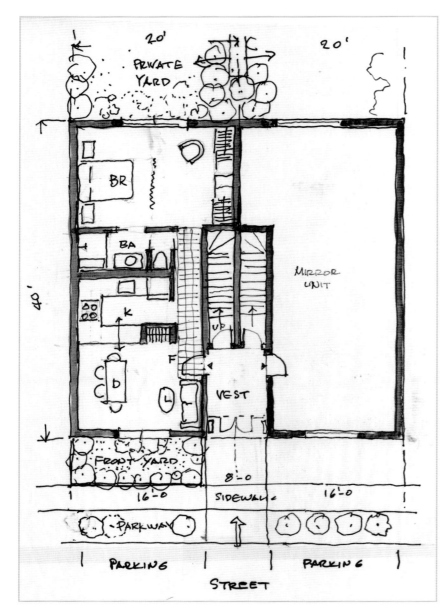

FIGURE 3.8C **Floor and Landscape Plans for Double Duplex.** With front and rear yards, all rooms give on to gardens.

FIGURE 3.8D **Plans for Level Two of Double Duplex.**

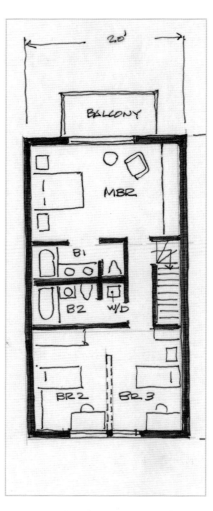

FIGURE 3.8E **Plans for Level Three of Double Duplex.**

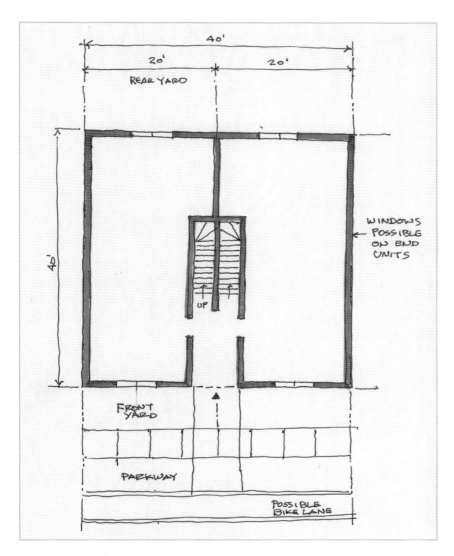

FIGURE 3.8F **Base plan.**

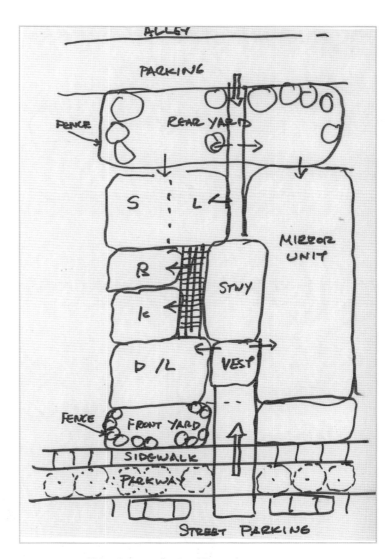

FIGURE 3.8G **Bubble Diagrams for Double Duplex.**

above. Doubling up the duplex for a total of four units provides a possible source of rental income for the owner.

Exercises
1. Create a space plan on the 20-foot basic base plan (**Figure 3.6a**).
2. Make a furniture layout using the space plan.

End Units
End Unit on a Corner Lot (Figures 3.9a–f)
This unit type is ideal for people who want a townhouse but with three sides exposed rather than just two. It allows for generous side entries and larger garden space.

Client Profile
The client family likes the townhouse prototype for the purpose of economy and perhaps a little more security than a single-family house

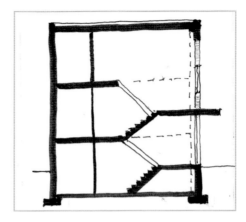

FIGURE 3.9C **Section.**

provides. They require a lot of light, so they opt for an **end unit**. This gives them three faces of exposure: front, rear, and side. They are avid gardeners and want to see trees, shrubs, and flowers from all the rooms in their home. They also want to walk directly from their living and family rooms onto a garden or patio. In addition, they prefer a generous private entry and the side facade can serve this purpose. They don't own a car, so yard space can be maximized. A **permeable** parking pad may be reserved for guests at the rear of the lot, near the alley. Using permeable materials allows the parking pad to appear as an element in the landscape when it is not used for parking.

Exercises
1. Create a space plan based on the given base plan. Include location of the windows.
2. Make a furniture layout from the space plan. Try a diagonal furniture layout to make use of the corner window in **Figure 3.8b**.

Side Entry at Mid-Level (Figures 3.10a–e)
This corner unit shows how to maximize yard space on the adjoining open space. Because it's located on the corner, the wide edge of the townhouse can serve as a grand front facade and entry.

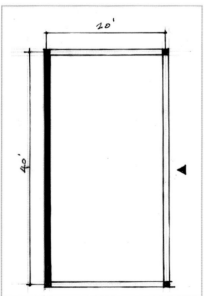

FIGURE 3.9A **Base Plan for End Unit.**

FIGURE 3.9B **Elevation.**

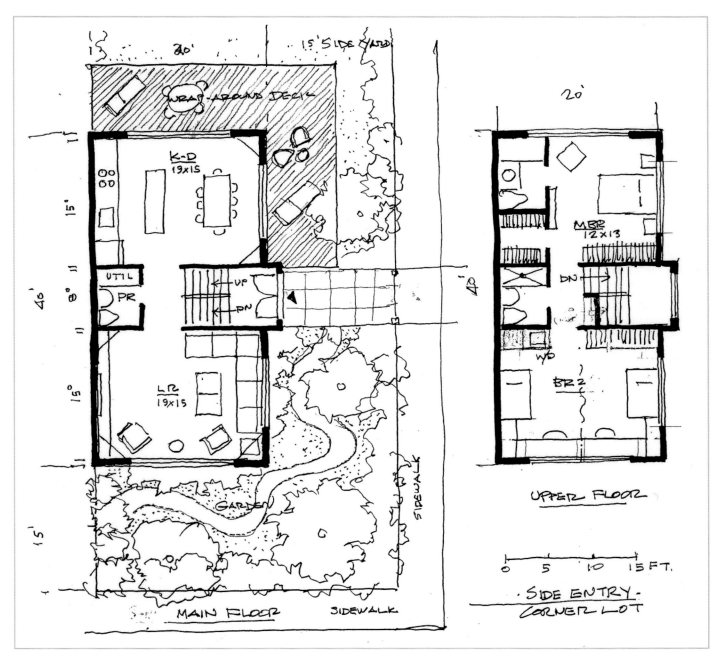

20'
15' SIDE YARD

WRAP-AROUND DECK

K-D
19x15

15'

UTIL

PR

UP

DN

LR
19x15

GARDEN

SIDEWALK

MAIN FLOOR   SIDEWALK

20'

MBR
12x13

DN

W/D

BR 2

UPPER FLOOR

0   5   10   15 FT.

·SIDE ENTRY·
CORNER LOT

FIGURE 3.9D **Floor plans.**

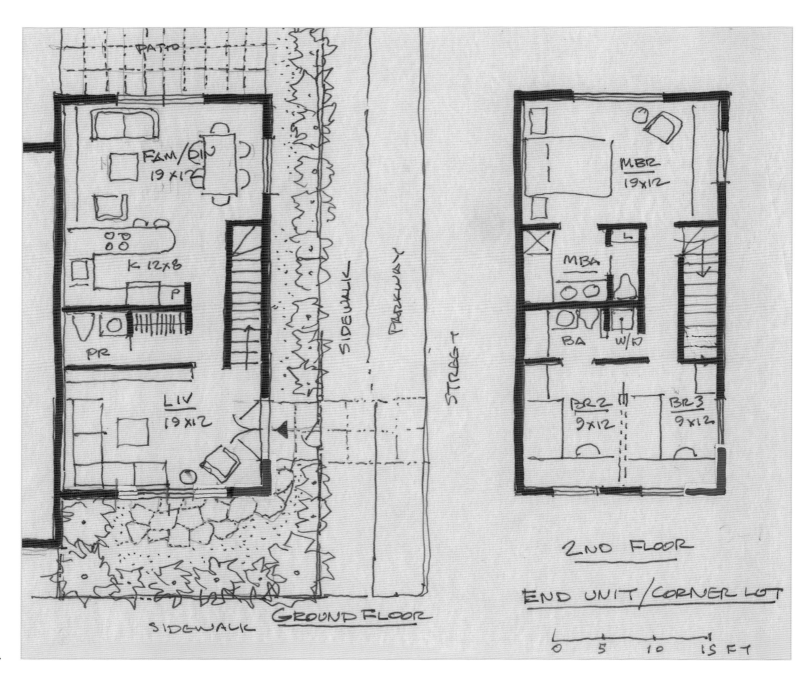

FIGURE 3.9E **Alternate
Floor Plans for End Unit.**

CASE STUDY 3.7

Rue de Chandon Housing Development

Paris, France
Jean-Paul Viguier, S.A. d'Architecture

This private housing development, built in 2007, is located in the Barbusse-Chandon sector in the north of Paris. The project utilized the existing street grid and fit into the height context of adjoining buildings on the street. The buildings are comprised of stacked units, so they connect the garden units to the higher units. The four- to seven-story buildings are linked by a road that runs alongside a garden, allowing for a radial link between the so-called green corridor, a pedestrian walkway that circulates through the development, and the Boulevard Claude Debussy.

front view

staggered balconies

continued on the next page

continued from the previous page

The townhouses have access to roof terraces that can be used as additional private garden spaces by residents. The buildings are set back from the edge of Avenue Chandon, allowing for garden spaces on the ground floor. The housing is organized around a large common park that is shared with the office building directly opposite. The landscaped garden space and the distance between the buildings allow for enjoyment of views, while maintaining privacy at the same time. The design of the facades allows for the double height spaces to be seen from the park and the street, while the glazed vertical circulation creates transparent views through the buildings to the garden spaces within.

Specifications

NUMBER OF UNITS: 121 dwelling units

AREA: 31,069 square feet

yard view

balcony screens

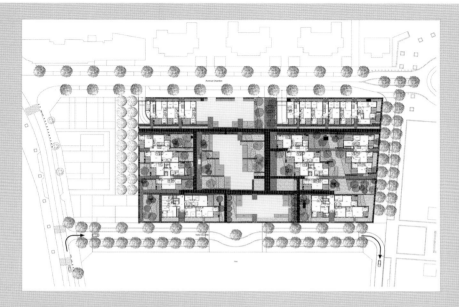

grade floor plan

streetscape

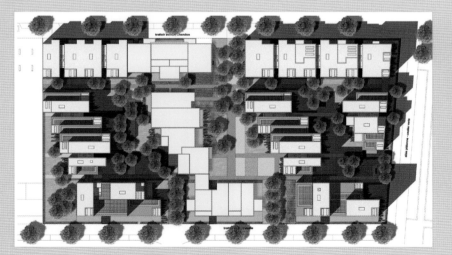

site plan

balcony

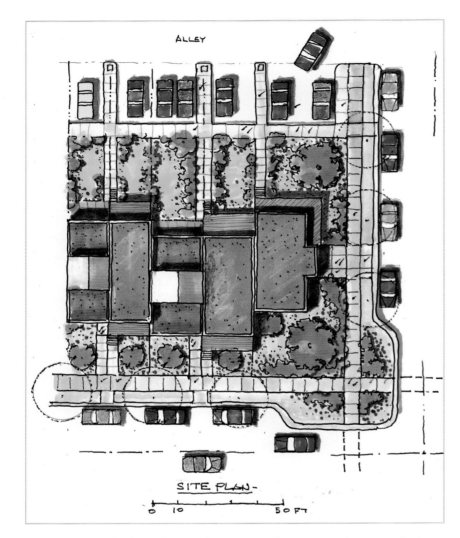

FIGURE 3.10B **Elevation for End Unit with Basement.**

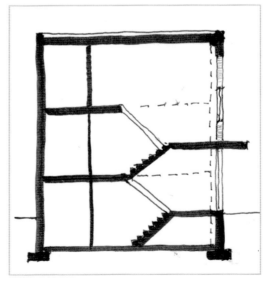

FIGURE 3.10C **Section for End Unit with Basement.**

FIGURE 3.10A **Site Plan for End Unit with Basement.** This prototype shows an end unit with central doorway and the entry at grade level. The main level is a half level up and the basement is a half level down. The second floor can be accessed without passing through living spaces.

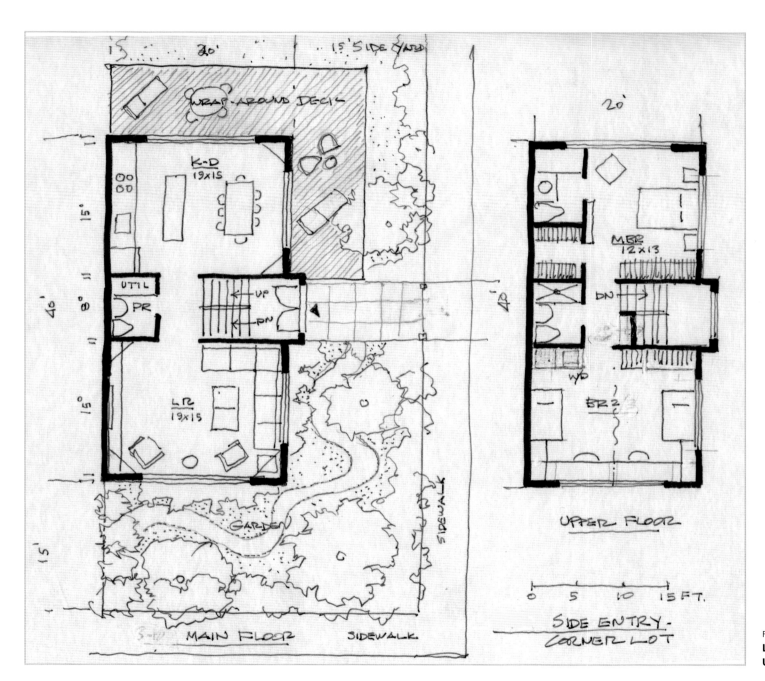

20'   15' SIDE YARD

WRAP-AROUND DECK

K-D
19x15

15'

UTIL

40'   8'   PR

UP

DN

LR
19x15

15'

GARDEN

SIDEWALK

MAIN FLOOR   SIDEWALK

20'

MBR
12x13

DN

W/D

BR 2

UPPER FLOOR

0   5   10   15 FT.

SIDE ENTRY -
CORNER LOT

FIGURE 3.10D **Floor and Landscape Plans for End Unit with Basement.**

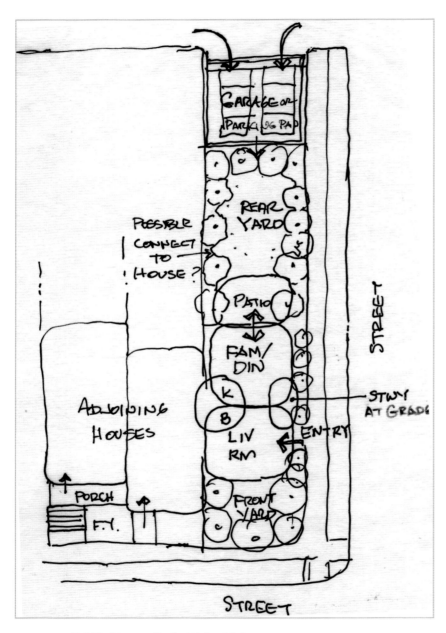

FIGURE 3.10E **Bubble Diagram for End Unit with Basement.**

Client Profile
The client requires a full basement, but does not want an exterior porch and stairway. Therefore, a midlevel entry at grade is required between the basement and the main level. The side entry is similar to the one in **Figure 3.9**, except that the basement requires an interior half-level entry stairway up to the main floor or down to the basement. This is not accessible for handicapped people, but it is very convenient for a client with a shop in the basement. They can either go up one half level to the main living space or down a half level to the shop.

Exercises
1. Draw a site plan at a smaller scale, showing the street, alley, sidewalks, and location of the house and yards. Show where the entry is located and include fences. Then draw a landscape plan. A simple designation of trees, shrubs, flowers, and patio areas is sufficient. How is this different from the site plan in Figure 3.9 with the entry at grade? What are the advantages and disadvantages of a mid-level entry?

End Unit with Garage Underneath (Figures 3.11a–e)
This double unit maximizes the economy of the site, providing space for two townhouses on one site.

Client Profile
The family consists of a soccer father, a lawyer mother, and two teenaged children. The family does not live near public transportation. One of the children drives. They require two indoor parking spaces as well as a parking pad on the site for the teenage driver and guests. They don't want the site to look like a parking lot, so the landscaping should camouflage the additional parking. Consider the use of the yard space when there is no car parked there.

Exercises
1. Create a space plan on the given base plan.
2. Make a furniture layout from the space plan.

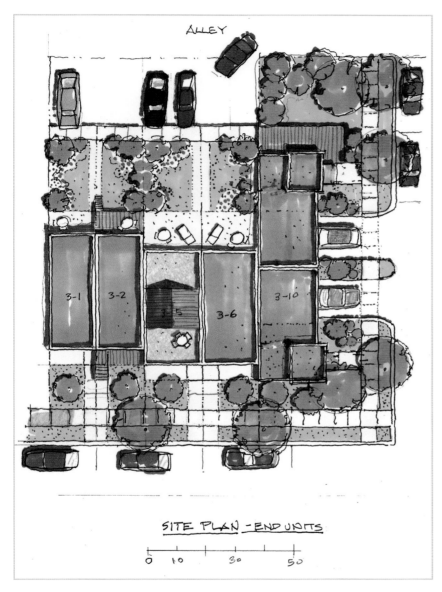

FIGURE 3.11A **Site Plan for End Unit with a Two-Car Garage at Grade Level.** The wide facade allows a two-car garage and curb cut. This is only recommended when an alley is not available for an end unit. The curb cut is an impediment for pedestrians. It may create a traffic hazard as well, with cars backing out onto the street.

FIGURE 3.11B **Elevation for End Unit with a Two-Car Garage at Grade Level.**

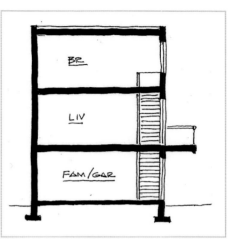

FIGURE 3.11C **Section for End Unit with a Two-Car Garage at Grade Level.**

Corner Store with Apartment Above (Figures 3.12a–c)
This prototype invites locally-owned businesses into the community. By providing lower overhead, a small business can be successful. It can also provide space for artisans and artists. A corner store can bring street life to most neighborhoods, and serve practical needs, like grocery store, pharmacy, or cleaner.

Client Profile
This prototype was very popular in the days before shopping malls, and it may be useful once again. As we will discuss in Chapter 9, there is a growing demand for local retail establishments that are accessible within a five-minute walk. Whether it is a convenience grocer, cafe, art gallery, candy shop, laundry, law office, or design studio, this type of store greatly enlivened the older urban neighborhoods of most cities. The client is a couple that owns an independent business. They don't want to work for a big company, and they don't want to waste time commuting. Previously, they owned their own cafe/bakery, specializing in homemade pastries. But as their neighborhood gentrified, they were driven out by rising rents.

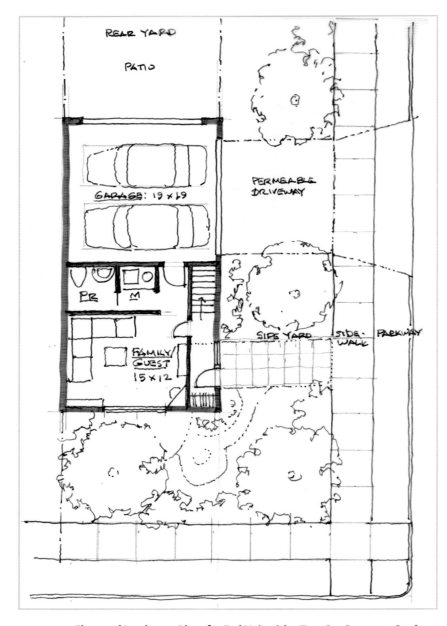

FIGURE 3.11D **Floor and Landscape Plans for End Unit with a Two-Car Garage at Grade Level.**

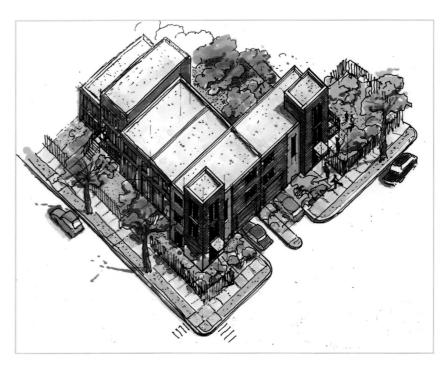

FIGURE 3.11E **Aerial Perspective of End Unit with a Two-Car Garage at Grade Level.**

This time, they vowed to own their own space in order to benefit from rising values.

The couple enjoys talking to people and they are happy to sell local products and promote local artists. Mixing an art gallery with a cafe or bookstore allows them a mix of products not found in most franchise stores. The corner store has an apartment above, which helps keep the overhead low. There should also be provision for a small office on the ground-floor retail space. Parking is available at the back of the lot and on the street, but since it is located near the town center, most people will walk to this store.

CASE STUDY 3.8

University Village

Chicago, Illinois
Pappageorge/Haymes Ltd., Architects

The program for this unique urban community was centered on the integration of greenways to connect the buildings to the neighborhood and provide safe and interesting passage throughout the development. The complex of 147 townhouses and condominiums exists within a pedestrian-friendly framework of tree-lined public streets, beautifully landscaped greenways, and three strategically placed neighborhood parks. The "village" is patterned after vintage Chicago styles and utilizing human-scaled materials and varying rooflines. Interesting outdoor spaces

above: corner view

next page: entry courtyard

are anchored by round turret bays. Highly articulated entries of masonry and stone, articulated stone accents, brick cornice detailing, brick arches, patterned Flemish bond accents, and corbelled bays are stylishly evoke and reinterpret the rich architectural heritage of the community.

Specifications

NUMBER OF UNITS: 147 Units
STORIES: 3 Stories

alternating bricks

continued on the next page

continued from the previous page

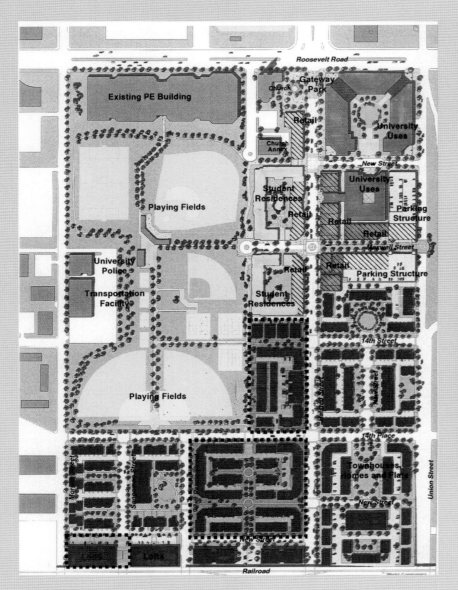

site plan

bird's-eye perspective

rendering: Bondy

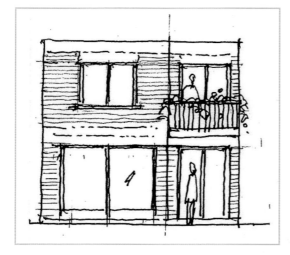

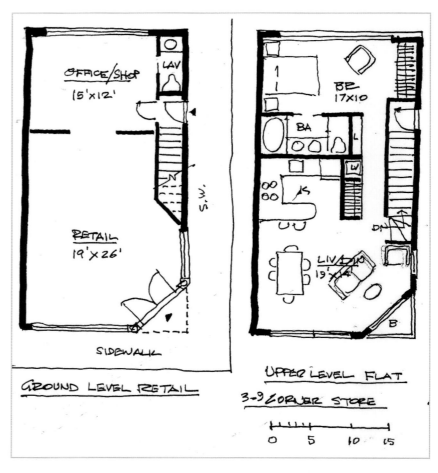

FIGURE 3.12A **Elevation for Corner Store with Apartment Above.** This live/work space has a corner store with an apartment above. This configuration can be an important element of walkability in urban design. It allows people to shop for food or other products and services within a five-minute walk. It also provides employment opportunities and cuts down on the need to drive. During the nineteenth and twentieth centuries this model was prevalent; it may once again become advantageous.

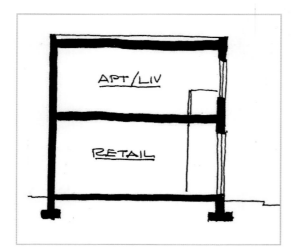

FIGURE 3.12B **Section for Corner Store with Apartment Above.**

FIGURE 3.12C **Floor Plan for Corner Store with Apartment Above.**

Exercises
1. Create a space plan on the given base plan. Make use of the corner as an entry.
2. Make a furniture layout from the space plan. Show how the outdoor space could be used to complement the business, as in an outdoor terrace.

Chapter Summary

This chapter charted the development of the attached townhouse, from humble nineteenth-century dwelling to a sophisticated and valuable part of the modern urban fabric. Students discovered the effect of the site plan on the interior layout of the townhouse. The site plan determines the width, the entry, the relationship to parking, and the window locations.

As with other housing types, the attached townhouse presents both opportunities and limitations. With the inevitable vertical stairway, accessibility can be a major issue. This type of house obviously does not work for the disabled. However, it lends itself to duplex units with independent and accessible private units at the ground floor and family units above. It can be useful as a multigenerational cohabitat, either for elderly parents or returning children.

Townhouse designs in this chapter were separated into 16-foot and 20-foot widths, because each represents a different set of opportunities, as shown in the prototype plans. Furthermore, the zoning of public and private spaces within the residence and determining activities that best suit lower or upper levels are important factors in space planning for townhouses. Also, the particular opportunities for light and air in the end units were explained.

These issues were explored further in the prototypes, which included examples of units 16 and 20 feet wide, as well as end units. Case studies of finished projects by prominent residential design architects provided real-life examples.

KEY TERMS

Party walls: Walls between townhouses that are shared by both houses.

Rowhouse: A row of similar houses attached to each other with no side yard between them.

Townhouse: The term *townhouse* is generic and indicates simply a house in town. It is usually a narrow front, multistory house. It may be detached in some cases. The term *townhouse* is used interchangeably with *rowhouse* in some cities. It's one of the inconsistencies one must learn to live with.

ENDNOTES

1. George Orwell, *The Road to Wigan Pier* (New York: Harcourt Brace, 1958), 51–74.
2. Charles Dickens, *Hard Times* (New York: Bantam, 1981).
3. Ibid., 180–188.
4. Wid Chapman and Jeffrey P. Rosenfeld, *Home Design in an Aging World* (New York: Fairchild, 2008). This book provides many good ideas in the evolving requirements of housing programs and designs as a growing number of people age in their own homes.

CHAPTER 4

Remodeling and Adaptive Reuse

The Sustainable Alternative

Chapter Purpose

This chapter explores the relationship between remodeling and sustainability. Several of the main remodeling prototypes are identified. Projects include client profiles that introduce the types of clients who might prefer to live in a remodeled house. In some of the projects, details about the regions, climates, and neighborhoods of the sites help students understand how these conditions affect the final design. Each project is followed by exercises so students may try out different ideas. A remodeling checklist that can be applied to all types of remodeling projects is provided. This tool will help the designer get started with the investigation, program, and design. Case studies illustrate how professional architects and designers have resolved various remodeling challenges.

Background

In the twenty-first century, most people think of remodeling or restoration as an homage to the elegant materials and construction methods of the past. Who among us has not admired the limestone lintel above a window or door of a red brick historic home? We also admire the fine craftsmanship that produced **quartersawn oak** cabinets; carpenter-built stairways, moldings, and trim; and polished hardwood floors, lovingly applied in herringbone patterns. Where can we find handmade stained glass windows today? Homebuilders who worked in the early twentieth

century were much more generous with materials, dating from a time when they were less expensive and more available. They built full 12-inch-thick brick walls with **English cross bond** and thick, solid-wood doors and frames with substantial bronze hardware. Brass light fixtures and porcelain plumbing fixtures can be repaired and are still in service today. Though many such homes have been demolished, a growing number have been lovingly restored to their original elegance, some of which have been updated with modern and energy-efficient materials and equipment.

It may be hard to believe now, but not so long ago anything old was relegated to the junk heap. Demolishing the old house and raising up the new was the norm. That was the slogan of urban renewal throughout most U.S. cities and small towns. Only a few people saw value in restoring these old homes and reusing them. There followed an era of reclaiming old and abandoned industrial buildings and converting them into lofts. This in turn led to the revitalization of many neighborhoods in cities across the country.

Remodeling and Sustainability

Remodeling is an important technique in current housing development because it is environmentally friendly. It combats global warming and keeps useful materials out of landfills. Remodeling has been called the ultimate sustainable building method. Since the foundation has already been built, the exterior walls and the roof structure are in place (assuming that they are in relatively good condition). The site work, including mature landscaping, is already done. Even if there is a need to replace windows and a substantial amount of the interior, it's still better, from the point of view of conserving materials, to remodel rather than to build new. Other considerations, such as location and client needs and preferences may come into play, but for conservation of materials alone, remodeling rather than demolition and new construction should be seriously considered. Industry experts have compiled the following data on the benefits of remodeling:[1]

- A 50,000-square-foot building requires the same amount of energy as driving a car 20,000 miles for 730 years.
- An average 2,000-square-foot home requires 3,000 pounds of wood, 2,000 pounds of drywall, and 600 pounds of cardboard. This translates to four pounds of waste per square foot. Only a small percentage of that waste is reusable.
- By 2030, Americans will demolish and replace 82 billion square feet of existing buildings. It is estimated that there are about 300 billion square feet of space in the United States. That means nearly a third of our building stock could be demolished in the next 20 to 25 years.[2]
- It takes as much energy to demolish and reconstruct 82 billion square feet of space as it would to power the entire state of California (the tenth largest economy in the world with a population of about 36 million people) for 10 years.
- If we were to rehab even 10 percent of this 82 billion square feet, we would save enough energy to power the state of New York for well over a year.
- Energy translates to gasoline. The energy in existing buildings is equivalent to about 5 to 15 gallons of gasoline per square foot. A 250,000-square-foot building is equivalent to 3.75 million gallons of gasoline.
- It takes between 35 and 50 years for an energy-efficient new building to save the amount of energy lost in demolishing an existing building.
- Debris from construction contributes 25 percent of the municipal waste each year.

Demolition of buildings in the United States generates **124,670,000 tons** of debris, according to the Florida-based Deconstruction Institute. "That would be comparable to a wall 4,993 miles long, 30 feet high, and 30 feet thick that could surround the entire coast of the continental United States." According to the National Association of the Remodeling Industry:

- The amount of embodied energy contained in an average, 2,000-square-foot home is 892 million BTUs, the equivalent of 7,826 gallons of gasoline, enough embodied energy to drive an SUV 5.5 times around the earth.
- About 5 million tons of carbon equivalent are annually released into the atmosphere as methane gas. This is the result of burying about 33 million tons of wood from demolition and construction debris in landfills and anaerobic microorganisms decomposing the lumber. This is the equivalent of emissions from 3,736,000 passenger cars.
- Total greenhouse gas reduction from recycling the 5,174 pounds of steel and 1,830 pounds of plastic in an average single family home would be equal to the yearly absorption of carbon dioxide by 114 trees.
- For each ton of wood remodelers reuse, they avoid creating 60 pounds of greenhouse gases from the development of raw lumber into a usable form for building.

Since residential construction, especially new construction, contributes so mightily to global warming, toxic landfills, and all forms of pollution, it is particularly important to preserve and restore the housing stock that can be saved. The designer must investigate and propose energy-efficient construction whenever possible. That includes using both passive and active solar energy, as well as wind power. Also, the designer should specify as many recycled products as possible.

Neighborhood urban design is another important aspect of sustainability. Retaining viable neighborhoods is important environmentally as well as historically. This is explained in Parts V and VI.

And there's plenty more where that came from. Say you don't like the style of a house, or it's not big enough, there are many possibilities for remodeling it or adding to it without substantial demolition.

Design and Sustainability

A good designer should understand and make use of the many advantages of remodeling, especially those that save energy, combat global warming, and recycle existing materials. Sometimes they may be able to save money for their clients in both short- and long-term costs.

There are several things that designers should remember when considering a remodeling project. For all remodeling and adaptive reuse projects, it is important to begin by taking inventory of the existing building. Measured drawings are essential. A photographic inventory can be very useful in preparing construction drawings and seeking product sources. The designer must carefully evaluate, sometimes in conjunction with other consultants and builders, whether the remodeling will be cost-effective. (This isn't a simple matter of finding the least expensive construction.) **Life-cycle** costs must also be considered. If it takes five years of energy savings to pay back added insulation or window repairs, it is well worth it. And a responsible designer must be able to inform the client as to the environmental costs of the new construction. (*Tip:* There are local consultants and engineers who specialize in sustainability and can help measure the environmental impact of various systems.)

Designers should be prepared to have backup research from the many governmental and private organizations that currently exist. Read reports from the Environmental Protection Agency, American Lung Association, The National Association of the Remodeling Industry, The National Trust for Historic Preservation, and the many builders, craftspeople, and materials suppliers that can help in this work. A well-stocked library of sources and reading materials is necessary for any designer interested in remodeling and sustainability.

Some clients will still be tempted to tear down all or part of a house and start from scratch. But they should be reminded that it would add to greenhouse gases, global warming, air pollution, or toxic landfill. After careful consideration, there are many clients who would be willing to pay extra to help the environment, especially when some of those costs may not be as great as they had feared. However, if the client decides to demolish a part of a house because it doesn't conform to current needs, the designer can counsel the client as to which parts of the building can be saved and recycled. This includes windows, doors, hardware, stair railings, finished wood of any type, light fixtures, copper wiring, bathtubs, and sinks. Framing wood, such as two-by-fours from demolished partitions, can be stripped of nails and saved for other work. Even old nails and screws can be melted down and recycled. There are a growing number of salvaging and recycling businesses, as well as on-line brokers, who can find buyers for building materials. The designer can add to services rendered by maintaining an up-to-date resource of these recyclers. Remember, recycling anything keeps it out of the landfill and helps prevent global warming.

Remodeling Prototypes
The "Gut": Demolition and Reconstruction

A common form of remodeling is the **gut** demolition and reconstruction. In this case, the exterior shell is maintained, but the entire interior is removed (see **Figure 4.1**). This may be done to remedy problems such as deteriorated materials or an obsolete layout. Designers must take great care to consult with a licensed architect or engineer to confirm which walls are structural. Proper methods of removing and disposing of electrical and plumbing materials must be followed. (*Tip:* Remember, all materials removed from the building must be transported by a licensed toxic waste handler to a licensed toxic waste dump. Try to avoid this by conserving as much as possible from the building.)

The house is a typically modest early to mid-twentieth century home of 720 to 1,440 square feet, depending on the number of floors. There may be an attic on the second floor.

Client Profile

The clients are a young recently married couple looking for a starter home. They chose the house because of the neighborhood, a small but dense college town in New England. They both teach at a nearby college

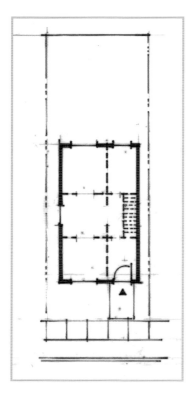

FIGURE 4.1 **Gut Demolition.** Some remodeling projects require complete demolition and reconstruction.

and are fond of the "old-time" feel of the place. The clients have no experience with buying or remodeling older homes.

Unfortunately, they didn't consult with an architect or residential designer prior to buying the house. When they started to inspect the premises after purchase, they found rotting wood in the walls, broken plumbing with lead piping, dangerous electrical wiring, an inadequate heating system, a leaky roof, and many other things that were invisible in the walk-through.

They then consulted with an architect and some local builders. Some suggested tearing the house down and starting from scratch, while others suggested substantial replacement to the structure. Neither of these alternatives was appealing to the clients and both were more expensive and time-consuming than they had hoped. Finally, they located a restoration design specialist who was highly recommended in the community.

They visited his projects and he convinced them to proceed with a compromise; preserving as much of the structure as possible, but doing a full interior demolition. By careful staging (and with a lot of takeout dinners) they were able to live on one floor while the other floor was being remodeled. They will never do that again! But when it was finished, they were very happy to finally be at home in their dream house.

Exercises

1. Plan this house as a single story of 720 square feet, 20 feet wide by 36 feet deep, with all rooms on the main floor.

Restoration and Preservation

Some homes are worthy of restoration. They were originally well-constructed and beautifully detailed, but may have fallen into disrepair. In most regions, there is a growing corps of craftsmen developing for this market. There are experts in historic preservation who can rebuild and replace parts of these historic homes to their original status. Craftsmen trained to make stained glass, ceramic tile, and historic hardware and light fixtures are springing up throughout the country. Paint and wallpaper can be examined with spectrometers to determine the exact original colors that were used. In many cases there are government incentive programs to encourage this kind of work. The National Trust for Historic Preservation is an organization that can help support projects in any part of the country.

This prototype house (**Figure 4.2**) is typical of many early twentieth-century houses. It has a raised front porch, a foyer, and a long corridor with three rooms to one side. Living, dining, and kitchen/family rooms are lined up. French doors at the center of each room line up so when all are opened it's one continuous space. This allows for large-scale entertainment, but the rooms can be closed off to create more private spaces such as a study or den.

Client Profile

The clients are a couple with no children. They have lived in the same Nashville, Tennessee, neighborhood for a while and have long admired this house. They are friends of the previous owner, an elderly gentleman. They told him that they hoped he could stay in the house forever, but if he ever decided to move he should let them know. They had fallen in love with the historic details and proportions of the house. They had stopped by many times to enjoy a drink on the porch and hear stories about the old times in the house. When the former owner decided to move into an apartment, he contacted the couple and they struck a deal.

The clients are generally pleased with the layout. There is no need to change the floor plan and the French doors between rooms will remain. Some conveniences can be added, such as a closet or **armoire** in the entry and perhaps some new plumbing fixtures. They know of a number of salvage and recycling shops in the area, so they have picked up some fixtures manufactured in the same time period as the house. A large amount of

deferred maintenance will have to be taken on, such as a new roof and some window repairs. They have decided to restore the old windows by reglazing the glass and replacing the cords with new chains. They have done much of the work themselves and have found skilled craftspeople to supply the parts.

Obviously, this takes a commitment of time and energy, as well as money, so the people who restore homes like this do it out of love rather than efficiency. The work of the designer on a project like this is to help the client research the time period and find examples of similar houses from the period. They can also help to locate local contractors and sources for parts and fixtures.

Furnishing a historic home should be done with the same care as restoring it. A designer can help identify the historic color schemes. Cost estimating is sometimes difficult in a project like this, but the designer and owner must agree on a budget and a time period for construction. Here are some practical exercises to help the student become acquainted with this type of work.

Exercises
1. Produce a set of measured drawings of a historic home. Find a cooperative owner who will allow measurement of the interior spaces (perhaps in exchange for a set of existing plans?). Usually two to three people are necessary for this job; one to hold the tape, the second to make the sketches, and the third to read the dimensions. The exterior dimensions can sometimes be obtained from an owner's survey or city records. Record the ceiling heights as well. This is an important part of every restoration job.
2. Take extensive photos of the house, including details such as stair rails, stained glass, cabinets, and doors. Place a yardstick in the photos for future reference to size. Create a photo inventory of the house from which it is possible to make construction drawings.
3. Search for sources. Use the Internet or word of mouth. Find out where the local suppliers are and start to assemble a project booklet of historic parts and furnishings. The project is in Nashville, but the student can research other areas as well.

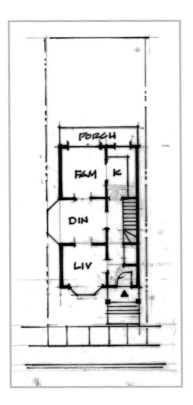

FIGURE 4.2 **Historical Restoration**. Most features in a historical restoration are retained and restored.

CASE STUDY 4.1

Harper Avenue, near the University of Chicago Campus

Hyde Park, Chicago, Illinois
Robert P. Gordon, Architect

There is an interesting story to this house. The architect lived in this Victorian house when he was a student. The owner was an architect in his late eighties. He had converted it to a boarding house and was forced by the city to put drywall over the beautiful wood finishing and stairway. He installed it in a way that made it easy to remove without damaging the wood. He thought that some day someone would buy this house and discover a treasure.

A number of years later, the younger architect was asked to remodel the house. He remembered the wood beneath the drywall. The result was a mixture of historic restoration with modern convenience. The rear of the house was opened with the installation of French doors that led to a porch and the backyard. Many different and interesting people have lived in this house over the years.

bathroom

facade

hallway

Additions

Some houses work fine for the owners at first, but families change. If a client likes the house and the neighborhood, they can add space by creating additions for many different types of spaces without purchasing additional land (**see Figure 4.3**).

Client Profile

The clients are very happy with their location in Minneapolis, Minnesota, but they have outgrown their house. There are a sufficient number of bedrooms and bathrooms upstairs, but the entry and general circulation were never adequately planned. This family has grown to include two children. The kids tend to track mud into the house and leave coats and books scattered throughout. Much of this can be controlled by a simple small vestibule addition to the front entry. The parents also appreciate the **air lock** provided by this vestibule, especially during Minneapolis winters. The designer can propose a place for hanging coats and a neat storage area for shoes and boots, as well as key rack. Each family member should have a place for his or her keys. Also, a table should be provided for staging morning departures.

There should be a separate place for the children to entertain their friends. A sunroom addition at the rear of the house would help to solve this problem. The room can be opened in the summer and enclosed in winter.

Other aspects and uses for additions include the following:

- Front porches. Screened in summer and enclosed in winter, can add usable space while greatly improving neighborhood conviviality and even security.
- Air-lock vestibules. When a door opens directly into the living room, there is a large draft and energy drain. It's more comfortable for inhabitants and more energy-efficient to build an enclosed vestibule. This can also be used as a **mudroom** for removing wet boots and coats. It's also a convenient and secure place for delivery of mail and packages. There is also added comfort for guests, who can await entry under a roof in an enclosed shelter. This is a relatively inexpensive project with many benefits.
- Older houses sometimes have very small kitchens and dining areas. In order to take advantage of backyard landscaping, a garden room, or sunroom, can be added. This is usually used as a family room, with generous table space and easy access to the yard. Sometimes it can be a screened in or enclosed with glass doors. The energy advantage of an additional glazed garden room is that the heat can be turned off when it is not in use. The room itself forms a barrier to outside wind and cold. Alternatively, it could be heated and used as a regular interior room. If it is large enough, it can accommodate a greenhouse for starting plants. There is great flexibility in a sunroom and it can be a source of great pleasure.

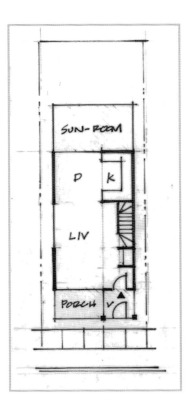

FIGURE 4.3 **Additions.** Smaller homes can be made more functional with the addition of key spaces.

Exercises

1. Act out in class the different activities associated with entering a house. Record them. Draw interior elevations of a vestibule, half-inch scale, of all four sides of the entry vestibule. Show in detail all hardware and cabinetry, such as coat hooks, cubbies for boots, caps, and keys (these will probably be custom built). Show lights and switches (a **three-way switch** would be useful here). That way, a person can enter the vestibule, turn on the light, then pass through the vestibule and turn it off at that point. The second switch can actually be inside the house so the owner can light the vestibule without going into it.

Bungalow Projects
Basic Postwar Bungalow
The typical postwar bungalow, sometimes called a ranch house, was very small at about 700 square feet (**see Figure 4.4a**). Everything was on one level. It was usually divided into thirds: the front section contained the living room and entry; the core held a bedroom, a bathroom, a storage room, and a coat closet or utility room; and the rear contained the kitchen and dining room. According to the family's needs, the rear area could be open, as a kitchen/family/dining room, or divided to allow for a small additional sleeping area for guests. As the family's needs changed, this partition could easily be put up or removed. All things considered, these homes were serviceable for thousands of families in the 1950s and continue to be so today.

Exercise

1. Try incorporating a flexible sleeping space in the family room without building a partition (i.e., a sofa bed or fold-down bed). Take advantage of the large room size when it is not being used for sleeping. Perhaps design as a guest room.

Evolution of the Bungalow: Second-Floor Addition
Over time, a family may expand beyond the capacity of their home. But they may not be able to afford a new home in their current neighborhood. Relocating far from their daily activities would necessitate buying a sec-

ond car, which would add additional cost to their housing budget. If the family stays put and avoids the additional transportation cost they may be able to afford an addition on to. Often, the only solution is to go up (**see Figure 4.4b**).

Client Profile
A family living in Levittown, New York, has recently added one child and is anticipating a second. It can no longer fit into the existing single-story space. They require two bedrooms, a second bathroom, and a study on a second floor. The study may be used as a third bedroom when the time comes. A bay window on the study can add additional space. Freeing up space on the first floor permits them to have a generous side entry with two closets and a large kitchen/dining room. Since the entry is on the side, the living room can also be used as a guest room. Compare this to **Figure 4.4a,** where the living room is disrupted by the entry and circulation back into the house.

Bungalow Evolution: Adding a Garden Room
By purchasing an adjoining lot, homeowners can add considerable utility and value to their existing house. The additional width can accommodate special rooms, such as garden rooms, greenhouses, libraries, conference rooms, or family dining rooms. If one doesn't already exist, the designer can add a side entry, or one through the garden room, which increases the privacy of the living room. A garden room can be added, adjoining the existing living room (**see Figure 4.4c**). Sometimes garden rooms are combined to make a larger living room. Otherwise they may be used as separate entries or connecting galleries.

It is also possible to make the garden room a separate private room, or guest room, unencumbered by entry requirements. A garden room can also provide live/work space. It's a very flexible and useful space.

Client Profile
A retired couple, living in a Seattle neighborhood, has recently invited an elderly parent to live with them. They hope to achieve additional space by adding rooms rather than by internal remodeling, because they must live

CASE STUDY 4.2

Brennan/Orelind Residence

Chicago, Illinois

Greene and Proppe Design, Architecture and Interior Design

The clients' program for renovating this 1908 stucco home located in the Lakewood Balmoral Historic District in Chicago was to create a rear addition to expand the kitchen, relocate the powder room, expand the master suite, and add a new stairway to the third floor. The kitchen was completely remodeled to include an eat-in area and new powder room. The master bedroom was expanded and received a new window seat and a large, luxurious bathroom. The stairway connecting the second and third floors was converted into a light-filled opening leading to the newly remodeled attic office and TV room. The final design has a four-story addition (including basement) totaling about 450 square feet.

The new kitchen has custom-built, craftsman-style, rift-cut red oak cabinets topped with two different granite surfaces, a basket-weave patterned ceramic tile backsplash, and generous storage. A sunny eating area overlooks a small deck that descends into a newly landscaped backyard. The exterior facade received a small

front view

living room

continued on the next page

continued from the previous page

bump-out and was designed and painted to visually reduce the scale of the home and reflect the style of a Swedish cottage. Adjacent to the kitchen, the powder room carries on the interior theme with an oak vanity table, concrete counter top, vinyl wall covering, and a sublime combination of track and pendant lighting. The new master bedroom has a slightly vaulted bedroom ceiling and a gabled, cantilevered, window seat bump-out. It features a beach-inspired bathroom with a floating maple vanity, blue glass tile floors and wall, heated floor, and a steam shower with a pebble rock floor surface. The entire house was redecorated with new paint colors and wall coverings, many new light fixtures, art glass windows, and custom window treatments.

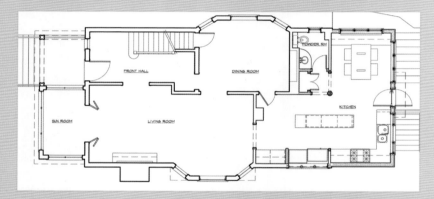

plan first floor

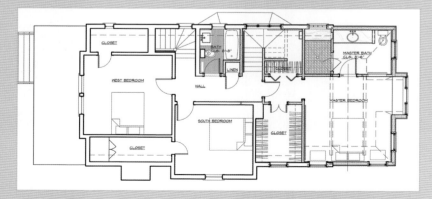

plan second floor

in the home while it is being renovated. The lot they own is 25 feet wide by 125 feet deep. They have purchased the empty lot next door, which is the same size. They love the outdoors, and the idea of being surrounded by trees is very appealing.

The addition of the garden room makes it possible to change the uses of the former spaces. The former living room can now be used for a library or guest room. The former kitchen and dining area can now be used as a kitchen/family room, for informal dining. Children might eat in the kitchen while an adult dinner party takes place in the garden room. The former living room can now be used as a library after the entry is moved to the side, through the new garden room. It could also become an accessible bedroom without disrupting the flow of the house. The rear patio, located directly off the family room, also extends the useful living space. There is a great view of Mount Rainier visible from the family room.

Exercise

1. Assume that the original house had a front entry from the street. Draw a street access the front entry with door and a small foyer. Then redesign the entry to open through the garden room, as shown in **Figure 4.4c**. Draw the coat-hanging space in both alternates and show any furniture, lighting, or floor tile that could be considered. Compare these two types of entries.

Bungalow Evolution: Studio Addition
Client Profile
Another client, with a similar house in the same neighborhood in Seattle, has seen the work the designer has done (**see Figure 4.4c**). They are impressed with it and engage the designer for a larger project. The client would like to explore the possibility of building a separate studio building to start a small pottery-making business. They have the opportunity to buy two adjoining lots, for an additional property width of 50 feet. There should be space for a work area, exhibition display space, and two offices. The kiln will be located outside of the studio, in an adjoining yard (**see Figure 4.4d**).

CASE STUDY 4.3

Shanahan Residence

Chicago, Illinois
Greene and Proppe Design, Architecture and Interior Design

This project included interior renovation, an addition, and exterior restoration of a 1904 Victorian shingle-style residence in Chicago's Lakewood Balmoral Historic District. The exterior restoration transformed this home from its dilapidated and aluminum-sided state into a home befitting its style and history. Spatially, the original first floor program called for the creation of a better relationship and flow between the kitchen, family room, and backyard. The owners also wanted to add a kitchen eating area, pantry space, improved storage, a desk workspace, and deck area. The second floor called for an improved master suite. The architect completed the design of additions to the kitchen, family room, and second-floor master suite, expanding each floor by 180 square feet. The finished product is another testament to historic restoration with the seamless incorporation of modern comforts, luxury, and personality.

The new kitchen follows in the Arts and Crafts tradition with custom-built, quarter-sawn, oak cabinetry. The dark green granite countertops are complemented by cabinets with hammered leaded glass panels. To complement the dramatic granite countertops, the island base is also painted deep seaweed green. A rift-cut oak top matches the surrounding cabinetry and offers a friendly casual dining surface. The kitchen also features a nine-foot desk, a mudroom area with matching oak woodwork, and a large walk-in pantry. Adjacent to the kitchen, the powder room continues the interior theme. The built-in washstand is crowned with an ebony-stained mosaic tile backslash and elegant vessel sink on a soapstone top. The original toilet and sink locations were switched during the remodeling. The redesigned family room enjoys a greatly improved connection with the new kitchen and boasts oak built-ins that reflect the kitchen's style and warmth. The second-floor master suite was completely remodeled and received a new balcony. The master bathroom features his-and-her vanity areas, a large walk-in shower, a freestanding Victorian soaking tub, and a separate toilet room for added privacy and functionality. The newly restored exterior of the home exemplifies the shingle style with added Arts and Crafts details and colors.

kitchen

continued on the next page

continued from the previous page

family room

powder room sink

fireplace

master bedroom

master bath

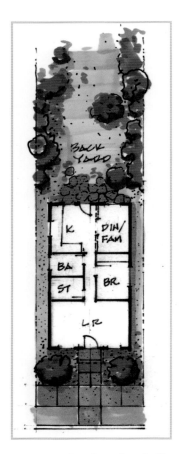

FIGURE 4.4A **One-Story Ranch.** The standard ranch house of the 1950s was typical of postwar housing.

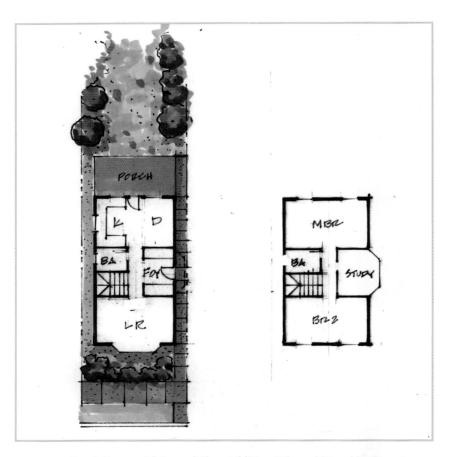

FIGURE 4.4B **Ranch House with Second-Floor Addition.** When additional land is not available, space can be added by building upward.

The client wants an enclosed access link between the two buildings in case of rain, as well as two clearly distinct entries: one for the residence and one for the business. The connecting corridor should also be usable as a gallery to exhibit finished work for sale. The yard outside the gallery, sheltered by a wide overhang, can provide additional display and sales space.

The business function requires a small, discreet parking lot, screened from the street so as not to disrupt the walkable character of the neigh-

borhood. The gallery acts as a window to the street, encouraging sales and providing an enjoyable view for passersby.

Within the original bungalow, the client would like to add an enclosed greenhouse or terrace in the back, to serve as a family room.

Exercise

1. Draw a circulation diagram explaining how people would move through the space. Design a connector space between the original res-

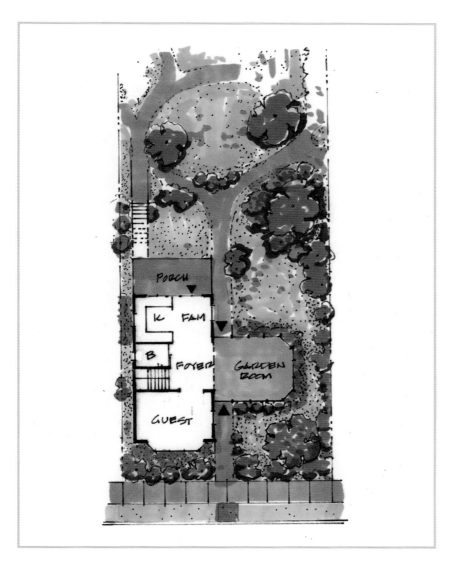

FIGURE 4.4C **50-Foot Lot with a Garden Room.** The purchase of an adjoining lot allows for the addition of a large garden room. This addition permits entry from the side as well.

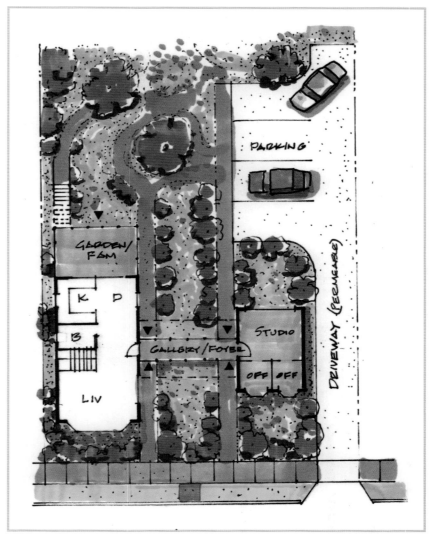

FIGURE 4.4D **75-Foot Lot with Added Studio.** Purchase of two adjoining 25-foot lots adds enough space for a separate studio and parking.

CASE STUDY 4.4

Haupt/Rosen House

Chicago, Illinois
Michael B. Rosen, Architect

This small, circa 1890 house, 1,400 square feet in its original state, has been remodeled and added to in stages since 1980 by the architect, Michael B. Rosen, for himself, his wife, and his two children. The original interior spaces were poorly planned, but the garden on the south side of the house made it attractive for remodeling. The first remodeling changed the main orientation of the house from the street to the garden by means of a large sliding glass door and a screened porch. In 1993, the living room was extended into the garden and a master bathroom was added above. The small, second-floor bedroom at the west end of the third floor was enlarged with a 3-foot "bump-out" to the south. The narrow house with large areas of glass to the south is economical to heat and cool.

porch

SECOND FLOOR PLAN

SCALE: 0   8'   16'

6. BEDROOM
7. BATHROOM

second floor plan

living room

dining room

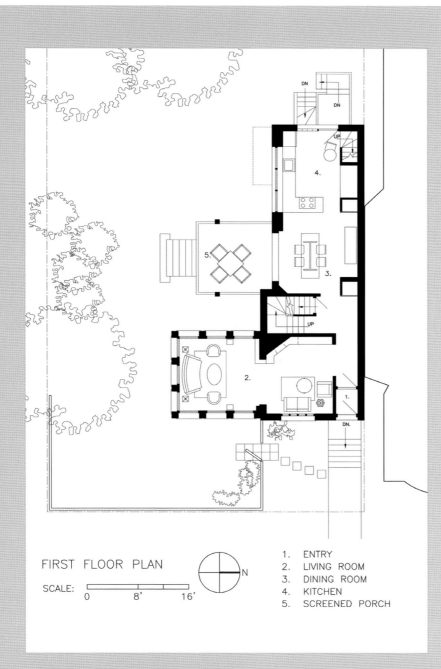

FIRST FLOOR PLAN

SCALE:
0   8'   16'

N

1.   ENTRY
2.   LIVING ROOM
3.   DINING ROOM
4.   KITCHEN
5.   SCREENED PORCH

first floor plan

idence and the new addition. This can also serve as a main entrance for both spaces. How can the pottery be displayed without blocking the light and garden view? Think of interior and exterior displays, as well as furniture for the space

Adaptive Reuse of a Small Industrial Building

A two-story industrial building, 30 feet wide by 60 feet deep, is adaptable for conversion to a residential live/work facility. The ground floor can be used for business purposes and the upper floor for residential. The business use is compatible with other buildings on the street, and helps provide a walkable environment for the community. Parking is in the rear, through an alley.

Map out the space allocation and circulation using the bubble diagram in **Figure 4.5a**. **Figure 4.5b** is a floor plan diagram showing the basic plan diagrams and section, without interior planning details. An open-plan loft is desirable for clients who want complete flexibility for interior space divisions, and it is a great challenge for the designer.

Client Profile

A young couple has bought a former bookbinding factory near the coast in Portland, Oregon, and hopes to convert it to a residential and working space. They have a successful photography and graphic design business. Currently it is just the two of them, but they expect to have a child in the future. They require flexible space and furnishing for a variety of projects. The building is large enough to accommodate both living and working, without being too large to afford.

- The front of the building should be inviting to customers, but must be acceptable to the adjoining mixed-use neighborhood. Minimal signage is allowed.
- Portland has great public transportation and there is a train station nearby as well as a farmers' market and grocery store. The couple works at home, so a car is not needed for daily activities. They rent a car for work. A garage or off-street parking is required for clients.

- Separate business and residential zones for the space are of utmost importance. Privacy for family activities must be maintained, so the residence should be located on the second level.
- The clients want to make use of the vertical space wherever possible. The plan should include at least one two-story space.
- Both people participate in cooking. The kitchen must be large, open, and accessible to all. Utensils must be visible and clearly placed.
- The dining room and living room should be open to the kitchen. A small office space should be attached to the kitchen for family book-keeping and recipes.
- A second bedroom is required for overnight guests.
- There must be a private conference room, apart from the main family room, for client presentations. A projector is used for business and entertainment purposes. This should be adjacent to or part of the media space.
- The 14-foot vertical space on the first level should be fully utilized for storage and additional workspace. A partial mezzanine may be added.

Region/Climate
- No flooding is anticipated, but there is considerable rainfall. Sunlight is highly valued.
- Heating is required, but not air-conditioning. Natural ventilation and sunscreens are important to avoid the need for mechanical cooling.
- Energy efficiency is a necessity. Passive solar design is required. Most of the year, the sun is greatly appreciated, but at times in the summer it can become quite warm. Solar or wind-generated electricity is highly desirable.
- Inside-outside living on both levels is necessary and should be part of the interior space planning.
- Water conservation is an integral part of design. Capturing and reusing rainwater is very feasible in this region.

Neighborhood
- Portland is a **smart growth** city, with building zones carefully interspersed with open space zones and a world-famous public transportation system.
- The subject neighborhood is located near the Willamette River, not far from Reed College and the Central area. It is a former residential area which has recently seen remodeling of abandoned industrial buildings into live/work spaces. It is zoned as a mixed-use industrial/residential/commercial neighborhood.
- The natural environment is very important in Portland and should be integrated into the streetscape.

Site
- 50 feet wide by 125 feet deep
- Green space is important. There are open views of the adjoining mixed-use neighborhood, including some old industrial buildings and a park.
- Windows on the side facades are necessary, so the views at the sides should be landscaped. Site privacy can be achieved with trees and shrubs or fencing.
- Front sidewalks must be comfortable for walking.
- Servicing, parking, and delivery entry are from a rear alley or service drive.

Area/Rooms
- The footprint is 30 feet by 60 feet. The total area is 3,600 square feet on two levels, not including an optional garage.
- Workspace and conference room are at ground level, with living space above.
- The first-floor ceiling height is 14 feet and the second-floor height is 9 feet.
- A waterfront-view terrace onto the rear yard adjoins the conference room. This is very important to the business function.

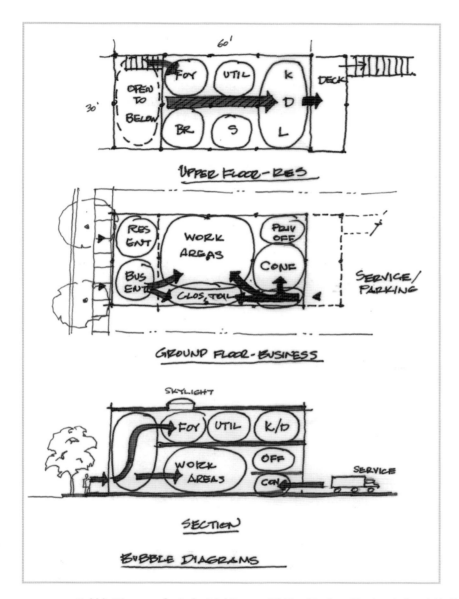

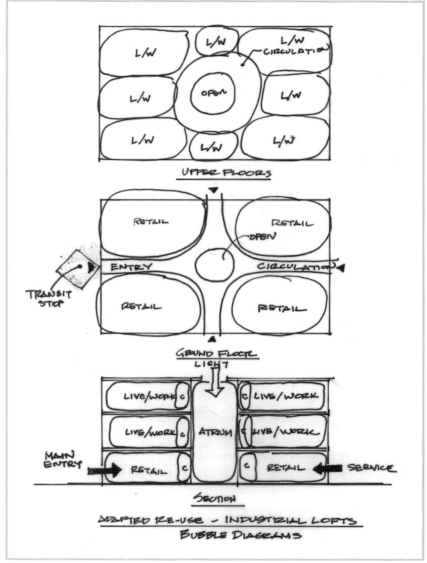

FIGURE 4.5A **Bubble Diagrams for Industrial Reuse with Two Stories.** Obsolete industrial buildings can be adapted to accommodate new live/work spaces.

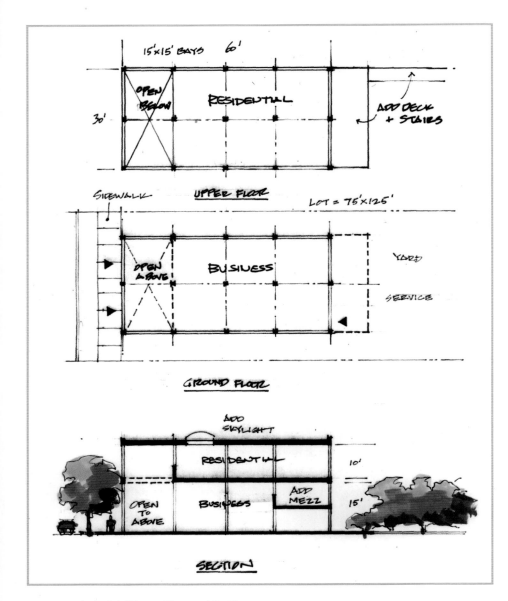

FIGURE 4.5B **Industrial Reuse Plans and Sections.**

- A generous entry mudroom with closet and a place to hang guests' coats. Separate delivery pick-up and drop-off space should be provided as well.
- A great room that encompasses the kitchen, dining, and living space is on the second level, with an adjoining roof garden.
- Also on the second level, there are two bedrooms, one master bath, and one guest bathroom. The guest bedroom could become the nursery in the future.
- A bicycle storage area is necessary near the entry. The clients use bicycles frequently for daily chores and there is a bicycle path in a nearby forest preserve.

Furnishings
- First level: Mid-twentieth century modern business furniture. Workstations should be flexible and mobile, preferably on wheels. Furniture must include a conference table and chairs, a pin-up wall for presentations, work tables, work chairs, and lounge chairs. The artwork to be hung includes examples from the couple's business.
- Second level: Eclectic residential furniture. Includes a mixture of inherited antiques and modern furnishings.
- Finishing includes sustainable durable materials for floors, with area rugs. (Concrete floor, slab on grade, with area rugs.)

Window covering to be shades or venetian blinds. Designer to determine type and color. Conference room must be capable of being darkened for presentations, but will normally be open with no obstructions.

Exercises
1. Obtain photographic views of the Willamette River and the natural environment of Portland. Better yet, visit the city. This is always a good idea when starting a project.
2. Incorporate these views as part of the project presentation to give a good feeling for the site and the active lifestyle of the clients. Photos of Portland's transit system and bicycle facilities are very important to the clients and help to determine their design needs.

CASE STUDY 4.5

The Spice Factory

Mandeville Wharf
New Orleans, Louisiana
SMNG-A Architects, Ltd.

The site for the repurposed Mandeville wharf spice factory previously housed Chef Paul Prudhomme's Cajun Magic spice warehouse in New Orleans. The project's approach included selective subtractions and additions. The archaeologies of the former place along with the modifications reflect the rich context of the neighborhood. Covered walkways, balconies, and overlooks were added to this ensemble to weave all levels of the complex together. This project had a very positive affect on the revitalization of the entire Vieux Carre Historic District of New Orleans.

yard

pool

3. Draw some perspectives of the interiors, both residential and business. Include furniture and window mullions. Collage or PhotoShop the exterior landscape view into the composition. Maybe you can see the Willamette River in the distance. This will give the client a good feeling for the space and help to determine the color scheme.

Medium-Sized Industrial Building

This three-story building, 45 feet wide by 75 feet deep, is located on a commercial street, also in Portland, Oregon. The ground floor is entirely dedicated to retail shops, with entries from all four sides of the building. There is a transit stop in front, which should be integrated into the main entry to the building. The two upper floors contain a mix of residential, office, and studio use (live/work). Since the building has a large volume, it is important to bring light into the interior, so an atrium is planned.

As shown in **Figure 4.6**, the retail stores on the ground level have angled walls to encourage circulation**.** The light from the skylight above is visible from the entry, and attracts the shoppers to the interior. Interior landscaping is also a feature of the central core, where it can be enhanced by sculpture and water.

The second-floor diagrams show possibilities for residential units of various sizes, a must for developer flexibility in sales. One buyer may want a small unit while another might purchase two and combine them.

Figure 4.6 represents the raw space of the building. It is a blank canvas for the designer and client. This is one of the attractions of loft space, along with restored natural timbers and brick.

Client Profile

The client for this type of project is generally a developer, but the designer can be very helpful in laying out the boundaries of the interior spaces. Different "proof of use" drawings can be shown to indicate how a space can be used. This is called **space planning.**

The designer can also be engaged by individual buyers in laying out each individual unit, space planning the actual rooms.

CASE STUDY 4.6

Byron Residence

Chicago, Illinois
SMNG-A Architects, Ltd.

This former industrial building was adapted for residential use. A two-story space with a stairway to the mezzanine above provides a dramatic great room. Heavy steel beams, exposed wood decks, and exposed brick walls

living room

maintain the industrial character of the space. Exposed ducts and a stainless steel kitchen complete the factory character. The living space is warmed by residential components such as wood cabinets, soft furnishings, and Native American carpets. Much of the space in this former power station was left "as is." The $250,000 renovation used existing features, such as white glazed brick, copper windows, and a distressed metal ceiling. The space (24 feet high by 35 feet wide by 125 feet deep) was divided into two units by new core elements (stairs, baths, and storage). An existing truss crane and a new platform adjusts to the owner's spatial requirements. Kitchen components were organized around an island and radiant heat in a new stained concrete floor completed the interior. Dramatic new openings were created along the side wall that opens to an adjacent newly landscaped lot. Hollow metal doors and large fixed aluminum garage doors with glass panels punctured the masonry wall in scale and sympathy with the rich material palette. (Photography John Faier.)

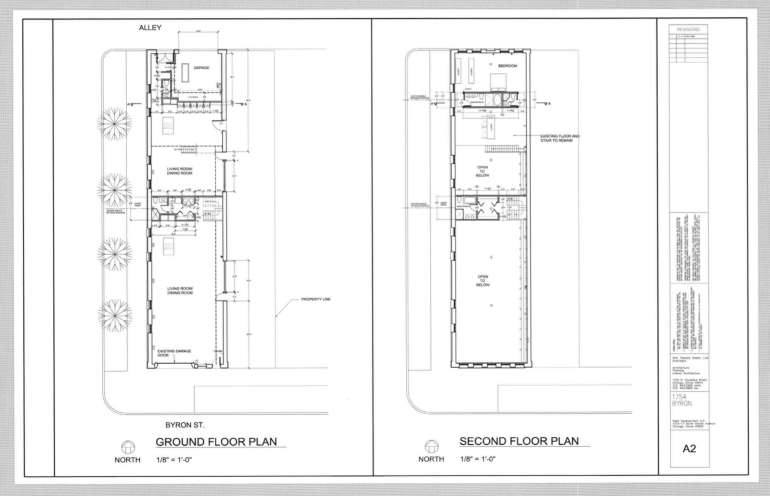

floor plan

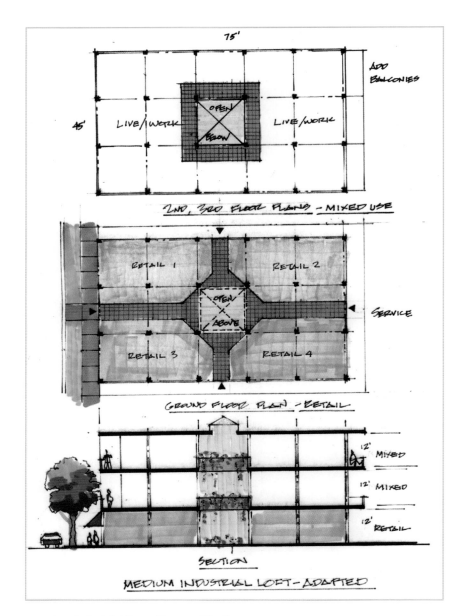

FIGURE 4.6 **Industrial Reuse Plans and Sections.**

Renovated Coach House

Chicago, Illinois
David A. Swan, Architect

Few changes were made to the ground floor of the 1899 coach house. The open space of the stable on the north side of the entry stair and a coach room for carriages on the south side was retained and reused as a garage and storage. On the second floor is a three-bedroom apartment. The exterior has not been altered since it was built, and the interior features of the carriage room and the stable are also pretty much intact. The architects were commissioned to add a small elevator.

front view

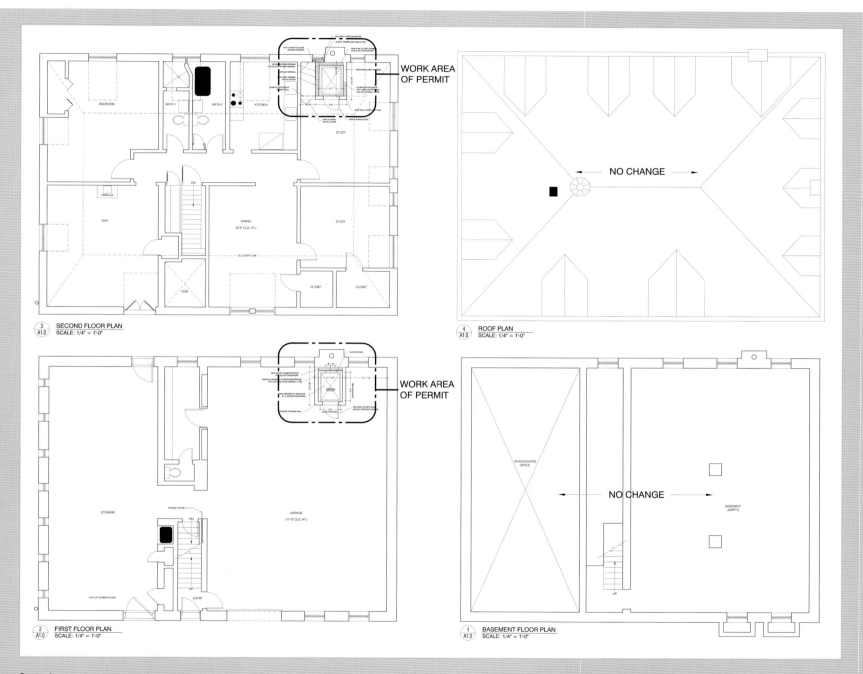

floor plans

Exercises

1. How many retail spaces can be accommodated at the ground level? Show options.

2. How many residential spaces, and at what combinations of dimensions, can the developer offer on the second and third floors? Work with the given 15-foot-square bay (225 square feet). There are fifteen bays; three are dedicated for circulation and an atrium. Twelve bays remain for net residential use. For example, two bays comprise 450 square feet, enough for a studio. Four bays could provide enough space (900 square feet) for a one-bedroom unit. Eight bays (1,800 square feet) could provide a luxurious three- or four-bedroom unit. Some possible combinations are three one-bedroom units at 900 square feet or two studios and two one-bedroom units. An 1,800-square-foot unit can be combined with a 2,700-square-foot unit. Think of other alternatives. Try a 225-square-foot studio apartment.

Chapter Summary

This chapter explained the closely intertwined relationship between remodeling and sustainability. It identified several of the main remodeling prototypes, including partial demolition, restoration, additions, and adaptive reuse of industrial buildings. For each project a client profile was provided to help the designer visualize the type of client for that particular project and to begin to assess their needs. The importance of considering regions and neighborhoods for designated project sites was discussed, so that the designer might take into account how climate and neighborhood context affect the final design. For example, a warm climate and a congenial neighborhood in the South might favor a wraparound porch. High ceilings help ventilate the space, encouraging warm air to move up and out. In New Orleans or other potential flood plain regions, raising the house on pilotis, or piers, is an option. On the other hand, a cold climate requires a secure vestibule to protect the interior from gusts of cold air. If there is an alley system in the neighborhood, parking can be in the rear, determining the entire entry sequence.

REMODELING CHECKLIST

☐ **Client's program and budget.** Include specifics on which areas are to be preserved and which are to be demolished.

☐ **Photographic inventory.** Pay particular attention to details and whether they are to be retained or removed.

☐ **Survey and measured drawings.** A client may provide a survey that came with the purchase of the property, or it might be found in city records. Take care to prepare accurate drawings for the use of the client as well as the builders. This is often handwork, but there are also some impressive measuring laser devices available at local hardware stores that can help speed things up.

Inventory of reusable details.

☐ **Inventory of items** that are not required for this project but should be saved and recycled for another project.

☐ **Furniture inventory.** Is there existing furniture to be retained in the building? If not, create a list of required furniture and determine the client's tastes.

☐ **Cost estimates.** Work with experienced builders and consultants who specialize in remodeling.

The exercises provided for each project should be critiqued by the instructor, practicing professionals, and perhaps a sampling of clients. The remodeling checklist can be altered to accommodate all types of remodeling projects. This tool aims to help the designer get started with the investigation, program, and design.

KEY TERMS

Armoire: A cabinet designed as a closet; common in Europe.

English cross bond: A method of laying brick with alternating header (short side) and ledger (long side) courses. It is considered to be the most resistant to cracking.

Gut demolition and reconstruction: Remodeling that requires the removal of the interior of a building, including walls, finishes, fixtures, plumbing, and electrical systems.

CASE STUDY 4.8

Bank Note Place

Chicago, Illinois
SMNG-A Architects, Ltd.

Bank Note Place is a 112-unit loft condominium conversion project in the South Loop section of Chicago. The project is composed of three buildings that wrap around to enclose a private landscaped courtyard at street level with a new underground parking garage below. Three floors have been added to the existing north building, carefully blending state-of-the-art construction with history. Unit plans vary from "shotgun" type to penthouse duplex homes with outdoor terraces.

plaza view

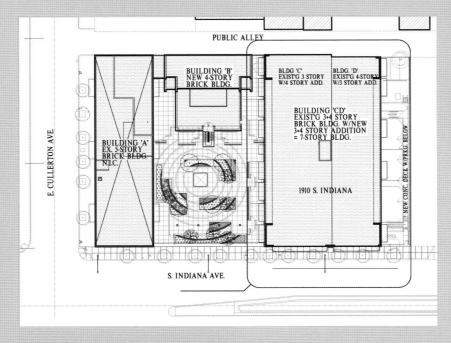

site plan

CASE STUDY 4.9

Gordon/Chappel Residence

Robert P. Gordon Architect

This house is a former neighborhood bakery, converted to residential use. The back of the building was opened to a private garden. For views, a triangular steel balcony was added to the back to enable access to the garden from the upper floor.

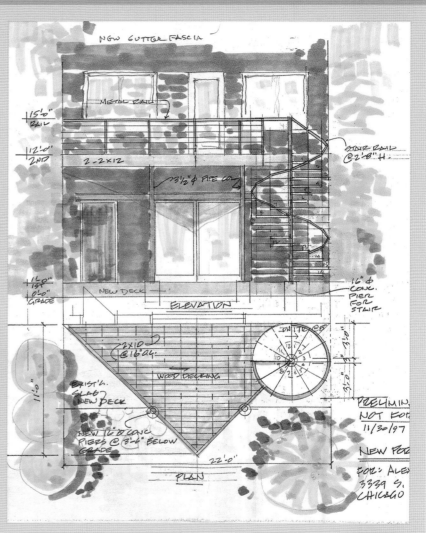

rear elevation, deck plan

yard

Printer's Row Loft

The South Loop
Chicago, Illinois
Robert Gordon, Architect

The South Loop in Chicago was home to the printing industry in the nineteenth century. Many people arrived at Dearborn Station from the south, found immediate employment, and never left the neighborhood. *The Wizard of Oz* and *Raggedy Anne* were printed in the historic Donohue Building. A group of architects, led by Harry Weese, helped to convert the entire district to a new use in the 1980s. Mr. Weese was a prominent Chicago architect, known for his sense of civic responsibility and concern for public spaces. He also led a successful campaign to save the Loop's old elevated tracks. The result was the revitalization of an area of the city near the Loop that had been abandoned.

The heavy beams and posts were necessary to support the printing presses and they remain a memory of this past use. Exposed brick walls show the structure throughout. The lofts were sold as raw space. Many artists, architects, and designers contributed their own labor and money to finish them in quirky and individualistic designs, but they all managed to maintain the authenticity of the original spaces. The space shown here is an open kitchen, dining, and living space for the architect. This project, along with many others in this book, illustrates the relationship between neighborhood and residence. If the neighborhood wasn't renovated and revitalized, these old loft buildings might have remained abandoned for much longer. Instead, the neighborhood revitalization made it possible to offer new residential opportunities, to preserve and recycle historic buildings, and increase the tax base for the city. Since these were existing buildings, no parking areas were built. The spaces that already existed on the street and in a few vacant lots and garages were renovated. Located in the South Loop, most residents have no need for an automobile for their daily activities, which is another benefit to the environment.

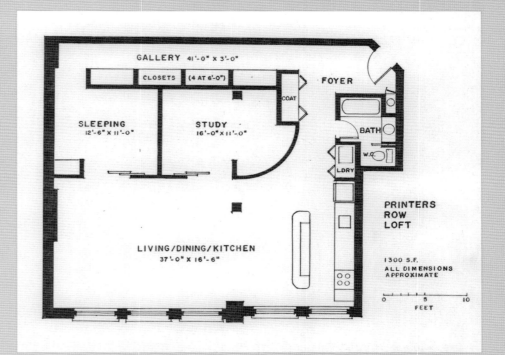

floor plan

continued on the next page

continued from the previous page

interior

entry

interior with shoji screens

Life cycle: The actual cost of a building component, as opposed to its initial cost. Takes into account long-term costs, such as energy efficiency and replacement time. Often a low initial cost is offset by short replacement periods and additional energy costs.

Quartersawn oak: Technique in which a log is cut perpendicular to the rings. It is considered a superior method of cutting wood and is prevalent in fine old cabinetwork. It produces a unique and characteristic grain.

Smart growth: A city plan that preserves natural zones alongside high-density urban development. This type of planning combats sprawl while allowing a healthy balance of development and transportation.

Space planning: A general layout of the spatial use of a space. Using bubble diagrams, consider various options for locating interior spaces, such as the living room, kitchen, dining room, bedrooms. This plan is simpler than a final floor plan to allow for changes and doesn't include construction details.

Three-way switch: A light switch that can be turned on or off at two different locations. These are useful for turning on the lights when entering a house, then turning them off from the interior. They are sometimes used in bedrooms so that lights can be turned on when entering a room and turned off from the bed. There are many uses for this very practical switch.

ENDNOTES

1. National Trust for Historic Preservation, "Sustainability by the Numbers: The Costs of Construction and Demolition," available at www.preservationnation.org/issues/sustainability/sustainability-numbers.html.
2. Ibid.

PART III

Important Spaces

44″
54–60″
30″
27″
36″

ROBERT GORDON

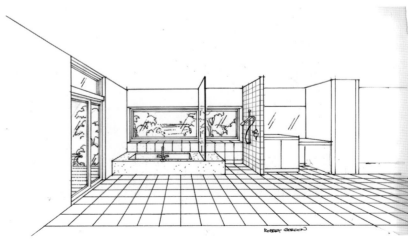

ROBERT GORDON

CHAPTER 5

Kitchens

Chapter Purpose

The purpose of this chapter is to help students understand the importance of the kitchen as a central space in residential design. Much of residential space planning is dependent upon how kitchens, and related dining rooms, are used. The kitchen-dining space may also be open to the living room forming a "great room" where all family or group activities take place. In addition, students will:

- Learn about the changing standards for kitchens, from historical precedents to the present.
- Study and observe the importance of accessibility in kitchen function and space planning.
- Discuss how family makeup is a factor in kitchen design. A family of one or two people may not require the same amount of cooking or dining space as a family of three or four people. A blended family with two sets of children from different parents presents additional problems. Do residents eat at the same time or on a staggered schedule?
- Discuss the requirements for preparing meals and cleaning up afterwards, including equipment and utensils.
- Analyze prototypes associated with the variety of clients who might use kitchens in different ways.
- Observe how different designers have interpreted the kitchen through case studies

Background

"Tell me what you eat and I shall tell you what you are," wrote Jean Anthelme Brillat-Savarin, one of the founders of French gastronomic literature, in *Physiology of Taste* (1825). This has become the familiar "You are what you eat." The kitchen is arguably the most important room in a home. Whether it is a 30-inch compact kitchen or a large restaurant-style complex, people congregate in and look forward to what's produced in this room: a fine meal and good chat.

In the early twentieth century, people cooked on open fireplaces. For the upper classes, there were maids and cooks to do the preparation in a separate room away from the dining area. But in a modest one-room cottage, cooking and eating was all done in one place.

As the century progressed, new technology developed, including refrigerators and electric ranges. Indoor plumbing became standard and social customs changed. Wartime K-rations led to the development of processed foods for the home. Women entered the workplace in greater numbers and the kitchen became a family domain with multiple cooks. Americans began to change their eating habits and kitchen design followed suit. Some of the most significant changes were as follows:

- In 1900, 95 percent of all flour sold in the United States was for home use.
- In 1910, 70 percent of all U.S. bread was baked at home.

- The first electric refrigerator was introduced in 1914. By 1937 more than two million American households had refrigerators.
- In 1925, the average American homemaker prepared all food at home. By 1965, 75 to 90 percent of all food had gone through some degree of factory processing.[1]

In recent years, there has been a movement away from processed foods. Increasing health concerns have led to a return to the use of whole foods such as nonindustrial grains, beans, rice, flour, potatoes, and vegetables. More of these foods are locally produced, bought, and stored in quantity.[2] Nevertheless, we still enjoy electric appliances and modern fixtures. Clients and designers alike enjoy browsing through catalogs, going to showrooms, and shopping for appliances. There is also a wide variety of materials and finishes, including stainless steel, marble, ceramic tile, and wood cabinets. These choices cause people to think about the kind of food they will prepare, and how they will cook it.

According to the American Institute of Architects, "Kitchens and bathrooms traditionally have been the areas in homes that get the most design attention. This trend is unlikely to change anytime soon."[3]

Kitchens perform many different functions in a household:

- Cooking. A kitchen must be efficient for receiving, preparing, cooking, storing, and cooling food, and sometimes serving it.
- Cleaning. Kitchens must also provide an area for cleaning plates of trash and washing dishes. Usually, a place to temporarily contain garbage is necessary.
- Recycling. A recycling space is now considered essential in most kitchens, with different bins for food remains, paper, metals, and plastics.
- Family or group meetings.
- Sharing of cooking and dishwashing responsibilities and the different functions and facilities required for different people (young, old, tall, short, and others).
- Service to the dining area.
- Bar service.

- Storage of additional products. The pantry is often overlooked and sorely missed. Sometimes a small cabinet adjoining a refrigerator serves this purpose. The size of this storage space depends upon how often the client shops and whether or not they stock up on large quantities of items such as paper products and canned goods.

Design Considerations

Clients know what they like to eat and how they prepare it. These are critical ingredients in kitchen design. The client's needs and wishes are important in determining the type and size of a kitchen, but the size and shape of the dwelling dictates the available space. For example, if the client wants a window, the kitchen must be located on an exterior wall. The choice of an open or closed kitchen is also determined by the client's needs and budget. But for all kitchen types, there are planning considerations that are widely recognized and should be followed. These are codified in *Planning Guidelines with Access Standards*, published by the National Kitchen and Bath Association.[4]

Client Profiles

The Epicurean

These clients love to cook and want every fixture, appliance, and gadget necessary to cook a wide range of menus. They have a wine cooler so that all wines are kept at just the right temperature. There are multiple ovens for baking and roasting. The cooktop is restaurant style and gas-powered. There is a strong exhaust fan and hood above the cooking surface. They want a pantry for storing bulk quantities of flour, grain, and produce. They enjoy entertaining, so the kitchen will be open, with an adjoining bar. This kitchen may cost as much as the rest of the house. An outdoor patio or terrace (or balcony in an apartment) is also very important to this client. Indoor/outdoor entertaining requires a barbecue at minimum and a preparation area/bar if space and budget permit.

The à la Carte Family

This is a family of modest means but very specific habits. Each family member knows what they like to eat and won't compromise. There may be pasta boiling on the stove, chicken roasting in the oven, and cheese sandwiches being prepared on the counter all at the same time.

The Microwaver

In contrast to the à la carte clients, microwavers don't like to cook. Period. They eat at restaurants, bring home takeout, or just pop a frozen meal into the microwave. They don't need an elaborate kitchen, but they do need well-organized and compartmentalized storage, as well as preparation space. Microwavers often eat standing up in the kitchen. Provide a stool. They rarely entertain, but might invite people up for a drink before going out to dinner.

Students

Students often have to share space in small, efficient quarters (see Chapter 8). Since they study a lot and play a lot, they don't have much time to eat, though they are frequent snackers. So why waste space on a large kitchen? There are prefabricated kitchens on the market that are 30 inches long by 25 inches deep. They include a two-burner stove, an under-the-counter refrigerator, and a small sink. Students also need a small table for preparation and eating. They may want a snack pantry for those late-night study sessions.

Kitchen Prototypes

Figures 5.1a through f. show the common kitchen types. When planning a kitchen, the **work triangle** must be taken into account. This is a simple means of diagramming the motions required to function in the kitchen. Draw a triangle to connect the refrigerator, sink, and range. The sum of the three travel distances should not exceed 26 feet. No single arm of the triangle should measure less than 4 feet or more than 9 feet.[5]

Even a **single-galley** kitchen has a work triangle. An optional counter can be added for preparation and dining.

CASE STUDY 5.1

Open Kitchen with Bar

Grant Place
Chicago, Illinois
Pappageorge/Haymes, Ltd., Architecture

An elegant open kitchen with wide island bar and serving area. Bar stools provide informal seating and a dining room table allows formal sit-down dining.

Kitchen Bar with Stools. (Courtesy of photographer Nick Novelli and Pappageorge/Haymes Ltd.)

The **double-galley** kitchen design is better for a more compact space. It is a good idea to use a bar for the outside part of the galley to protect visitors from the range. A bar is also a good divider between the kitchen and the living/dining space. Dirty dishes and pots and pans can be hidden during dining. It can also be useful for serving drinks and aperitifs. A good bar height is 42 to 45 inches above the finished floor. (I prefer 45 inches because it hides more and provides a better barrier to the kitchen.)

The **L-shaped** kitchen is another common layout. Some people prefer this compact arrangement of appliances. However, there is unusable space in all corners, though some cabinetmakers offer special designs for this situation.

The **square L** uses the corner for the sink, midway between the range and refrigerator. The other, open corner is a good place for a breakfast table or additional counter and cabinet space.

The **U-shaped** kitchen is the largest, though not by much. The main advantage of the U-shaped kitchen is that it accommodates a full 60-inch diameter turning circle for a wheelchair in the center.

Where space and economy are extremely important, the prefabricated all-in-one kitchen is a simple solution. The overall dimensions of 30 inches wide by 25 inches deep make these kitchens very popular for small studios and dorm rooms. The price ranges from $700 to $1,300, plus hook-up.

The plans and details shown in the NKBA *Planning Guidelines*[6] can greatly assist the designer with laying out any kitchen types. The relationship of workspaces, such as the range, sink, and refrigerator, and the distances between them, are carefully illustrated. The clearances required for passage in a kitchen and up-to-date accessibility standards are also provided.

It is also important to incorporate principles of universal design, even though there may be no one with disabilities in the client household. As people age, they hope to remain in their homes. So the kitchen plan should take accessibility into consideration. Also keep in mind that children may be using the kitchen. A universal kitchen will require more space than a conventional kitchen.

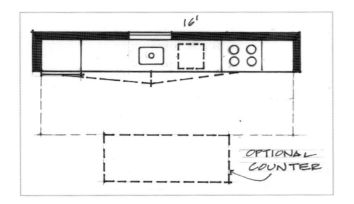

FIGURE 5.1A **Kitchen Plan: Single Galley with Optional Counter.**

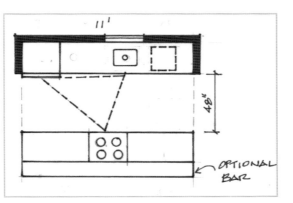

FIGURE 5.1B **Kitchen Plan: Double Galley-Range on Opposite Side.**

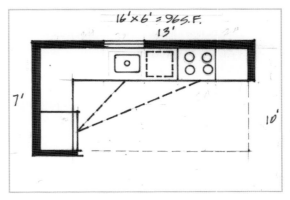

FIGURE 5.1C **Kitchen Plan: L-shaped.**

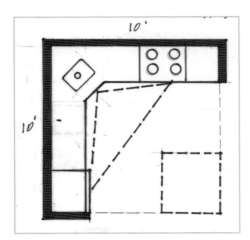

FIGURE 5.1D **Kitchen Plan: Square L.**

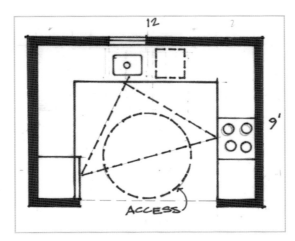

FIGURE 5.1E **Kitchen Plan: U-Shaped.**

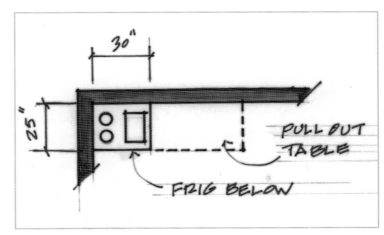

FIGURE 5.1F **Kitchen Plan: Corner Kitchen.**

CASE STUDY 5.2

Kitchen Made for Entertaining

Del Canto Kitchen
Chicago, Illinois
Rodrigo del Canto, Architect

This elegant kitchen combines the best of professional cooking with informal family and guest dining. The cooking surface is on the granite island so that guests are an integral part of the preparation experience. A large stainless steel hood with lighting ventilates the gas grill. The space is comfortable for small groups and large parties. The architect/owner is a chef and his art collection from around the world warms the area. The overall plan of the house is shown in Chapter 2.

kitchen

dining

Kitchen Elevation: Double Galley with Granite Bar. (Courtesy of Rodrigo del Canto.)

CASE STUDY 5.3

Open Kitchen with Garden View

Rosen/Haupt Kitchen
Chicago, Illinois
Michael B. Rosen, Architect

The owner/architect and his wife wanted an open kitchen, but with adequate separation for cooking. Since the kitchen/dining area faces a large south garden, it was important to cut a window under the wall cabinets. This allows adequate storage but with abundant natural light on the surface. A porch was added to the dining room, making indoor-outdoor dining a great pleasure.

Rosen-Haupt Kitchen. An open kitchen with window to garden view. (Courtesy of Michael B. Rosen.)

The standard kitchen counter height is 36 inches. A serving bar can be placed on one side of an open kitchen at 42–45 inches in height. This hides the clutter of the preparation area from guest view (**Figure 5.2a**).

In order to accommodate under-counter access, make up the necessary cabinet space elsewhere, perhaps in a pantry (**Figure 5.3b**).

Another factor to consider is natural versus artificial lighting. Many people want a window over the sink. Accommodating this request depends on the size and shape of the dwelling. Plenty of natural light

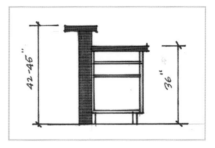

FIGURE 5.2A **Kitchen Section: Standard Counter and Bar.**

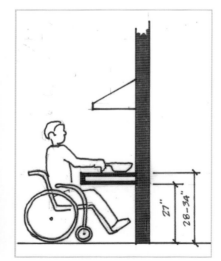

FIGURE 5.2B **Kitchen Section: Accessible Cook Surface.**

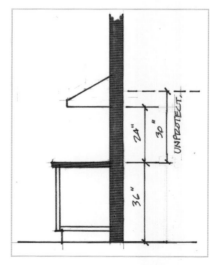

FIGURE 5.2C **Kitchen Section: Minimum Vertical Clearance Between Exhaust Hood and Cook Surface.**

CASE STUDY 5.4

A Chef's Kitchen

Winnetka Kitchen
Michael B. Rosen, Architect

The client was a professional chef and had a full understanding of the requirements for the kitchen. A large collection of pots and pans hangs over the work surface for easy retrieval. The dining space is nearby and faces the garden. A nearby pantry allows substantial space for storage.

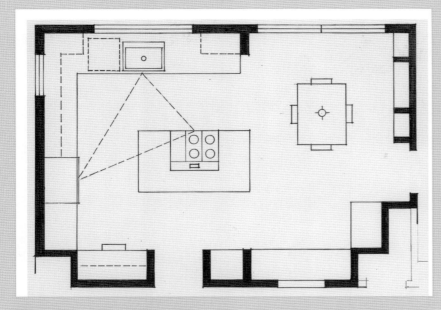

floor plan

Winnetka Kitchen. A professional-style kitchen with island. (Courtesy of Michael B. Rosen.)

CASE STUDY 5.5

A Functional L-Shaped Kitchen

Robert P. Gordon, Architect

This urban apartment offered a compact space for the kitchen, so that the dining and living areas could remain generous and open. The owners, Robert Gordon (the author) and his wife, Nancy Turpin, do a lot of cooking so the utensils and tools must be visible and within easy reach. Glass doors on the cabinets allow for quick visual access and organization. A nearby pantry takes the load off of storage. A high bar covers the preparation area. This creates a clean look for entertaining without having to remove clutter. Task lighting on the counter provides good visibility during preparation. Separate recycling bins are available for trash, metal, and plastics.

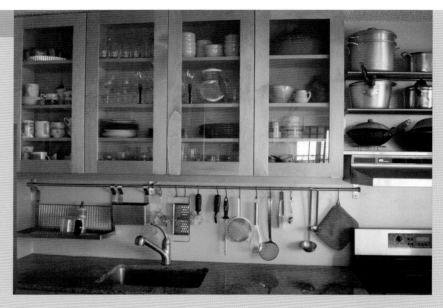

Kitchen Cabinets with Tools Visible for Easy Access. (Courtesy of the author.)

kitchen/dining room with pantry

range with pot storage above

Galley Kitchen with Bar Counter. (Courtesy of the author.)

continued on the next page

continued from the previous page

spices

tools

Under-Cabinet Lighting. (Courtesy of the author.)

Trash Bins Illustrating Separate Recycling Bins. (Courtesy of the author.)

hidden bins

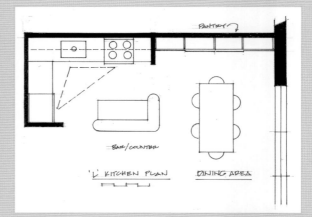

floor plan

should reach the kitchen area whenever possible. There should also be task lighting over all preparation and cooking surfaces. Under-cabinet lighting is perfect for this. If there are no cabinets, spotlights overhead will work.

Appliances and Fixtures

Selection of appliances is important. Energy and space efficiency are key considerations. Europeans have long understood the usefulness of smaller appliances, such as 24-inch refrigerators and ranges. This depends to a great extent on the availability of shopping. If daily shopping is possible, there is no need for large appliances. When meals are prepared daily, smaller pots and pans can be used, so a smaller cook surface is acceptable, especially if space is tight. However, if the client intends to shop for a large family, or to drive a distance for daily food, they will need larger storage and refrigeration spaces.

The local appliance store and manufacturers' representatives can be very helpful in obtaining brochures and pricing. The designer can help the client by assembling a good library of different appliance brochures. Visible plumbing fixtures, such as sinks and faucets, are another important part of kitchen design and should be carefully researched.

Kitchen Utensils and Small Appliances

For serious cooks, the kitchen designer must take into account the many different utensils and small appliances that make up the modern kitchen. An extensive description of these tools and devices is provided in *The Essential Kitchen*, by Christine McFadden.[7]

After consulting with the client to determine which utensils and small appliances will be needed, a means of storing them must be included in the design. Tools that will be used on a daily basis should be placed near the appropriate work station. For example, spices and spatulas should be near the range, and dishes and glasses near the sink and dishwasher. Some cooks prefer to hide the small appliances in an "appliance barn" on the countertop, and put tools away in drawers and cabinets. In a busy kitchen, especially one shared by many people, it might be desirable to have these items visible and ready for action

It is also very convenient to place the recycling bins in slide-out cabinets. Plastics and glass can be separated from perishable foods.

The Pantry

At this point in planning the kitchen, one is painfully aware of the balancing act between needs and available space, as well as budget. It sometimes seems impossible to include all of the preferred elements, especially in a modern compact dwelling. Here the designer must become super clever. Incorporating a pantry within or near the kitchen is an excellent solution.

In the twentieth century, the pantry diminished in size. The widespread availability of packaged and frozen foods in the 1950s meant the end to pantries and servants in most homes. Beginning in the 1960s, many renovations completely removed these vestiges of the past in order to enlarge the kitchens or provide a breakfast area. Conversely, buyers in the early twenty-first century started demanding more storage space for the kitchen. Today, there is a trend toward using whole foods, or bulk foods. New ways are needed to store these items without taking up too much space. Cabinetmakers have devised clever slide-out storage units that can be installed alongside a refrigerator. These are ideal for storing small objects (**Figure 5.3a**).

It is also possible to build a 12-inch-deep shelf system, enclosed by sliding or folding doors at the end of a dining room. This type of unit accommodates a significant amount of storage, even a broom closet (**Figure 5.3b**).

Home Office

There is also a growing need for space that accommodates telephones, computers, calendars for appointments, cookbooks, recipes, and even personal files. The family member in charge of the kitchen may be in charge of many other household activities. It's really a management center and serves a very important function in a household without servants. Sometimes this won't fit into the kitchen itself, but the designer can find space in a corridor or adjoining room. Since it can be a messy space, the client may wish to close it off from other activities with sliding or folding doors (**Figure 5.4**).

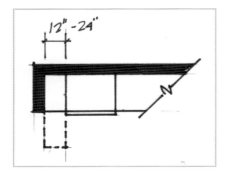

FIGURE 5.3A **Slide-out Storage.**

FIGURE 5.3B **Narrow Pantry.**

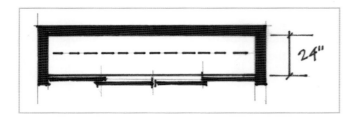

FIGURE 5.3C **Mini Home Office.**

Cost Estimates

Kitchens are a very expensive part of a homeowner's budget, so careful attention should be paid to estimating their cost. A lot of this information, such as the price of cabinets, fixtures, appliances, lighting, and flooring can be obtained from manufacturers. Labor costs are provided by bids from local contractors. This is often the same contractor who is building the house. It can be very helpful to prepare the client with a detailed estimate so that they are aware of the cost implications when choosing elements of the kitchen. A cost estimate form is provided, comparing estimates to actual costs. Using an Excel spreadsheet, the designer can keep track of the costs while assembling the kitchen specifications.

Exercises

1. Create a meal diary for all daily meals for a week or two and categorize the appliances and utensils used. Add to the list any others you would like.
2. Assemble a catalog of equipment and appliances to be used in kitchens.
3. For the five basic kitchen plans (**Figures 5.1a–f**), draw large-scale elevations (1/2 inch = 1 foot) of all interior kitchen walls. Include cabinets, lights, switches and outlets, plumbing fixtures, and wall finishes. Give dimensions for counter and cabinet heights. Show door swings for cabinets.
4. Collect samples of materials to use for kitchen planning. Prepare a "material board" showing actual pieces of tile, paint, hardware samples, and photos of plumbing and lighting fixtures. Include cabinet samples and catalog cut sheets of built-in cabinet lighting.

Chapter Summary

In this chapter, the student learned about the importance of the kitchen in the household. The modern kitchen must accommodate multiple functions that the designer must keep in mind when starting to work with a client.

A client profile and checklist were provided that can be used when designing a kitchen. This checklist takes into account family size, the number of people who participate in cooking, accessibility requirements for residents, types of food normally prepared, location of kitchen within the dwelling, whether it is open or closed, and the types of utensils and small appliances required.

Examples were provided of five common kitchen prototypes, giving information on sizes and shapes. The functions of these plans were amplified with corresponding section drawings.

CASE STUDY 5.6

A Great Room and a Great Kitchen

Bryon Kitchen
SMNG/A, Architects, Ltd.
Photography: John Faier

A great room with an open space to the upper mezzanine provides a dramatic setting for this kitchen. The industrial loft is softened with Native American carpets and crafts. This open kitchen with a large stainless steel serving island is ideal for cooking and serving. The dining space has the added advantage of a full-length pantry with translucent glass doors to provide an abundance of storage.

kitchen

Kitchen/Dining Area, Byron Residence. A long narrow cabinet works as an attractive pantry and storage area. (Courtesy of SMNG-A.)

Kitchen/Great Room, Byron Residence. The kitchen can be an integral part of a large-volume great room. (Courtesy of SMNG-A.)

Mini Home Office Near the Kitchen

Robert P. Gordon, Architect

This convenient home office serves as a personal staging area but is hidden from view by sliding doors.

Home Office. A narrow workspace can be hidden from view with sliding doors. (Courtesy of the author.)

home office open for work

Students also learned the purpose of the pantry in kitchen planning, and the specifics of storage in the kitchen/dining area.

Case studies of finished kitchens were provided to show students examples of good kitchen design.

A sample cost estimate was provided.

Upon completion of this chapter, the student will be familiar with the design process for kitchens, and will be prepared to give creative and practical design consultation to clients.

KEY TERMS

Double galley: Type of kitchen layout, similar to a single galley but with an aisle and a second aligned work surface.

Single galley: Type of kitchen with a single linear alignment of fixtures and appliances.

Work triangle: The triangle formed by placement of the refrigerator, sink, and the range/oven.

ENDNOTES

1. Beverly Bundy, *The Century in Food* (Collectors Press, 2002 Portland, Oregon), 25, 47, 69.

2. Michael Pollan, *The Omnivore's Dilemma* (New York: The Penguin Press, 2006).

3. Kermit Baker, PhD, Hon. AIA Chief Economist, *Residential Architects Report Strong Design Focus on Kitchens and Baths*, AIArchitect Quarterly Home Design Survey, Feb 2006, p. 1.

4. National Kitchen and Bath Association, "Planning Guidelines with Access Standards, 2007," available at www.nkba.org/guidelines/kitchen.aspx.

5. Ibid.

6. Ibid.

7. Christine McFadden, *The Essential Kitchen* (New York: Rizzoli, 2007).

#	ITEM	ESTIMATE	BID	NOTES
	KITCHEN COST ESTIMATE		DATE	
1	Stone countertops			
	78/25	800.00	850.00	Under-mount sink
	36/25	300.00	300.00	
2	Refrigerator: Stainless steel Kenmore 30"	629.00	629.00	
3	Dishwasher: Stainless steel Kenmore	249.00	249.00	
4	24" Stainless steel sink, below counter, Kohler	236.00	236.00	
5	Faucet: Kohler Fairfax 12177-CP single control	180.00	180.00	Pull-out
6	Base cabinets			
	18" 3-drawer: 2 @ 133	266.00	266.00	Ikea
	30" sink cabinet	133.00	133.00	(Assembled by owner)
7	Wall cabinets			
	18" 1-dr: 3 @ 83	249.00	249.00	
	36"	160.00	160.00	
8	Stainless steel utensil rod: 120"	100.00	100.00	
9	Utensil racks (Plates, spices, knives, soap)	100.00	120.00	
10	Cabinet hardware (13 pulls)	260.00	260.00	
11	Backsplash tile 10' 6 x 2" = 21 square feet	240.00	250.00	Installed
12	Electrical			
	Light strip w/3 blue shade pendants	200.00	210.00	
	Below cabinet (east wall)	150.00	160.00	
13	Construction/Labor			
	Level floor under base cainets - east wall	100.00	200.00	
	Install new base and wall cabinets	500.00	550.00	
	Add diagonal wood flooring near frig (6 s.f.)	100.00	150.00	
	Thresholds (2)	100.00	150.00	
	Install sink and dishwasher	250.00	250.00	
	Install light track, outlets and switches	250.00	250.00	
	Install new outlets on dry counter	200.00	200.00	
14	Finishing			
	Paint by owner	200.00	200.00	
	Refinish entire wood floor (owner)	1,000.00	1,000.00	
	Estimated Cost	**$6,952.00**	**$7,302.00**	**Actual Bid**
	ALTERNATE ADD:			
	Folding door cabinets - 122" long + shelves	1,000.00		

FIGURE 5.4 **Cost Estimate**

CHAPTER 6

Bathrooms

Chapter Purpose

The purpose of this chapter is to demonstrate different bathroom layouts that might be effective for different individuals and households. The prototypes provided are associated with the variety of clients who might use them. Some of the most intimate and private human functions take place in bathrooms, and so the rooms must reflect the basic attitudes and wishes of the owner. Family makeup is also a factor. A family of one or two people may not require the same amount of privacy as a family of three or four people, or even a blended family with two sets of children from different parents. Case studies illustrate how different designers have interpreted the bathroom.

Background

Throughout the greater part of history, humans in Western cultures found little reason to bathe inside their homes. Public bathing was common in ancient Rome. There are many examples dating from 500 B.C. to 500 A.D. in Rome and in its territories. There are also examples of public baths in Japan. In other places, people would just take a dip in a river or take a sponge bath using a bowl. Body odors were a part of daily life. Until about 1800, prior to the industrial revolution, elimination of human waste was relegated to a hole in the woods. In more advanced settlements, people built **privies**. These permanent structures were situated a good distance from the main shelter. People in early agricultural communities gathered waste from the privies to fertilize their crops. They learned to recycle waste with care in order to combat disease, the full effects of which were not known until well into the nineteenth and even twentieth century.

The modern water closet has a long history of development. Flushing of human waste dates back to 3000 B.C., on the island of Crete. The water closet was flushed by rainwater or cisterns built for that purpose. Waste was drained into great stone sewers. Evidence of flush toilets also exist in India from 2500 B.C., and in Egypt, and Ancient Rome. From 500 to 1500 A.D. in Europe, there was a regression in human hygiene. Castles and walled cities disposed of human waste by flinging it into the street yelling *gardez l'eau!* (This meant "watch out for the water!" a phrase that might have led to the popular term *loo*). Ultimately, it wound up in the moats surrounding the cities and probably in the food supply. In 1596, Sir John Harrington invented the water closet and installed it for his godmother, Queen Elizabeth I (perhaps the derivation for the term "the John"). Men and women used separate toilets for the first time at a dance party at a restaurant in Paris in 1739, and in 1824 the first public toilet appeared in Paris. A big breakthrough came in 1861, when Thomas Crapper, an English plumber began marketing his patented silent valveless water waste preventer, the first effective flushing device (Crapper was the name-sake of a common term for this device).[1] The room we know today as the bathroom is a hybrid. Historically, places for human waste elimination were separated from areas used for washing and bathing. Using one room for all of these functions is a fairly recent development. In this chapter we will rethink the functions of this room and consider the possibility of separating some of them.

Modern Bathrooms

The functions of washing, bathing, and waste elimination are combined in bathrooms for the sake of efficiency and cost. This does not always benefit the users, however. This confusion is evident in the various names used for this room: bathroom, washroom, toilet room, water closet, men's room, ladies' room, restroom, and powder room to name a few. The preferred term, and the one that will be used in this chapter, is *bathroom*. The term *water closet* is used to indicate a separate room that contains only a toilet.

After World War II there was an attempt to create the most efficient bathrooms at the lowest possible price to serve the rapidly expanding supply of new homes. This very important space, which shared many important and sensitive functions, was designed to occupy 35 square feet. In a home of 1,000 square feet, that was only 3.5 percent of the total floor area. Since that time bathrooms have become more spacious, accommodating a number of functions with room to spare.

As bathrooms become more complicated and luxurious, designers should consider dividing the functions, rather than housing them all in one room. Separate rooms can be created: one for the toilet (the water closet) and another for bathing and washing up. This would lead to less competition between family members for use of the bathroom at peak times.

Builders often emphasize the quantity of bathrooms provided, but they give little attention to how people use them. There should be adequate space at the entrance to the bathroom and between the fixtures to accommodate disabled family members. The sizes and shapes of fixtures don't always fit the people using them. Designers should pay careful attention to the heights and locations of the fixtures within the bathroom.[2] An increase of the bathroom area to 45 or 70 square feet would make a vast

difference in the comfort, convenience, accessibility, and pleasure of bathroom use. More elbow room also makes bathrooms safer. The U.S. Bureau of Product Safety once estimated that 275,000 people are injured annually while using showers and bathtubs.[3]

The Modern Water Closet

From 1900 to 1932, the U.S. patent office received 350 applications for water closet designs In 1992, The National Energy Policy act required new toilets to be made in order to conserve water. This is our present day toilet.[4] The water closet is now present in virtually all urban dwellings. In fact its use has vastly proliferated, and it is not uncommon to find multiple toilets, even one for each family member. This is a trend that will probably reverse in the future, due to energy conservation and housing economics.

Design Considerations

There are a number of factors that should be considered in the design of any bathroom, including family size, budget, and guest usage, as well as overall budget. First, consider the number of bathrooms and fixtures required. This depends on family size as well as the budget. It also depends on whether or not the client anticipates having guests for extended periods of time.

Take accessibility into account in bathroom plans for size allowance[5] and types of fixtures. It is important to know whether or not there is an accessible bathroom on the ground floor to accommodate the handicapped. If a stairway is planned in the dwelling, it is not necessary to provide accessible bathrooms on the second floor. There should always be at least one bathroom that can be accessed from the living area without climbing a stairway. Everyone who uses the living room will appreciate the convenience. Natural light is very important in bathrooms.

Unfortunately, designers don't often include this in modern bathroom design. An operable window provides fresh air and helps to prevent mold. It also makes it possible to keep a plant in the room. Artificial lighting is also important in bathrooms, both for safety and aesthetic reasons. Lights around a mirror are important for shaving and grooming.

CASE STUDY 6.1

Master Suite with Adjoining Bathroom

Rodrigo del Canto, Architect

An elegant ensemble of spaces, bedroom, walk-in closets, and compartmentalized water closet, bathroom, shower room, and double sinks. The bathroom suite has generous windows and faces onto a roof terrace and mature landscaped yards.

two sinks

freestanding tub

continued on the next page

continued from the previous page

shower with lighted floor

separate water closet

Heating a bathroom is a very good idea because people are often undressed in the bathroom. A switched heater would be very useful, so that energy can be conserved when the room is not in use. All bathroom receptacles must be protected by **ground fault circuit interrupters** that automatically cut off when splashed. Accessibility for people with disabilities is one of the most important considerations. The entry width, door handles, space between fixtures, grab bars, walk-in or roll-in showers, appropriate lavatories, basins, water closets are fundamental to all bathroom designs.

Finally, as in all parts of the residence, cost is an important factor. Though they are small spaces, bathrooms can be very expensive. Since they are important to owners, the budget may be relatively high. Nevertheless, it's a good idea for the designer to obtain estimates for the various fixtures and cabinets. The sample bathroom cost estimate form below will help the designer and the owner keep track of the costs so as to maintain the budget throughout the project.

Bathroom Prototypes

In the housing boom that followed World War II, builders developed an unprecedented quantity of new homes in the United States. Facing the return of large numbers of GIs, the emphasis was on building homes quickly and efficiently. The standard bathroom was 7 feet by 5 feet. It became known as the GI toilet (**Figure 6.2**). As families grew, traffic jams at the bathroom during morning "rush hour" became a fact of family life. With four to six people getting ready for work and school at the same time in the morning, there wasn't enough time for father to shave, children to brush their teeth, and teenagers to shower. One person spending too much time in the bathroom could throw off the entire family's schedule.

Gradually, as families grew during the postwar period, the cramped quarters of the GI bathroom became inconvenient. There was a need for more elbow room, and bathrooms grew very slightly larger in size, to about 8 feet by 5 feet (**Figure 6.3**). This increase of 5 square feet was helpful, leaving more space between the sink and tub, but it didn't adequately extend the usefulness of the facility for multiple family members.

#	ITEM	ESTIMATE	BID	NOTES
	BATHROOM COST ESTIMATE DATE _____			
	MATERIALS			
1	Kohler "Tea for Two" tub	1,200.00	1,200.00	White
2	Tub Faucet: Grohe -Single Control	225.00	225.00	
3	Spout: Grohe	225.00	225.00	
4	Stone Countertop: 59/22	600.00	600.00	
5	Lav - below counter	200.00	200.00	Under-mount sink
6	Lav faucet	300.00	300.00	
7	Floor and wall tiles	500.00	500.00	
	Base Cabinet:			
8	2 @ 24" (3-drawer base and 2-door base)	500.00	500.00	
9	Hardware - 3 pulls, 2 handles	100.00	100.00	
10	Sliding door, mirror	250.00	250.00	
11	Electrical: New outlet, new in-wall heater	200.00	200.00	
	Total Materials	**4,300.00**	**4,300.00**	
	CONSTRUCTION			
	Carpentry:			
12	Install new base cabinet	200.00	300.00	
13	Install towel bars, t.p.	100.00	100.00	
14	New 1 5/8" studs, 1 1/2" Durock - tub area	500.00	600.00	
15	Install Sliding Door	200.00	200.00	
	Plumbing:			
16	Re-route piping	1,000.00	1,150.00	
17	Install tub, new faucet, shower, spout	1,000.00	1,200.00	
18	Install lav, faucets	200.00	250.00	
	Electrical:			
19	Install electrical heater, outlet	300.00	300.00	
	Total Labor	**3,500.00**	**4,100.00**	
	DEMOLITION			
20	Remove tub, tiles, dry wall in tub area	300.00	300.00	
21	Remove lav, cabinet	150.00	200.00	
	FINISHING			
22	Paint - Owner	100.00	100.00	
23	Install floor and wall tiles	500.00	600.00	
	Total Misc	**1,050.00**	**1,200.00**	
	Estimated Cost	**$8,850.00**	**$9,600.00**	Actual Bid

FIGURE 6.1 **Cost Estimate**

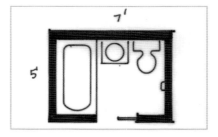

FIGURE 6.2 **Bathroom Plan: GI Bathroom.**

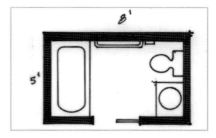

FIGURE 6.3 **Bathroom Plan: Bathroom with Additional Clearance.**

CASE STUDY 6.2

Compartmentalized Bath/Shower

Robert P. Gordon, Architect
Alex Gordon, Artisan, Owner

The Bathroom has been compartmentalized to allow privacy for the adults to shower while the children are using the bath tub.

custom sink cabinet

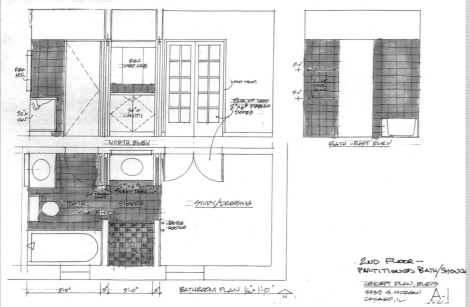

floor plan

separate shower room

separate family bathroom

shower floor with granite mosaics

The Americans with Disabilities Act (ADA) of 1990 set standards for uses, sizes, and types of fixtures and layouts of both public and private bathrooms (**Figure 6.4**). Though not required in all private bathrooms, these standards are now seen as a benefit even to people without disabilities. A seat built into the shower can be a great comfort. It is very practical for washing feet and shaving legs. The ADA dictated larger clearance spaces, grab bars, and more comfortable fixtures and fittings. (Designers should be mindful of the location of grab bars for baths and toilets, as well as towel bars and toilet paper holders. They are useless if incorrectly placed.) Bathroom renovations that were a result of the ADA also brought a new awareness of the bathroom as more than a utilitarian space. Bathrooms in general became larger and more spacious.

Privacy and Luxury

As people became more affluent, they could afford, larger and more compartmentalized bathrooms. Double sinks became more prevalent, with the bath and water closet in a separate area. Two people could use the sink while a third was bathing. A separate shower stall could be provided.

In Europe, many homes have the toilet in a room separate from the sinks and bathtub. These water closets (**Figure 6.5**) can be used while another family member is using the shower or tub and someone else is shaving or making up at the vanity. The addition of a separate water closet would be a big improvement for a minimal addition of area and cost.

The washing and bathing functions can be placed in two independent spaces (**Figure 6.6**). A separate shower allows two people to use the bathroom at the same time, one in the tub and the other in the shower. Two sinks are also provided. A pocket door gives privacy without swinging in the way. A double sink and counter allows two people to wash up and apply makeup at the same time. A linen closet and a place to hang robes keep things organized. For a luxurious touch, consider using a heated towel bar or towel rack.

A master bedroom suite includes a "master bath" that is adjacent to the sleeping area. **Figure 6.7** illustrates the privacy gained through the use of separate rooms for water closets and sinks as well. A large soaking tub with a window and a separate shower completes a luxurious bathing area.

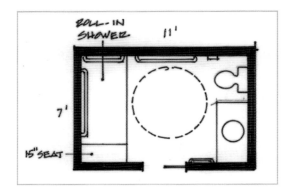

FIGURE 6.4 **Bathroom Plan: Accessible Bathroom.**

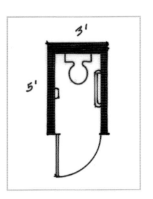

FIGURE 6.5 **Bathroom Plan: Separate Water Closet.**

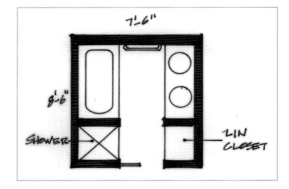

FIGURE 6.6 **Bathroom Plan: Extended Bathroom.**

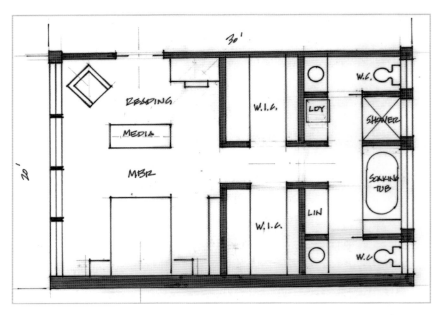

FIGURE 6.7 **Master Bedroom Suite with Master Bathroom.**

There is also space provided for a laundry room and a linen closet and walk-in closets for both individuals who use this bathroom.

An alternative to the master suite is shown in **Figure 6.8**. A shower room with a sink and countertop that is separated from the main bathroom area allows adults to get ready for work while children are getting ready for school. A study separates the compartmentalized bathroom from the master bedroom, to create a zone of privacy for adult family members.

Bathroom Sections and Details

Most bathroom countertops are set at uncomfortable heights for adults. Standard bathroom cabinet counter heights are 32 or 36 inches high. Other heights are custom sizes. For adults, specify 36 inches for comfortable use. For children, 32 inches is a better height, but they can also use stools. For wheelchair accessibility, a height of 28 to 30 inches is best, with open space below the counter.

A person should be able to stand comfortably with hands extended and slightly lowered when they wash their hands. When washing the face, one should not have to go into contortions to cup the water for rinsing. There should always be a towel bar nearby. A setup with a sink, countertop, and built-in cabinet is ideal because there are many items that are stored in the bathroom, such as soap, toilet paper, cleaning brushes, and buckets (**Figure 6.9**). A generous mirror with the top measuring to 6 feet in height should be mounted above the sink. Be sure to provide adequate

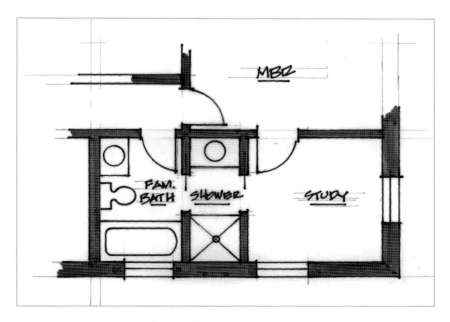

FIGURE 6.8 **Compartment Bathroom Plan.**

floor toward a lower drain area removes the need for a curb. Water naturally flows away from the bathroom floor. This is especially useful for people with wheelchairs or walkers.

Grab bars are also very important for any user, and should be set about 36 inches high. The shower control should be near the shower entry so that one can turn on the faucet before stepping in. Finally, a built-in seat is a great comfort and convenience. It can also prevent accidents in the shower, as people can wash their feet and lower legs while sitting instead of balancing on one foot.

A soaking tub can be the focus of the entire bathroom, with ample space for a spa-like experience. Soaking tubs, which are common in Japan, can be a center for relaxation as well as bathing (**Figure 6.13**). Typically, one showers before entering and exiting the tub. American plumbing fixture manufacturers are providing a growing number of large tubs for use by more than one person at a time. By using the shower first, a number of people can use the tub and thus conserve water. In a luxury installation,

lighting around the mirror. Many people request a built-in medicine cabinet for extra storage.

It's important for the designer to pay close attention to the location of accessories for the water closet (**Figure 6.10**). A toilet paper holder should be placed on the wall next to the toilet, about 7 to 9 inches in front of it and at least 15 to 24 inches above the floor. If a grab bar is required, it should be at least 42 inches long and be mounted 36 inches high. A second grab bar might be needed behind the toilet if "**transfer**" sitting is required.

A walk-in shower (**Figure 6.11**) is wheelchair accessible and can be customized with multiple showerheads for a luxury experience. When two people share a shower, one might prefer using the hand shower while the other is using the normal shower. There are also people who enjoy being sprayed from multiple angles at the same time.

Designers should consider a curbless floor with a slope toward a trough drain (**Figure 6.12**) along the shower wall. Sloping the shower

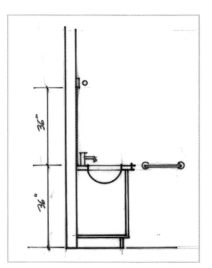

FIGURE 6.9 **Bathroom Section/elevation: Sink, Countertop and Mirror.**

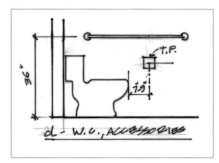

FIGURE 6.10 **Bathroom Section/Elevation Elevation: Water Closet and Accessories.**

CASE STUDY 6.3

Separate Bathroom and Shower Room

Robert P. Gordon, Architect

Two adults can enjoy the privacy of separate bathrooms. All surfaces are natural tile and the floor is unpolished, nonslip slate. One bathroom has a large marble countertop and mirror, which creates the illusion of ongoing space. The second bathroom has a smaller countertop and contains a walk-in shower.

bathroom with full-height mirror above counter

walk-in shower

slate tile floors

marble top with cabinet lights reflected

tub with side faucets

sink, counter, mirror, and lights

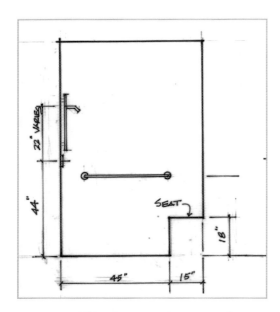

FIGURE 6.11 **Bathroom Section/Elevation: Roll-in Shower.**

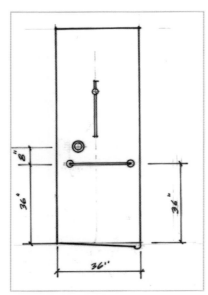

FIGURE 6.12 **Bathroom Section/Elevation: Trough Drain.**

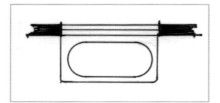

FIGURE 6.13 **Bathroom Plan: Soaking Tub.**

Completed bathrooms were illustrated in case studies and exercises rounded out the practical application of bathroom design ideas. Students should choose exercises to complete, culminating in the presentation of their projects to a jury of professional practitioners. Developers and salespeople as well as end users should also participate in the jury.

Bidet: A low basin commonly used in Europe, used specifically for washing one's private parts. It promotes cleanliness and health and many health practitioners believe it should be used more widely.

Ground fault circuit interrupters: Type of electrical outlet that protects a circuit if it gets wet, in which case the receptacle automatically shuts off.

Privy: An outhouse.

Transfer: A method of positioning oneself on a toilet or in a tub in which a grab bar is used and one's weight is transferred from one leg to the other. This is necessary for some people with disabilities and is convenient for all.

Water closet: A small room containing a toilet.

consider a built-in sound system. It can greatly contribute to the relaxation and sense of well-being.

Chapter Summary

This chapter provided an overview of the evolution of the modern bathroom. Prototypes for bathroom designs including a minimalist GI bathroom, various extensions, and a separate water closet room were reviewed. Design considerations for planning a bathroom were presented, which included issues of accessibility.

EXERCISES

1. Draw 3 different plans for fixture arrangements in a bathroom that is 6 feet by 8 feet. Include space for a linen closet (inside the bathroom). Discuss the advantages and disadvantages of each.
2. Design a luxurious master bathroom that includes a soaking tub, shower, two sinks, a generous mirror, and a **bidet**. A bidet is a fixture that is common in Europe. It a low basin used for washing one's private parts and is considered healthy and hygienic.
3. The water closet should be in a separate compartment. Provide space for a chair and reading area. The bathroom should be completely

CASE STUDY 6.4

Spa Bathroom with Soaking Tub

Michael B. Rosen, Architect

A grand room with abundant natural light is dedicated mainly to bathing.

soaking tub

wheelchair accessible. Include a generous window for viewing the exterior. Which views are compatible with bathtub use? If there is an issue with privacy, consider translucent glass.

4. Collect samples of materials to be used for bathroom planning. Prepare a material board, showing actual samples of tile, paint, hardware, and photos of plumbing and lighting fixtures.

ENDNOTES

1. Bindeshwar Pathak, "History of Toilets," paper presented at the International Symposium on Public Toilets, Hong Kong, 1995. As cited in *The Chicago Tribune*, February 1, 2004.
2. Alexander Kira, *The Bathroom* (New York: Viking, 1976), 39, 48, 53.
3. Ibid., 49.
4. Pathak, "History of Toilets."
5. National Kitchen and Bath Association, "Planning Guidelines with Access Standards." Available at www.nkba.org/guidelines/default.aspx.

CHAPTER 7

Bedrooms
A Safe Place to Sleep

Chapter Purpose

More than any other residential space, the bedroom is called upon to perform many important and often conflicting duties in people's lives. The family makeup and individual choices also affect bedroom planning. This chapter explores the multiple functions of modern bedrooms, as well as the different types of clients who require specialized room plans.

In the current marketplace, a diverse array of clients demands a wide range of approaches to the design of this important space. This chapter describes historic as well as personal and emotional influences on current bedroom design. This background will help the designer to better understand present-day social constraints: At what age should a child be sent from the parents' room to a nursery? When should children be separated by gender? What about blended families? Are children present when adults are entertaining or must there be a separate social space for them? These factors all contribute to the planning of the bedroom. They can also offer a wider range of ideas to better solve the client's needs in planning this very important space. The designer should be aware of the many choices that are available to clients. As in the other chapters, there are prototype plans that illustrate various room types and address the issue of accessibility.

Close attention is paid in this chapter to the size and layout of bedroom closets. Separate closets for two people sharing a bedroom can be a good idea. One person might be messier than the other, which can lead to arguments. The designer can propose different ways of keeping a mess out of sight. A client checklist is provided at the end of the chapter. This will help the designer understand the activities planned for each bedroom. It will serve as a guideline for design and serves as an official record of the initial client-designer interview.

In My Room

For some people, such as those who live in small city apartments, the bedroom is their entire residence. For others, it's a refuge away from the fray of family or communal life, a place to study, read, or just be alone. When people come home from a long trip, they are usually glad to sleep in their own beds again. More than any other space in a home, the bedroom should make people feel calm and secure.

Bedrooms are a key component of space planning for an entire residence. They have a lot to do with how people feel about their homes. An individual's mental and physical health can be traced to their environment, particularly the bedroom. The decisions the client and designer make regarding the purpose and design of the bedroom may affect the basic sense of security the client has about the home, such as whether a garden view helps to soothe or heal?[1] And the relationship between people who share a bedroom can be enhanced or inhibited by the design.

The bedroom plan also affects the layout of the other rooms. The client may not be aware of the many choices available to them in planning a bedroom and the effect a bedroom environment can have on their sense of well-being. For this reason, it is very important for the designer to understand the emotional and practical considerations that go into bedroom design, as well as the history behind our notions of proper bedrooms.

Evolution of the Bedroom

Bedrooms were not always separate spaces within a residence. As with other things in prehistory, people made do with what was available. Hunters and gatherers lived in rudimentary and crude shelters such as caves and huts. Their nomadic lifestyle required little more. There was no central heating, so people (and sometimes their animals) slept around fires and snuggled together to keep warm. The same fire was used for cooking.

In permanent medieval agricultural communities, a two-story barn was an upgrade from the hut. Servants often shared sleeping space with the family and animals on the (warmer) ground floor while the upper floor was used for storage. Children, rich and poor alike, were typically sent away from the home as apprentices or to find work at about the age of seven. Most daytime activities occurred in the main room on the ground floor. It was furnished with a table and chairs in the center and additional chairs were pulled up when required. The beds and other furniture were placed at the walls. At night, everyone—owners, servants, and livestock—slept in the same room. It would be a long time before the farmhouse would be developed as a separate building.

In the early fifteenth century, a merchant class emerged in European society. This middle class—the bourgeoisie—lived in relatively large, comfortable homes of about 1,500 square feet. They had several rooms and sometimes a second story. The number of bourgeoisie increased through the sixteenth and seventeenth centuries. Their homes grew to encompass more servants and more spacious accommodations for all.

A typical seventeenth- or eighteenth-century bourgeois home might accommodate the following under one roof: the family business, a stable, a barn, a hayloft, and a large main room for dining, entertaining, and sleeping for family members. Families often slept together in one large bed. Separate sleeping chambers for older children and servants might be found on the second floor. Separate bedrooms for the master and mistress of the house, children, and servants, were not standard until well into the eighteenth century.

The King's Bedroom at the Palace of Versailles

The bedroom was a relatively public place even in the royal chambers. In the late seventeenth and early eighteenth century, King Louis XIV of France, also known as the Sun King, slept in a canopied bed where he entertained his courtiers. At that time, some people slept sitting up for health reasons. This also made it easy to visit with people while taking a little snooze. The king's bedroom measured 9.7 by 9.15 meters and the ceilings were 10.15 meters high (about 33 by 31 by 34 feet).[2] It wasn't cozy, but the canopy around his bed kept out the cold air.

There were adjoining anterooms, or waiting rooms, where people lined up for an audience with the king. Daily ceremonies took place in the king's bedroom, such as the ritual awakening and dressing of the king in the morning, called the rising, and the evening undressing and putting to bed of the monarch. The bedroom was a public space in the palace, and was considered a very important instrument of state. The bed was located in an alcove separated from the rest of the chamber by a decorative railing. Anyone passing by the alcove showed respect; women curtsied and men bowed. Entry into the alcove had to be authorized by the king. The king's chamber served as a profit center as well. People paid for the privilege of an audience with the king at these private times. The king's bedroom foreshadowed the luxurious bedrooms to follow, albeit without the royal trappings.

The Industrial Bedroom: Overcrowding in the Tenements

Life in rural and bourgeois households did not change dramatically in the early nineteenth century, but people who lived in the very crowded conditions of industrialized cities were forced to share bedrooms. Urban bedrooms were small and had to double up as kitchens and workshops because space came at a premium. Parents often shared a bedroom with their younger children and that room became a kitchen/dining room in the morning. Older children shared the parlor, or living room, which became a workroom by day. Dramatic examples of this type of bedroom have been preserved in New York's Lower East Side Tenement Museum. (Tenements are described more fully in Chapter 8.)

The Beginning of Privacy and Intimacy

It wasn't until the nineteenth century that the idea of privacy for a bedroom took hold. "A heavy veil was thrown over the least manifestation of sexuality. As a result, the master bedroom became a sacred place, a temple consecrated not to voluptuousness but to procreation."[3] The nineteenth century saw a major change in space planning for sleeping quarters: for the first time, the parents had a right to privacy. This had an indirect affect on the other bedrooms. Younger children needed supervision and their older children required a place to study. Gender issues had to be addressed. The configuration of the bedrooms was no longer a simple question of sleeping arrangements. These changes marked the beginning of multipurpose bedrooms.

Modern Sleeping Quarters

From these earlier times, our notions of the functions of the bedroom would evolve and hybridize. The master bedroom is now a central element to home design. Some people prefer the master bedroom to be an intimate place, used and seen only by the owners. It can include a workspace, a media center, a cosmetics table, and other related functional elements. If there is room and the budget allows, most people prefer a private bathroom that adjoins the bedroom with no access for guests or other family members.

Children's bedrooms almost always include a study desk, bookshelves, and storage for clothes and objects. When two or more children share a room, issues of turf and privacy arise. The design and furnishings must reflect this need. These rooms might best be described as sleep/study/entertainment spaces, but most people still call them bedrooms. Besides sleeping and studying, bedrooms might also be needed for recu-

peration. There is a need to create a space where a sick person can have visitors without feeling they are intruding.

Site Influences

Location of the bedrooms within a residential unit became more important as specialized uses developed, particularly in cities. Adults demand privacy and tranquility in their bedrooms. A quiet night's sleep is important to personal health and well-being. A view of the backyard is desirable.

It's said that children can sleep through anything, so noise may be less important to them. They might be given the street side of the dwelling for their bedrooms. But direct sunlight in the morning might be an annoyance. Sleeping spaces should be planned with solar orientation in mind. In all bedrooms, there should be a good flow of air. Even in an air-conditioned or heated home, natural ventilation through windows or ducts is a must.

Design Considerations

As with any other project, the needs of the client must be determined. A client checklist is provided at the end of this chapter to start the process. Several personal interviews may be required, as well as visits to the clients' present home. What bed size will be required for each individual? How much storage do they have now and how much more will they need? Measure rod lengths or hanging space, as well as shelf or drawer space. Only clothes and related objects should be stored in the bedroom closet. Storage for other items, such as a utility closet or storage room, should be provided to avoid junk overflow. How do the clients feel about walk-in or separate closets? Are they a necessity? Will there be a master bathroom accessible only through the master bedroom? Do the clients wish to watch television or listen to music while in bed? This would require a cabinet and electrical provisions, as well as additional space. If the clients read in bed, a separate light for each is indispensable. The lights should be small and directed.

If one or more of the adults wants to use the bedroom as a home office, it is very important to keep this separate from the sleeping space. Clutter from an office can destroy a peaceful night and make it difficult to sleep. Consider a cabinet or closet with doors to close off the space when it's not in use.

All bedroom spaces should be accessible. Everybody can enjoy the advantages of larger clearances and hardware that is easier to use. In the prototypes in this chapter, all spaces around beds as well as aisles between furnishings and walls are at least 36 inches wide. In some bedrooms, a full 60 inches is provided for wheelchair turnaround.

Outlet placement is an important issue in any room. The furniture plan should be completed, and then the outlets for lamps, media, and other electrical equipment can be set. Also, it is very convenient to use three-way switches at the bedroom entrance. A wall switch turns on one of the night table lamps, which can then be turned off at the lamp itself. (*Tip:* It's better to have some extra outlets and not use them than to not have enough.)

Furniture is also a fundamental design consideration. Take an inventory of the clients' present furniture—what they intend to keep and what new furniture they will need. Make accurate measurements. This greatly affects space planning. Some important pieces for a bedroom include beds (of course), side tables, a reading or tea table, dressers, cosmetic tables, lounge or reclining chairs, snack bars, sofa beds, and desks and chairs.

Prototype Bedrooms and Client Profiles
The prototypes that follow progress from a minimal single sleeping space to a master bedroom "spa" suite. They recognize the many different functions of bedrooms and the options available to different clients. Living in a minimal bedroom may enable people to live in cities or neighborhoods they cannot otherwise afford. The small size is compensated by access to public spaces. Larger bedrooms allow for entertainment activities to take place that might otherwise require a separate study or media room.

Some of these examples show how the use of the room can change over time. Changes in a family over time will alter the purpose of a bedroom, such as when a child grows up and leaves the home (or returns) and when parents move in with their children.

Please note that doors are not shown in the diagrams for visual simplicity. They may be swinging or pocket doors. Pocket doors take up less room space and are very practical for small rooms. In all cases, pay close attention to the layout of the closets and how people enter the bedroom. This will vary in different residential layouts. Closet doors may be sliding, bi-fold, or hinged doors, depending on the wishes of the client. Door sizes should be based on inside closet divisions for easier access. (See **Case Study 7.1** for closet layout and photo.)

Also, pay close attention to the location of the windows in a room, sometimes given in a residential plan, and how it affects the placement of the bed and other furniture.

The Bare Minimum: Single Sleeping Space
The minimal sleeping space shown in **Figure 7.1** is enough for a single bed with 36-inch clearance on one side. There is a 36-inch-wide window and a possibility for a small desk. This room could be used for a single person, adult or child, budget hotel room, or monks in a monastery.. Though the room is small by any standards, it can and should be attractive. Decorative floor tiles, a colorful paint job, comfortable window coverings, and an attractive view add to the pleasure of any room. If this room were to look out on Central Park, the Luxembourg Garden, or the Eiffel Tower it would be acceptable to many people who ordinarily would not consider such a small space. Personal artwork hung on walls, a radio or TV, and some storage under the desk help to make even a small room comfortable. A small room in not for everyone, but access to a neighborhood and reduction in commuting time can compensate for the inconvenience.

There is a fundamental economy to small rooms, so the users can compensate by spending more money on other things. If one spends little time in the bedroom, using it mainly for sleeping, then a small room is acceptable, at least for certain periods in a person's life. The rest of the time can be spent at work and play; in cafes, on the streets, at movies, or visiting friends who have larger apartments.

This room can be extended another few feet to accommodate a closet, with coat hooks on the opposite wall. A private closet and efficient storage space are essential. Even with the closet, the room has a modest area of 80 square feet. A pocket door to enter the room can help create a sense of spaciousness. A swinging door would take up valuable space.

Client Profile

Our client is a recent college graduate with a job in Manhattan, who rarely stays in his room. He's generally out on the new pedestrian promenade in Times Square, enjoying a Broadway production, eating dinner in an Asian restaurant near Houston Street, or enjoying an espresso in the West Village. He buys fresh food at the farmer's market in Union Square. There is no need to pay for additional space. Who needs a living room or a kitchen?

Exercises

1. Draw an elevation of the top wall as shown on plan. Assume an 8-foot-high ceiling. Now draw an elevation placing the window on the left wall along the access space. How does this affect the feeling of the room?
2. Draw an elevation of the bed wall, maximizing storage. Show under-bed storage drawers and shelves above the bed.

Double Sleeping Space

Bedrooms with two single beds (**Figure 7.2**) are typical in family homes. A space that is 10 feet by 10 feet can accommodate two beds off of one central 36-inch access space. There is also room for a closet for each person. With bunk beds, four children could share this room, but there would only be enough space for one desk and two closets. This would be an extreme condition, but could be useful for temporary guests.

Client Profile

The client has two children of the same gender. There are other spaces in the residence that can be used for studying or entertainment, so the

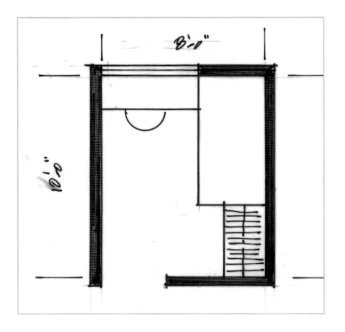

FIGURE 7.1
Minimum-sized single bedroom.
Includes closet and desk.

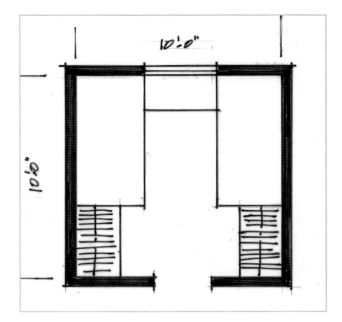

FIGURE 7.2
Minimum-sized bedroom for two single beds.
Includes two closets.

CASE STUDY 7.1

Gordon Residence

Bridgeport, Chicago, Illinois
Master Bedroom Suite
Artisan, Designer: Alex Gordon

This master bedroom suite is associated with the bathroom suite in **Case Study 6.2**. A tiny alcove (6 by 8 feet) was originally planned as an adjoining nursery for a newborn child. As she outgrew her space, the alcove was converted to a combination closet, dressing room, and reading room. The bedroom has a private terrace facing the garden. The alcove became available for other uses. It remains a connector between the bedroom and master bathroom suite. A full-height closet was designed by the owner, an artisan and designer, and built in his own shop. Since the ceiling is nine feet high, conventional sliding doors wouldn't reach the ceiling, leaving a "dust shelf" above the closet. The designer decided to fabricate lightweight shoji screens to solve this problem. Closet storage now goes all the way up to the ceiling.

alcove near bedroom

Bedroom Suite. A spacious and elegant bedroom, bathroom, and closet suite with terrace view.

bedroom closet alcove with shoji doors closed

Bedroom Closet. This closet features full-height shoji screens as closet doors. View of hanging space.

bedroom will mainly be used for sleeping. There is room for one table between the beds.

Exercises

1. Draw an elevation of the top wall in the plan showing the window above the table.
2. Draw a second elevation showing a high window going across the entire wall. What should the sill height and head height of the window be? How will it open for ventilation?
3. How much storage is available below the beds and what kinds of things would be stored there?

Large Single Bedroom

A residence contains a number of large, generous bedrooms, each intended for one person (**Figure 7.3**). Each bedroom has enough space for a full bed, a desk, and a full-height bookshelf. There is 10 feet of closet length, which provides a generous amount of storage space. There is also a large picture window for light and air.

Client Profile

The clients are a group of adult professionals who share an apartment in San Francisco. This household has adequate disposable income, but they don't want to spend it all on a private residence. Each bedroom comfortably accommodates one individual and can also accommodate two with a double bed.

Exercises

1. The plan is shown with a single bed, 39 inches wide. Some individuals might prefer a larger bed. Draw the plan with a single bed and then one with a full bed, 54 inches wide. How does this affect the furniture layout? Does the single bed provide enough additional floor space for additional furniture? How much storage space is lost with a full bed?
2. Draw the plan with the bed perpendicular to the left wall, with a window on the right wall. Rearrange the shelving. What are the advantages and disadvantages of each plan?

Dorm Room or Bedroom for Multiple Children

The room in **Figure 7.4** builds on the ideas presented in **Figures 7.1** and **7.2**. It can accommodate four beds. With a wall divider between the two pairs of beds, the rooms can be closed off for privacy.

Client Profile

A co-housing household refers to a home occupied by a blended family: several adults, and possibly some children. The clients may have different family structures; some have older children and some have infants. There may be a need for a nursery for the infants. In some cases, it may be necessary to sleep groups of children, dormitory style, in one or two large rooms. Flexibility is very important. When four beds are occupied by two different families, or genders, the room can be closed off and made private by use of a pocket door. Otherwise, it could be left open as one room. This room, or suite, could also be used for adults, or as sleeping space in a vacation cabin. Private storage cabinets for each person would be useful.

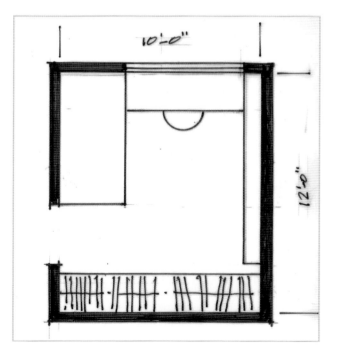

FIGURE 7.3 **Large Single with Study.** Large single bedroom with desk, shelves, and large closet.

The important feature is that the space can be divided into two rooms if the circumstances require it.

Exercises

1. Draw an arrangement of cabinets along the corridor; one for each child. There should be at least as many cabinets as there are beds. These could be individual small "cubbies" for each person. Remember, this storage is also used by children who may not be spending the night. Should the cabinets be accessible from the corridor or from inside the room? What is the reasoning for this decision?

2. Draw an elevation of the top (window) wall, showing an optional high window across the entire room, or a conventional window at the desks, with a 30- inch sill height. What are the advantages and disadvantages of each?

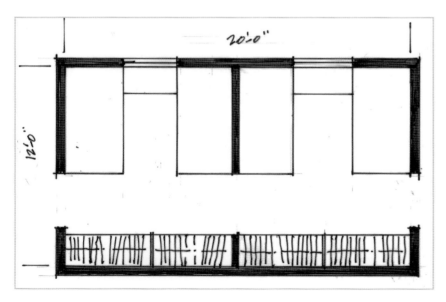

FIGURE 7.4 **Multiple Occupants.** Room for multiple beds and occupants, as in a dorm room. Separate closet provided for each.

Double Bedroom

A minimal master bedroom for two people has a full-size bed that measures 54 inches by 75 inches and includes a full closet that could be shared by two individuals (**see Figure 7.5**). If the couple adds a baby to their family, the closet can be left partly open for cradle space. When the child moves to his or her own room, the owner can again use the space as a closet. The room is large enough to accommodate two night tables, or small desks, with windows above. There is no additional space for a lounge chair or media center, though a media center with flat screen TV can be mounted on the wall facing the bed, between the two closets. This room has the possibility of two separate entry doors.

Client Profiles

- Client A: A recently married couple expecting a baby
- Client B: The same couple, but older. The child has moved out and each parent has his or her own closet.

Exercises

1. Design this prototype with the window on the right-hand wall instead of above the night tables.

2. Assume this is a corner room. The top wall and right wall have large windows. Reposition the bed. What are the advantages and disadvantages of this arrangement?

Accessible Master Bedroom

This large master bedroom (**Figure 7.6**) is completely wheelchair accessible, with a 60-inch diameter turning space in the room. Two 12-foot-long closets flank the bed, providing generous storage. There is a set of double doors facing the bed, either French or sliding doors. This room adjoins a living room. If the client wishes to mount a flat-screen TV on the wall at the foot of the bed, the doors can be placed to the side, flanking the wall, rather than in the center. If the designer has control of the exterior walls, another option would be to place a large picture window on one of the side walls or on the wall at the foot of the bed.

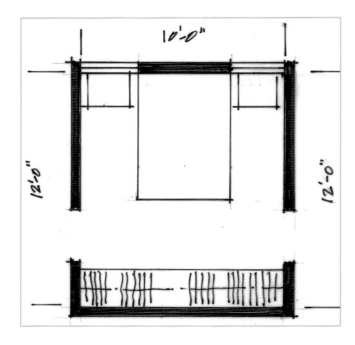

FIGURE 7.5
Minimum Bedroom with Full-Sized Bed. Includes a large closet.

Client Profile

The client is a middle-aged, affluent couple in Chicago, who want generous passage space as well as substantial closet space. The clients feel claustrophobic in a closed room and prefer an open floor plan. The clients want to enter the room through glass doors (with curtains) so that the room feels larger and can borrow light from other space. Though the couple is in good health, they want to provide space for the future in case one of them needs a wheelchair. Accessible spaces are a positive feature at any time, as they are larger and more spacious.

Exercises

1. Measure and draw the closet space. Include the hanging space, both single and double height, as well as shelves. Envision the items that will go into each area of the closets, such as shirts, jackets, trousers, dresses, shoes, hats, and undergarments. Estimate the amount of space needed for each type. Do a survey with people you know. This

exercise can be repeated no matter what size the bedroom and closet space.

2. If the client prefers a larger table or desk space alongside the bed, draw a plan with shorter closets and two generous tables with storage below. How much closet space is lost? Is there a more efficient way to arrange the closets?

Master Bedroom with Bay Window

The bedrooms shown in **Figures 7.7a and b** are similar to the previous prototype (**Figure 7.6**), with the addition of a bay window. The additional space can be used for a reading table with two chairs. The location of a single door on the left wall allows a specific use for each closet. The one nearest the reading table could be used for media. The client would be similar to the one in the previous example. When considering a bay window in an apartment building, or condo, permission must be secured

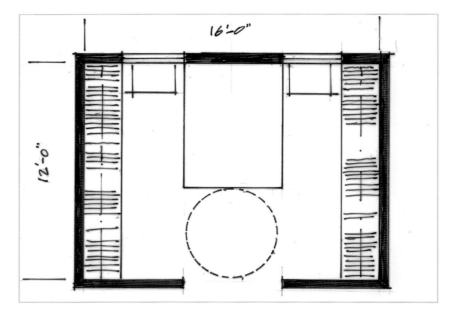

FIGURE 7.6 **Accessible Bedroom with Queen Bed.** Includes two large closets. Wheelchair radius is 60 inches.

from the association and the services of a licensed architect should be secured.

Exercises

1. The bedroom in **Figure 7.7a** has two doors, maximizing circulation. Show how the inward-facing closets can be turned and made into walk-in closets so that there are no doors opening into the bedroom

2. If there is only one door into the bedroom, as in **Figure 7.7b**, what are the possible uses for the extra space? A longer closet is shown on the right-hand wall, with two smaller closets flanking the door. These could be used for specialized storage, such as shelving or media. Draw different options for these specialized closets, including elevations. Measure objects to see that they fit.

3. Extend the bedroom by means of a bay window. What different types of uses, and furniture, can be planned for the new space? Draw alternate plans. Specify furniture. Present catalog cuts of possible furnishing.

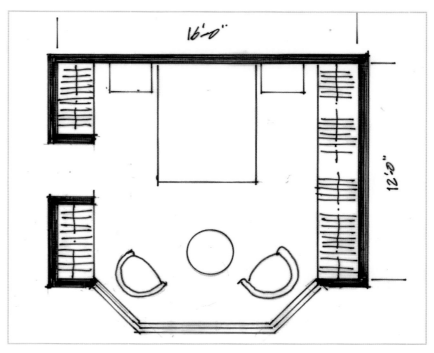

FIGURE 7.7B **Master Suite with Bay.** Same as 7.7a but with a bay window and entry from one side only.

Master Bedroom Suite: The Spa

The master suite in **Figure 7.8** contains all of the features of a luxury resort. It is a private and self-contained bedroom suite, complete with king-size bed, media center, breakfast table, lounge chairs, and a bay window or balcony. Sometimes the residents enjoy cocktails or breakfast in bed, so there is a mini-fridge and a hot plate for tea and coffee. A writing desk and two generous night tables also grace the room. (Louis XIV might have enjoyed this room.) Each individual has his or her own walk-in closet and a separate sink with vanity and toilet. The large soaking tub, with an adjacent glassed-in shower stall, completes the suite.

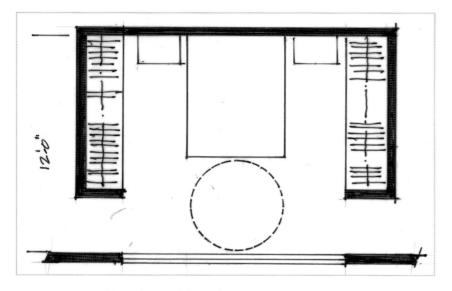

FIGURE 7.7A **Accessible Bedroom with Window.** Accessible bedroom with a queen-sized bed, two large closets, and large picture window.

Client Profile

An elderly couple in rural Massachusetts lives in a large home. They enjoy frequent overnight guests, including their many children, grandchildren, and friends. If there are guests in the house, they like to maintain their privacy. They want a large luxury master bedroom and bathroom suite with a mini-bar so they can get away from the fray for a while. The view is very important, and a bay window or balcony is necessary.

Exercises

1. Is there a better way to position the bed? Draw it at an angle toward the bay window. What do you do with the leftover spaces?
2. Should there be different floor finishes for the sleeping and entertaining parts of the bedroom? Perhaps hardwood with an area carpet under the table and lounge chair? Or carpets in the bed area with tiles in the front bay window area? Show different floor finishes for the sleeping area, walk-in closet area, and the bathroom suite. Draw plans showing these finishes.
3. Draw a soffit with recessed spot lights above the bay window.
4. Draw soffits with spot lighting at the top and bottom walls as well. This leaves a volume ceiling in the middle. Discuss the feeling of the room with varying ceiling heights.

Flexible-Use Bedroom

The so-called guest bedroom (**Figure 7.9**) is often used as a TV room or study. By using a sofa bed or a fold-down **Murphy bed**, the space can be open and useful most of the time. Multipurpose furniture is very important for the comfort of the owners as well as the guests.

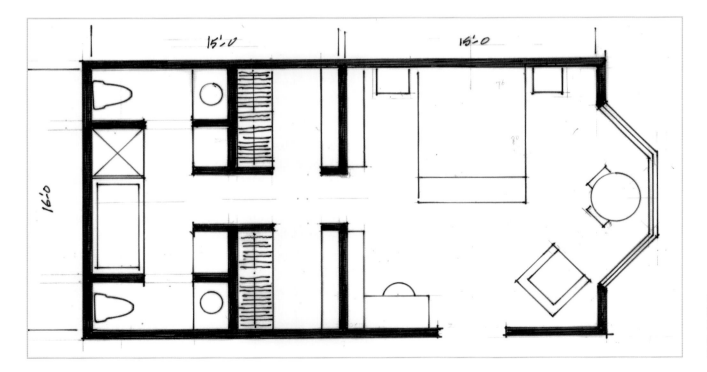

FIGURE 7.8 **Master Suite.** Large master bedroom suite with a king-sized bed, lounge chair, bookshelves, desk, and sitting area. Adjoins private master bathroom suite.

CASE STUDY 7.2

Master Bedroom Suite

del Canto Residence
Chicago, Illinois
Rodrigo del Canto, Architect

The bedrooms in this house **(see Case Study 2.5)** include an elegant and luxurious master bedroom suite, two single-bedroom suites for the daughters, and a guest bedroom suite. The corresponding closets are shown here (adjoining bathrooms are also shown in **Case Study 6.1**). The master bedroom is large, accommodating the bed and surrounding artwork, two bedside tables, and a floor-to-ceiling bookcase. Custom-built walk-in closets line the back wall of the bedroom and lead to the master bath, which in turn leads to the terrace. The room also includes a fireplace and sitting area. There is a large window with views of the neighboring landscape. (See second-floor plan and photos, **Case Study 2.5**.)

The walls are adorned with rich warm wood panels and the owner's extensive art collection. Lighting is directed toward the artwork by two bedside lamps. The daughters' bedrooms are on the same floor, but on the other side of the large hallway and stairway. Each daughter has her own suite, including closet, bathroom, and study area. The house also includes a separate guest bedroom suite.

bedroom art

Bedroom Suite. A walk-in closet adjoins the bedroom and bathroom.

continued on the next page

continued from the previous page

Bedroom Suite. This view features the bed with artwork and bookshelves.

bedroom sitting area

child's bedroom

walk-in closet

child's study area

Client Profile

An individual living in a small two-bedroom apartment in Philadelphia sometimes invites guests to sleep over. Most of the time however, he needs the additional bedroom for a study and extra clothes storage, as well as a TV room. He also needs bookshelves. The desk should be large enough to double as a cocktail table or snack bar. A sofa bed or Murphy bed is essential so that there is more floor area when the room is not used for sleeping.

Exercises

1. Compare the sofa bed to the fold-up bed. What are the advantages and disadvantages of each type?
2. In the fold-up bed, there is about 12 inches of depth in the finished cabinet. What can be designed to make use of that space alongside the bed cabinet? Bookshelves? Storage cabinets? Draw them in plan and elevation.

Chapter Summary

This chapter provided background on the different types of bedrooms and their many functions in the modern residence. It called attention to the relationship between family makeup to bedroom planning. It also provided some information on the emotional place the bedroom occupies in the minds of clients. The importance of site and view and their influence on the bedroom layout was discussed and different types of furniture used in bedrooms were identified. The importance of accessibility in bedrooms and many examples of clearances and wheelchair turnarounds were described.

A client checklist was provided, which can be reviewed with clients before starting the design process. It is the key to developing a program for the floor plan. In the classroom, this can be developed further as an assignment. Nine different prototype bedrooms, ranging from a minimal "monk's cell" to a luxurious master bedroom spa were detailed. Each prototype identified the type of client who might want a particular type of bedroom. Tips were given for locating electrical outlets by following the furniture plan. Through these prototypes, the student has been shown the wide range of bedroom types and clients for whom the residential designer may be working.

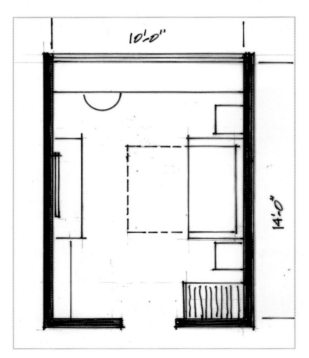

FIGURE 7.9 **Convertible Guest Bedroom/ Study.** This room can be used for family, TV, and storage when not in use as guest room. Sofa bed or fold-up bed is essential.

CLIENT CHECKLIST: BEDROOMS

1. Household composition: gender, relationship and age.
2. How many people will use the dwelling unit and how many bedrooms will they require?
3. How will this change over time?
4. Are any of the people in the household disabled?
5. Check which activities will take place in the bedrooms:
   - ☐ Sleeping
   - ☐ Romance
   - ☐ Studying
   - ☐ Watching TV
   - ☐ Reading
6. Will there be guest access to the bathroom through the bedroom, or will there be a private bathroom?
7. Quantify the clothes storage necessary, for example, lengths of closet poles and shelves.

Will closets be within the room? Are walk-in closets preferred?

8. Site Restrictions: Where can bedrooms be located in floor plan? Corner room? Garden view? Street?
9. How important is the view? Large windows or small?
10. Privacy factor: Is there a clear view or will neighbors be able to look into the bedroom? If this is the case, window coverings will be important.
11. Floor finish: does the client prefer wood, carpet, or sustainable materials?
12. Furniture:
    - ☐ Bed(s): twin, bunk beds, full-size bed, queen, or king?
    - ☐ Will there be under-bed storage?
    - ☐ Night tables
    - ☐ Lamps/switches
    - ☐ Desk/chair
    - ☐ Bookshelves
    - ☐ Cubbies for children's toys or armoires
    - ☐ Lounge chair
    - ☐ Media center
    - ☐ Breakfast table/chairs
    - ☐ Mini-fridge
    - ☐ Coffee/tea maker(s)
    - ☐ Coffee table
    - ☐ Window coverings: blinds, shades, curtains. For privacy or just for light protection?
13. Electrical requirements
    - ☐ Lamps
    - ☐ Switches
    - ☐ Outlets
14. Media requirements
    - ☐ Built-in speakers
    - ☐ Cable TV connection
    - ☐ Telephones

KEY TERM

Murphy bed: A bed that folds up into a wall cabinet. This allows the floor space to be used for other purposes during the day.

ENDNOTES

1. Esther M. Sternberg, , *Healing Spaces: The Science of Place and Well-Being* (Cambridge, Mass.: Belknap Press, 2009).
2. Gerald Van Der Kemp and Pierre Lemoin, *Versailles et Trianon, Châteaux et Jardins Guide,* (Paris : Réunion des musées nationaux, 1990), 74–78.
3. Phillippe Aries, Georges Duby, and Michelle Perrot, *From the Fires of Revolution to the Great War* (A History of Private Life, vol. IV, Arthur Goldhammer, trans.) (Cambridge, Mass.: 1994), 368.

PART IV

Multiples: Walkups, Midrises, and Towers

CHAPTER 8

Apartment Buildings

Chapter Purpose

This chapter describes the design opportunities inherent in apartment buildings, the clients who may prefer living in them, and the different variations on this type of residence. In this chapter, the needs and functions that are specific to apartment living are identified. Background on the history and evolution of the apartment building and prototypes for the various styles are provided. The modern history of the apartment building—how it developed, what we can learn from the past, and how we can improve apartment designs in the future—is discussed. Through the use of apartment prototypes, client profiles, and case studies of existing buildings, the student will begin to understand the unique and exciting design opportunities provided by apartment buildings. Exercises at the end of the chapter present an opportunity to learn by doing.

Background and Characteristics

For the purpose of this book, the term *apartment* refers to units in walk-up buildings, courtyard buildings, garden apartment complexes, and high-rise towers. Normally, an apartment is built on a single level, though there are exceptions, such as duplex apartments with internal private stairways. The single-level arrangement is advantageous for many people, especially for older occupants and people with disabilities.

Perhaps the main difference between apartment buildings and single-family residences or townhouses is that apartment dwellers share common entries, yards, and sometimes parking spaces. This mixture of public and private spaces creates a unique opportunity for designers of apartments and their clients. The **entry sequence** presents a variety of possibilities for handling the issues of security and convenience, as well as sociability. The lack of private yards can be an advantage, as maintenance is also managed in common so residents don't have to shovel snow or cut grass. Some apartment complexes have private tracts for residents who like to garden, providing the best of both worlds.

It can be argued that the apartment buildings were the first sustainable residences. Apartment buildings share common walls, minimize energy usage, and help to create dense, walkable communities. Though crowded apartments existed in ancient Rome, the modern version did not come into use until the nineteenth century. The earliest European version is typified by buildings found in Paris. Due to the scarcity of land in urban areas and the remnants of defensive city walls, residential construction moved upward. A typical Parisian apartment building consisted of a ground floor retail space and a *bel étage*, the level just above the retail space that was considered a prime residential location. Four residential stories were built above the bel étage, and the maids' quarters, or *chambres des bonnes*, were built just beneath the four-sided, steep-sloped roof. These roofs were referred to as the **mansards**. Often, dormers are punched into the roof to provide headroom and help make the space more useable. The French architects who defined this style were very influential in the United States, particularly in New York and Chicago.[1]

Apartment buildings, which were called **tenements** in the nineteenth century, got off to a rough start. Though the word *tenement* derives from *tenancy*, which simply means occupancy, it became a derogatory term for apartment buildings. Despite the splendor of many Parisian examples and their appeal to the bourgeois and upper classes, this term continued to be used negatively to describe the squalid conditions in ramshackle ensembles of shacks that comprised workers' housing in rapidly industrializing cities.[2] These dwellings were most often unplanned, with rooms added haphazardly to the back and rented out to large numbers of people. Open privies were provided in the backyards and were shared by everyone. Since the buildings were connected, it was not uncommon to walk hundreds of yards to the end of the block to get to the privy and then to wait in a line in the cold, damp air. The results were overcrowding and unsanitary conditions.[3]

As cities rapidly developed in the nineteenth century, even single people of the upper and middle classes needed places to live, so respectable **boardinghouses** were built and rented out, usually separated by sex. Hot meals were included in the rent. Gentlemen's clubs and ladies' lodging houses provided more security and a more genteel lifestyle than the tenements. However, the conditions in these houses quickly became overcrowded, with several people sleeping together or in shifts in one bed with no closets or storage space except their own trunks.[4]

The **residential hotel** became popular for wealthy families. The first building of so-called **French flats** in Chicago was the Beaurivage, built in 1878. These luxurious buildings had grand lobbies and other amenities. The apartments themselves had all the luxuries of the country mansions of the rich, with large living and dining spaces for entertaining. This appealed to the newly ascending merchant class.[5]

For the middle classes, more modest apartment buildings began to sprout up in most cities. They attempted to imitate the residential hotels, but were more modest and affordable. When this type of building became

FIGURE 8.1A **Chambres des bonnes with Mansard Roofs and Dormers.**

FIGURE 8.1B **Parisian Apartment Building.**

FIGURE 8.1C **Corner Window, Paris.**

FIGURE 8.1D **Paris Apartment Building Facade, Entry.**

more common, and more respectable, new forms of ownership were developed. The first **cooperative** development in New York City was the eight-story Rembrandt building on West 57th Street, built in 1881. The Chelsea and The Dakota soon followed.[6] Co-ops were popular through the 1930s, but the postwar housing boom favored individual ownership. The **condominium**, with fewer restrictions on buying and selling, became the most popular co-ownership structure. Some older apartment buildings converted to condominium ownership, and soon there was an industry of new construction of condominiums, which persists to this day.

Apartment Site Plans

It is generally felt that variety in apartment building sites and site plans adds to enjoyment for residents of the community. New housing types mix with each other and with older buildings and commercial buildings, creating a richer community life and more enjoyable walking (see Chapter 10, Urban Planning and Design). A few different patterns for apartment building sites are shown in **Figures 8.3a–d.**

Exercises

1. Devise different site placement diagrams to show a mixture of building layouts. Make cut-outs of different apartment buildings and move them around on the site plan, taking care to locate building entries, parking, landscaping, and recreation.
2. Make study models of the different buildings at various heights. Photograph them to show the effects of the sun and the view corridors.

Lobbies

The lobby is a key element of an apartment building. It is the first room one sees, and so it imparts a strong first impression. Lobbies also serve a number of different functions. A doorman can provide security, mail and packages are delivered and safeguarded in a special room, and tenants wait for a ride or meet their neighbors.

As discussed, in early apartment buildings an elegant lobby was an important sales tool. It conveyed a sense of grandeur to middle-class ten-

FIGURE 8.2A **Nineteenth Century New York Tenement.**

FIGURE 8.2B **Tenement Interior, Lower East Side Tenement Museum, New York City.** (Photo: © Kevin Fleming/Corbis.)

ants. What they might not be able to afford in their own apartments was at least available to them in the lobby. No cost was spared for elegant furnishing and ornamentation.

Even modest and smaller buildings require important, safe, and well-lit lobbies. If there is no doorman, a video intercom might observe guests and buzz them in.

Exercises
1. Draw bubble diagrams and space plans for different lobby configurations based on a 90-foot-by-90 foot building footprint or some of the apartment buildings in this chapter. Consider entries to the street (public) and to the parking garage. The streetscape is affected by the lobby and is an important consideration.
2. Draw a bubble diagram showing a grocery or convenience store adjoining the elevator. It should be located out of the range of building security so as to be shared with the public.

Apartment Prototypes
Apartments come in all sizes and shapes. The variety of clients directly affects the design of these spaces. Apartment sizes range from studios to large luxury apartments. This section looks at how the various units in a building relate to each other. In the interest of sustainability and economy, we begin the prototype studies with modest spaces for human habitation in dense urban communities.

In the future people will probably be living in smaller spaces. But they don't have to give up everything if they move from a 3,500-square-foot suburban house to an 1,800-square-foot apartment in the city. They have to become clever about the use of space and the arrangement of furniture. That's where the designer comes in. Remember, the location of the apartment may compensate for some of the objects and furniture that one no longer has space for in the living area. It's important to remember that "living small" has its advantages. If one is out in the city enjoying movies, restaurants, music, theater, and other public spaces then a large private space is less important. A smaller space also saves time on cleaning and maintenance, so one has more to time for enjoyment.

Small Apartment Buildings
Mini-Duplex Apartment Building
Figure 8.4a and b illustrate a modest two-unit apartment building, or duplex. It closely resembles a townhouse except that there are two units, one on each floor. These types of buildings are either detached or share party walls with another two-unit structure. The building is 20 feet wide by 40 feet deep. Because it contains only two units, it can be built as in-fill (a small site between existing buildings) on a flexible schedule and for a small budget.

This is a very flexible home. It can be a starter house with a single owner who rents out the second unit, which can be remodeled later in the case of an expanding family. Or there could be two owners, as in a condominium. There is a private vestibule for entering the building, which may include mailboxes or even a place to hang coats.

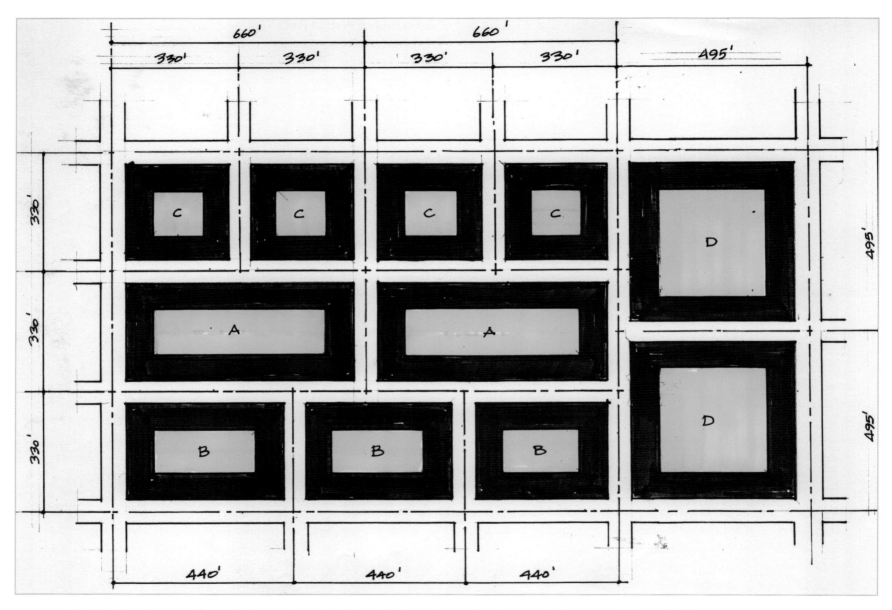

FIGURE 8.3A **Site Plan: Variations on a Block.** This diagram shows the different block sizes that can fit within a standard street grid, allowing for different sizes of buildings and a variety of spaces between them.

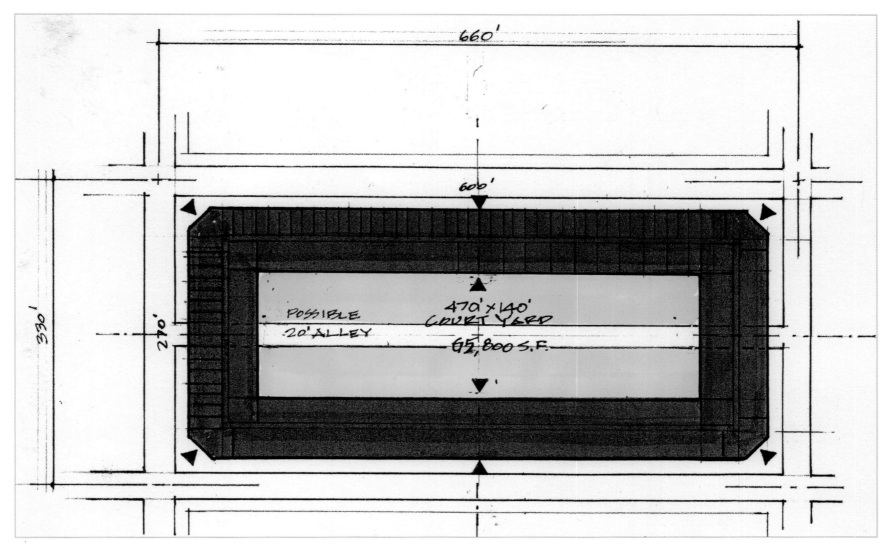

660'

600'

330'

240'

POSSIBLE
20' ALLEY

470' × 140'
COURTYARD

65,800 S.F.

FIGURE 8.3B **Site Plan: Apartment Building on Standard Block with Internal Courtyard.** This diagram shows a courtyard building around the entire perimeter of a city block. Entries and vertical circulation (stairways and elevators) are indicated by triangles. Local building codes govern the distances between them. The central courtyard garden can include a service alley with landscaped parking areas or, in higher densities, parking can be built underground so that the entire courtyard can be landscaped.

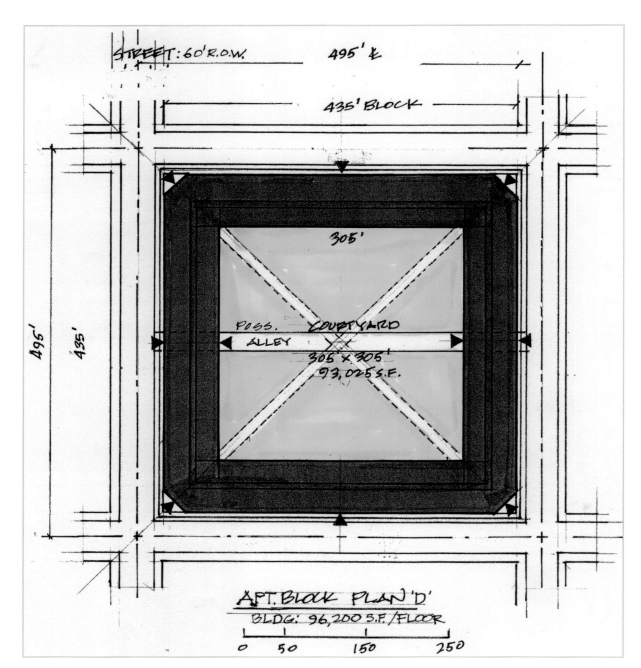

STREET: 60' R.O.W.   495' ₡

435' BLOCK

495'

435'

305'

POSS.   COURTYARD
ALLEY
305 × 305'
93,025 S.F.

APT. BLOCK PLAN 'D'
BLDG: 96,200 S.F./FLOOR

0   50   150   250

FIGURE 8.3C **Site Plan: Courtyard Apartment Building on Square Block**. This diagram shows a courtyard building on a square site with diagonal walkways in the interior garden and a possible service alley. If the alley is not frequently used, the client can use it as recreational space.

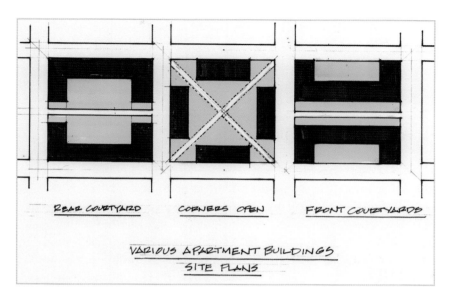

FIGURE 8.3D **Site Plan: Alternate Placements.** This site diagram shows three different apartment building footprints: Rear courtyard, open corners, and front courtyard. These footprints can be used on adjoining sites to contribute to the variety of the neighborhood. There are also other building types and site plans that the planner and designer can combine to create diversity in streetscape.

Client Profile

A young couple has purchased a lot (25 feet by 75 feet) from a developer. They have no immediate plans for children, but one of them has elderly parents who could benefit from sharing the new home. They are all independent people who require privacy, so separate entries are necessary for each unit.

The young couple has a good income but little in the way of savings. The parents have the necessary capital to buy the lot and finance the down payment. Though they are currently in perfectly good health, it is important for the parents' apartment to be accessible. A layout consisting of a ground-floor unit for the parents and one on the upper floor for the young couple would be ideal.

Program

Parents' Unit: Ground Floor (750 square feet)
- A combined kitchen/dining/living space with a media wall and shelving for books or additional storage
- Bedroom with sitting area, walk-in closet for two people, desk, shelves, possibly a television
- Laundry space
- One bathroom

Young Couple's Unit: Upper Floor (800 square feet):
- Combined kitchen/dining/living space
- Master bedroom with sitting space and walk-in closet

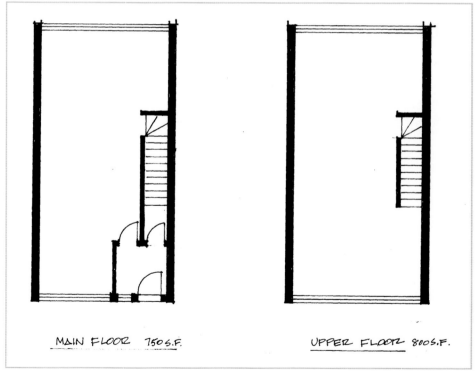

FIGURE 8.4A **Base Plan: Duplex Apartment.**

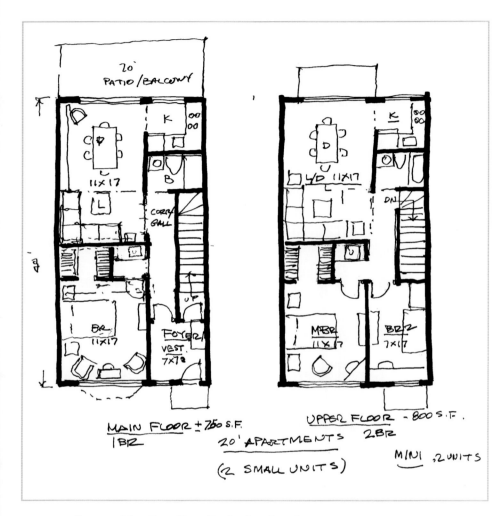

FIGURE 8.4B **Space and Furniture Plans: Duplex Apartment.**

- Second bedroom that can be used as a study
- Laundry space
- One bathroom

Exercises

1. From the base plan, lay out an interior space plan and furniture arrangement for both units.

Three-Story Apartment Building

The six-flat, three-story, walk-up apartment building can be a very useful prototype. There are many of these buildings constructed in different neighborhoods within large cities, including a large number in Chicago (see opening photo montage). They create a reasonably dense community that is walkable and active. In addition, they don't require elevators. A disadvantage is that a stairway must be mounted for the upper floors. However, by designing a ground-floor unit, one-third of all units can be accessible. With integrated terraces on the upper floors and access to yards at the ground floor, these units are sometimes referred to as garden apartments.

Site

Six units can be built in clusters with common grounds, or on an in-fill, on individual 50-foot lots. This lot size allows a full 20-foot width for each unit plus an entry lobby, a central hall, and stairway separating the two units on each floor. The site is 125 feet deep, with a service alley and parking at the rear. This is deep enough to provide yard space in the back and a front yard setback as well. There is guest parking on the street.

Client Profile

A developer has built several six-unit buildings for condominiums or rentals, depending on market conditions at the time of sale. The market for these units includes people of different ages and family types. Some families may have young children or teenagers. The units must be flexible enough to accommodate people at different stages of their lives. A study can become a nursery, then a child's bedroom, then a guest room.

Another option is that one owner can buy the entire building, live in one unit, and rent out the remaining five. This can be very efficient for operations and maintenance, though there may be disadvantages of close proximity between tenants and landlords.

Program

- Each unit measures 20 feet by 50 feet, or 1,000 square feet. The generous 20-foot width, with entry and stairway to the side, makes it possible to include two bedrooms or a bedroom and study on one end of the space. Great room: living/dining/kitchen that includes entertainment area and bookshelves
- Master bedroom
- Extra large bathroom with separate toilet off of master bedroom

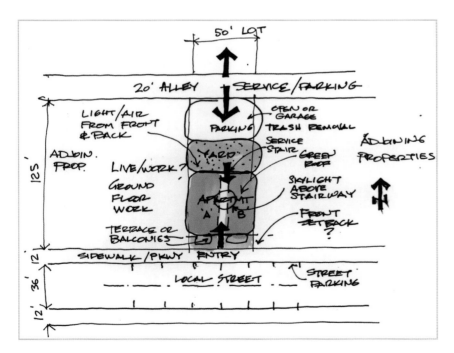

FIGURE 8.5A **Site Diagram.** This diagram shows front access, yard, and rear parking from alley for a site of 50 feet by 125 feet deep and a building footprint of 50 feet by 50 feet.

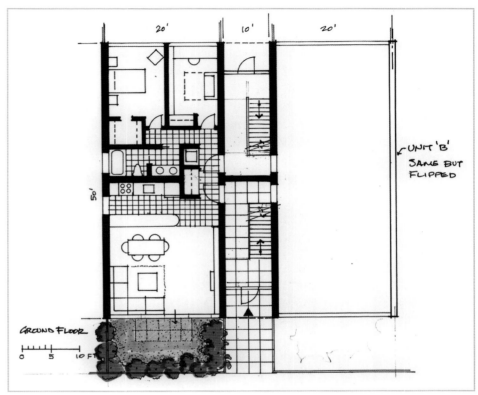

FIGURE 8.5B **Space Plan and Furniture Layout: Ground Floor.**

- Guest room/study
- Separate closets for two occupants. One can be in guest room.
- Coat closet
- Laundry space

Exercises

1. From the base drawings for the ground floor and upper floor shown in **Figures 8.5d and e**, sketch several bubble diagrams to show different options for apartment layout, according to program.
2. Choose one diagram and complete the space plan and furniture layout.

Large Apartment Buildings

Structural Notes for Large Apartment Buildings

In the following projects, the apartment sizes depend on the **structural bay** of the building. The bay is the distance between columns in both directions. In other words, one bay might be 24 feet wide by 24 feet deep, which is then repeated throughout the floor plan, forming the **structural grid.** For apartments over a parking garage, a grid that is 30 feet by 24 to 30 feet may be required. The bay size depends on whether or not the building is set above a parking garage. The apartment layout flows directly from this grid, but the grid has been developed because it reflects the

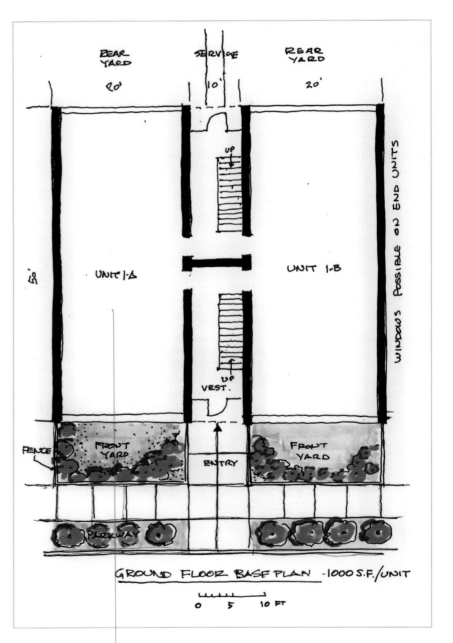

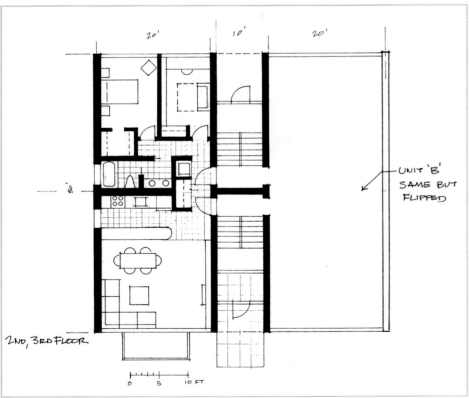

FIGURE 8.5C **Space Plan and Furniture Layout: Upper Floors.**

FIGURE 8.5D **Base Plan: Ground Floor.**

CASE STUDY 8.1

Grant Place

Pappageorge/Haymes Ltd., Architects
Chicago, Illinois

Eight spacious condominiums, each larger than 4,000 s.f., are housed this concrete-framed structure. Sheathed in sweeping expanses of bronze glass, the units range from two to five bedrooms and feature high ceilings and generous, flowing floor plans, as well as private outdoor terraces and patios. Common amenities include underground parking, a basketball court and a furnished roof deck with skyline views and a fountain near the entrance.

front view

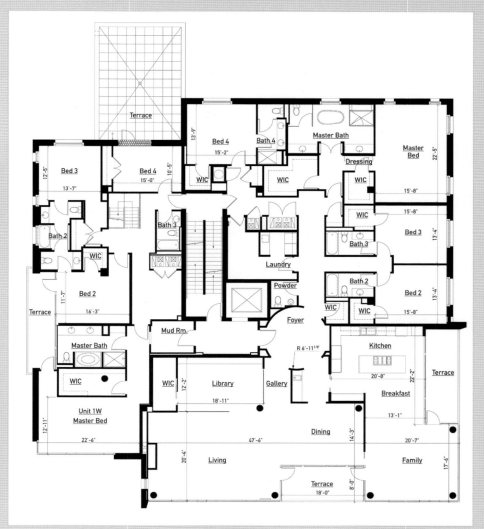

floor plan

continued on the next page

continued from the previous page

interior (photo courtesy Nick Novelli)

front foyer

kitchen (photos courtesy Nick Novelli)

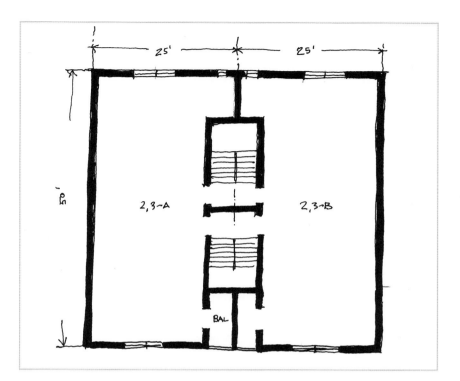

FIGURE 8.5E **Base Plan: Upper Floor.**

usage requirements of apartment spaces, as well as parking below. The two are mutually intertwined.

Many of the construction issues, including heating, cooling, and ventilation, have been resolved on the basis of the structural grid (see Case Studies 8.1–8.4). They are an integral part of the economy of the building, as well as the conventions of the construction industry. The actual size, shape, and height of apartment buildings are based on the urban design context (see Chapter 10).

Exercises

1. Lay out a rectangular structural grid 180 feet long and 54 feet wide, with a 6-foot-wide corridor in the center. That would make fifteen

bays, each measuring 12 feet by 24 feet, on either side of the corridor. Determine different apartment configurations and mixes. In other words, how many studios, one-bedroom, and two-bedroom units would fit. What are the design choices? Consider the type of clientele likely to prefer each apartment size.

2. Repeat Exercise 1 for a grid that turns the corner. How can the corner unit be laid out to take advantage of the views? What about the interior corners? Place the stairways at a distance not to exceed a 100-foot travel distance to the exit. Observe that the inside corner will yield less available window space, so it's a good place for stairways, garbage chutes, or elevators.

3. Design several different unit combinations. How does a studio fit into the structural grid with a one-bedroom unit? When combining two units into one larger unit, an extra kitchen or bathroom may not become available, because the plumbing stack is there. What use can be made of the additional kitchen? Perhaps a bar, or service sink? If two individuals are sharing one apartment, as in the student client profile, perhaps each could have a separate small kitchen instead of one large one.

Basic Apartments

Bays 24 Square Feet: Studios and One- and Two-Bedroom Apartments

Assuming a very compact 24-foot-square structural grid system (**Figure 8.6a**) there are many options for incorporating different sizes of apartments, including a special corner unit. **Figure 8.6b** illustrates the wall divisions, or base plans, for three different apartment sizes. These include a small studio of 288 square feet, a one-bedroom unit of 576 square feet and a two-bedroom/two-bathroom apartment of 864 square feet. All of these base plans are all functions of the bay size of the building, and are based on real market needs. From these base plans, the designer creates the space plans and furniture layouts (**Figure 8.6c**).

Site

The site for a large apartment building, while based on a structural grid, should also be based on the urban design pattern for the neighborhood. Great pleasure can be derived from planning a variety of apartment types, densities, and block layouts. Buildings can be laid out around courtyards or facing the street. The contextual streetscape must be taken into consideration. Many block sizes, as shown in **Figure 8.3a** are possible, which allow a variety of lengths and offsets.

Typically, the building will turn a corner. Special corner units are designed with windows and terraces to take advantage of greater panoramas and views at these locations. Parisian architects have built many apartment buildings with a great richness and variety of corner windows (see photo montage at the start of this chapter and Figures 8.8a–c for basic corner units).

Apartment buildings can also be laid out as double-loaded slabs, with the corridor in the center and apartments on the exterior faces. These can stretch as long as a city block. In many building codes, the travel distance to a stairway is a maximum of 100 feet. (Elevators do not count as required vertical exits due to the possibility of power failure during a fire.) Most importantly, limits are set on the length of these slabs based on how comfortable and convenient it is for pedestrians. Don't make the building so long that it is difficult to walk around it. *Tip:* Multiple corners and offset streets create more lively streetscapes and encourage walking.

Client Profiles

There are a variety of potential clients for a residential designer in the field of apartment buildings. Besides individuals remodeling single units, developers require the services of architects, interior designers, and urban designers. These professionals provide guidance for the overall shell of the building, determining the location of elevators, fire stairways, and exits, mechanical and structural systems, and the space plans for the units. Interior designers help to create model apartments, which are very important for sales. This is a specialized field and requires very intense market research to find the potential clients and determine what type of model will be effective.

CASE STUDY 8.2

Bercy Park, Paris

Jean-Paul Viguier, S.A. d'Architecture

This building is part of the project conceived by the City of Paris to construct a new residential area bordering the recently created Bercy Park. The city's architectural directives determine its form and organization. Apartments were to be created based on a relatively classic plan. The architectural effort was concentrated mainly on creating a full-height, layered external wall along the line of a winter garden. In order to increase the habitability of the apartments and to reinforce the acoustic and thermal comfort, the facade is modulated by sliding clear glass panels suspended from a rail fixed to the underside of the balconies. The movement of these panels by the residents creates a facade that changes depending on light conditions and reflections.

The building at the heart of the block is joined to the main body by a glass bridge. The two upper levels are designed as "rooftop" houses. These detached two-story units have large terraced areas framing superb views over the park and Paris. At ground level, duplex apartments lead directly off a small internal garden.

facade

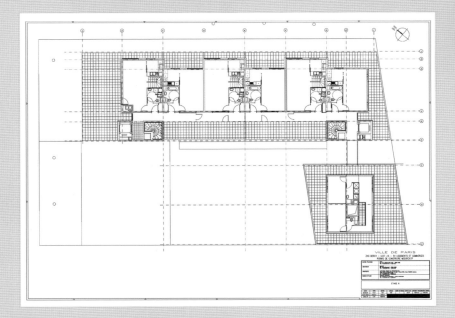

floor plan

continued on the next page

continued from the previous page

balcony

balconies

interior

continued on the next page

continued from the previous page

facade closeup

facade front

side facade

Another area of opportunity for designers is combining units, where one owner may buy two or three units and combine them for a single user, or for a live/work space. Sometimes a potential buyer approaches the developer and asks for a larger apartment than what has been planned or even built. It is up to the developer and designer to reconfigure the unit for the client. The developer may also ask the designer to propose alternate plans for potential buyers. Sometimes the building can be adapted during construction.

For younger designers starting out, there are opportunities to design the interiors of condominium apartments. They work with individual buyers to determine the space requirements as well as the furniture and finishes. It is a good idea to establish a relationship with the developer and offer these services as part of the sales and design team, so that they can be coordinated with construction.

Studio in Manhattan for a Retired Couple

A retired couple has moved back to the city to enjoy the cultural activities. They still have individual activities, but real estate prices being what they are, they have to fit within a studio space. (**See Figure 8.6c, left image.**)

In a small studio, it is imperative to maximize the use of all space, particularly wall space. This must be achieved without giving up the critical functions required in all living spaces. People have to do with less, it's true, but they still need a place to hang coats, store bed linens, towels, and blankets. They also need kitchen storage for canned goods, dry foods, and perishables. Storage is the critical issue. It's important to distinguish between the types of storage required, considering whether the use is temporary or long term and what is being stored. For example, it might be possible to make 3-inch shelves for canned goods. Books come in all sizes too. Paperback books are about 4 inches by 7 inches, so it makes sense in some cases to build bookshelves 4 inches deep.

Program

- A strategy must be devised to allow a certain amount of individual space for each person. This may be achieved through sliding doors, screens, curtains, and built-in furniture.

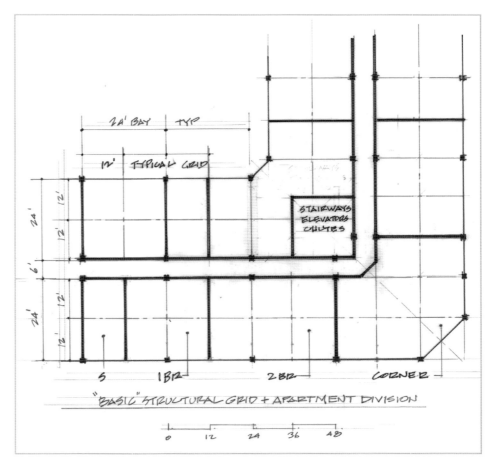

FIGURE 8.6A **Basic Structural Grid.** This building layout shows a basic bay, 24 feet wide by 24 feet deep. Adaptable for units without parking below.

- Both residents participate in cooking. The kitchen must be small but efficient. It can be closed when not in use.
- The bed must be a built-in or sofa bed.
- Overnight guests would not be comfortable.

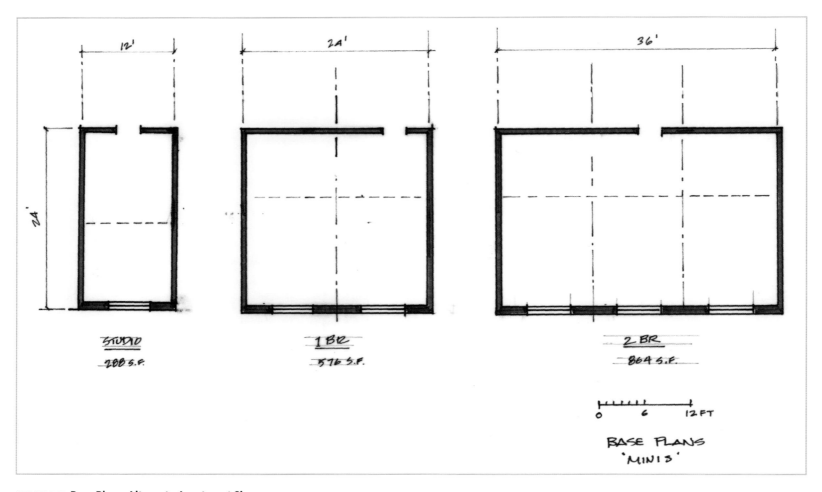

FIGURE 8.6B **Base Plans: Alternate Apartment Sizes.**

Area/Rooms
- Total area is 288 square feet, about 12 feet wide by 24 feet deep
- A balcony is required.
- The front entry foyer must be very efficient, with a coat closet and space to hang guest coats.

- The ceiling is 12 feet high, so inactive storage may be provided with a ladder.

Region/Climate
- New York City (four seasons)
- Heating and air conditioning are required.

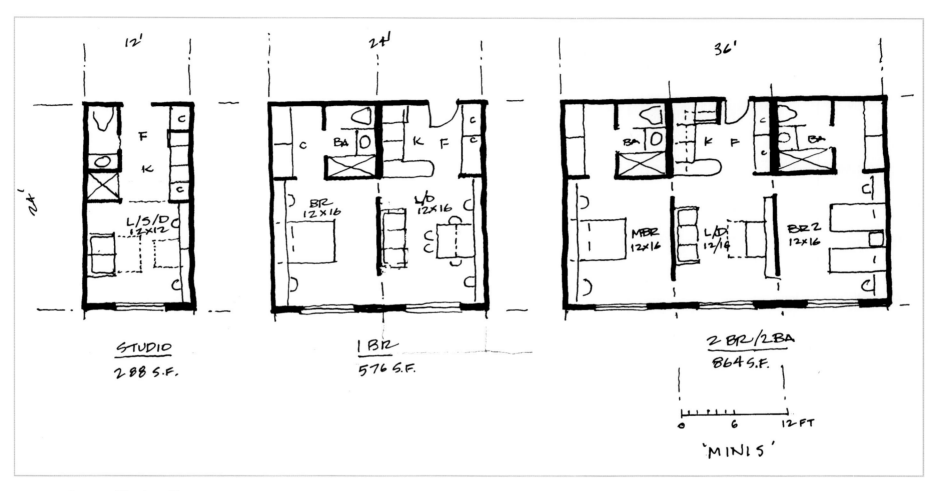

FIGURE 8.6C **Space and Furniture Plans.**

- Energy efficiency is a necessity.

Budget (Interior)
- $100,000, including all built-in furnishing, appliances, furniture, and finishing materials.

Community
- Manhattan
- Mixed-use zoning
- School, daily shopping, and community center are within walking distance.
- Public transportation is available within walking distance.

- There is a bicycle path in a nearby park, so the building must provide bicycle parking. They take up too much space inside a small apartment.

Site
- The building takes up most of the site space. There is a small courtyard for services and trash cans.

Furnishings
- Strictly modern; small and light
- Bookcases are required to the full extent possible.
- Artwork is minimalist and framed, with special lighting.
- Sustainable durable materials for floors and area rugs are preferred. Ceramic or stone tile at entry, with wood or bamboo for the remaining rooms.
- Window covering to be shades or venetian blinds. Designer to determine type and color.

Exercise
1. Draw interior elevations with emphasis on storage space. Take advantage of 12-foot ceilings. What kinds of objects can be stored up high and how can they be made accessible?

One-Bedroom Unit for Two Students

The clients are two students. As an investment, the parents of one student have purchased a one-bedroom apartment downtown near campus rather than paying for a room in the dormitory. Another room will be rented to someone else for additional income. (**See Figure 8.6c, middle image.**)

Special Requirements
- Each student requires a private room, which must accommodate sleeping, closet and study space, and possibly entertainment, including TV and stereo. This may be achieved through the use of conventional or sliding doors, but they must be soundproof.
- Each student cooks individually, though they may occasionally share a meal. The kitchen must be small but efficient, with a nearby dining table.
- A small sofa and coffee table in the common room would be useful for entertaining the occasional guest. No big parties anticipated.
- Overnight guests would not be comfortable.

Area/Rooms
- Total area is 576 square feet, about 24 feet wide by 24 feet deep.
- The entry foyer must be very efficient, with coat closet and space for hanging guest coats.

Region/Climate
- Chicago, four seasons
- Heating and air conditioning are required. Individual controls are desirable so that heat can be greatly reduced when students are away.
- Energy efficiency is essential.

Budget (Interior)
- It is assumed that the space is "raw," with no walls, kitchen or bathroom.
- $50,000, including all built-in furnishings, appliances, furniture, and finishing materials.

Community
- Chicago, central area
- Mixed-use zoning
- School, daily shopping, and a community center are within walking or bicycling distance.
- Public transportation is available within walking distance.
- A room for bicycle storage is needed in the building.

Rue de la Convention

Paris, France
Jean-Paul Viguier, S.A. d'Architecture, Architect

This residential development knits itself perfectly into the urban pattern of Paris. It respects the streetscape of this neighborhood, while creating a rich garden in back for the residents. Through the careful placement of buildings on the site, pedestrians can also see and enjoy the garden. It is also a green building. It uses roof gardens to protect the roofing membrane, doubling its life to 40 years. Rainwater is retained and stored in basins for irrigating the garden. Green facades also keep the building cooler in the summer and keep continuity with the garden. The height of 9 to 10 stories creates sufficient density to reserve space for the garden.. The pedestrian walkway in the garden maintains and improves the connectivity of walking typical to the city of Paris. There are also walkways and "passarelles (suspended walkways)," bordered by planters, and suspended gardens, which create a visual continuity between the residences and the community.

green facade

perspective

continued on the next page

continued from the previous page

Specifications

NUMBER OF UNITS: 128 subsidized units

78 builders units

1 commercial space

1 nursery school

1 children's hospital

1 center for the handicapped

TOTAL UNITS: 206

TOTAL RESIDENTIAL AREA: 174,375 square feet

AVERAGE UNIT SIZE: 846 square feet

perspective close up

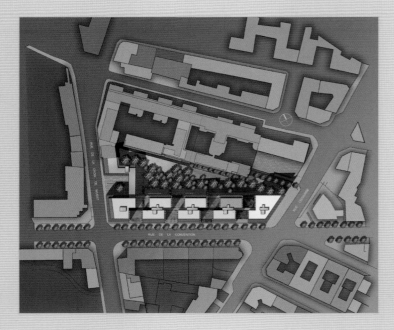

location map

panorama

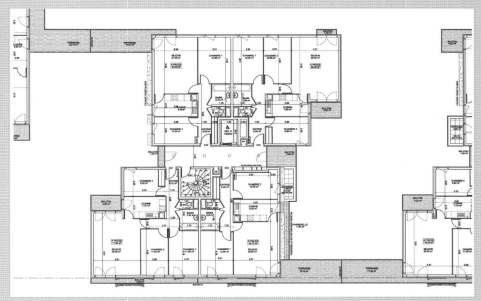

floor plan

perspective

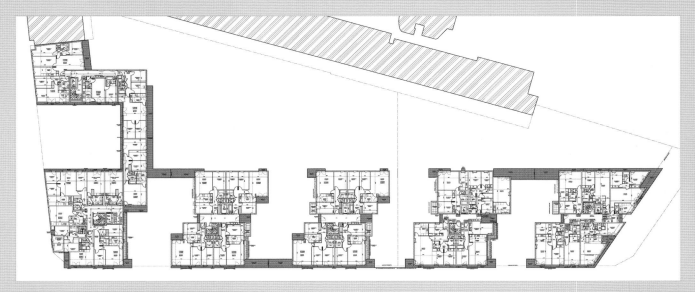

floor plan

continued on the next page

continued from the previous page

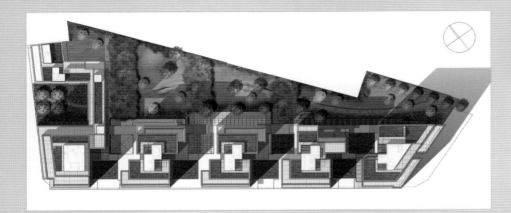

site plan

site model

front facade

interior

perspective balconies

perspective garden

Site

- Apartment building takes up about 50 percent of the site but there is a small yard in the rear that can be used for entertaining, as well as a garage and alley at the rear.

Furnishings

- Strictly modern; small and light
- Bookcases are required to the full extent possible.
- Student artwork is unframed, so a tack board is desirable.
- Sustainable durable materials should be used for floors.
- Window covering to be shades or narrow venetian blinds. Designer to determine type and color.

Exercises

1. Make a scrapbook of lightweight and inexpensive furniture (from IKEA, Target, or thrift shops). Include plans, photos, and prices to help prepare budgets.

Two-Bedroom Split Unit for Two Working Professionals
See Figure 8.6c, right image, *Split Two-Bedroom Unit*
The client is a working couple. They like living in the city, but each needs independent space. The space must also be flexible. They can only afford a small unit, but it's very important that they have a guest room because they like to entertain family and friends. The guest room must be separate from the master bedroom, with its own bathroom. The second bedroom will be used as a den or study, and the second bathroom will be used by one of the owners when it is not being used by guests. There should also be a small desk and chair in each bedroom. This implies flexibility in the type of furnishing.

Program/Area/Rooms

- Area: three basic bays; a total of 864 square feet
- A **split plan** is necessary, with the kitchen/dining/living room in the center and the two bedroom suites at the ends. Entry should be from

the center bay. Make use of pocket doors wherever possible to conserve space.

Exercise

1. The guest bedroom is used as a study or a den when there are no guests. Which would work best, a sofa bed or a fold-up bed? Why?

Basic Corner Units

Corner units are the most valuable units in an apartment building, and should be designed accordingly. Generally, there are no studio apartments at the corners. These spaces are the largest and most luxurious on each floor. They offer panoramic views in three directions. The great room can be a truly impressive space, and should include a terrace. Parisian architects have recognized this and most apartment buildings in Paris have an angled window.

Though this apartment is designed on the modest, or basic bay, there is still ample space, nearly 1,200 square feet, to provide luxury in the space planning.

In **Figure 8.7a,** the corner great room is flanked by a kitchen on one side and an entertainment room, or library, on the other. This allows for a little privacy adjoining the large space. The bedroom suites are located at the ends of the unit, divided by the kitchen/dining/living space. A central entry at the corner of the exterior corridor allows for efficient circulation. A large central foyer distributes the circulation to all spaces.

Figure 8.7b shows the limits of the apartment, the glass walls, and the central foyer. A possible space plan/furniture layout is shown in **Figure 8.7c.**

Exercises

1. If this were a live/work space, how would the office relate to the residential quarters? Show a reception desk and privacy arrangements.

Standard Apartments

Bays 30 Square Feet

The grid for a basic unit (**Figure 8.6a**) is very tight and might not be large enough to satisfy some buyers. A *standard apartment* (author's term) is based on a larger grid of 30 feet by 30 feet, which also adapts to the standard parking grid. The structural grid required for an underground parking garage can also form an orderly grid for typical room sizes in the apartments above it. This works out to be about 30 feet between columns, with an apartment depth of 30 feet as well. The depth of the column spacing is based on the optimum locations for the parking bay. **Figures 8.8a and b** show a depth for column spacing of 22 feet. This bay size also corresponds to a convenient location for structural columns within the unit (**Figure 8.8b**). Base plans for units of three different sizes are shown in **Figure 8.8c**.

In laying out the bubble diagrams for these three units, note that bathrooms and kitchens should back up to each other for economical plumbing connections. Otherwise, general planning rules for residences, as discussed throughout this book, also apply for apartment layouts. Layout preferences still depend upon the client's wishes and budget, as shown in **Figures 8.8d and e**.

Exercises

1. Using the client profiles provided for the basic units (**Figures 8.6a–c**), design a space plan and furniture layout for the 30-foot base plan grid (**Figure 8.8c**). Compare the spaces designed for the standard grid to the smaller spaces of the basic grid. Note the advantages of the larger grid for accessibility and easier circulation.

2. Seek cost estimates on a square-foot basis from some local home-builders and apply them to the two grids, basic and standard. What is the difference in price between them? For example, if the construction cost in an area is $150 per square foot, then the 540-square-foot studio in the larger grid would cost $81,000 to build. The 288-square-foot studio on the smaller or basic grid would cost $43,200 to build, a considerable savings of $37,800. Check this with actual builders based on various plans. It will certainly affect the client's ability to

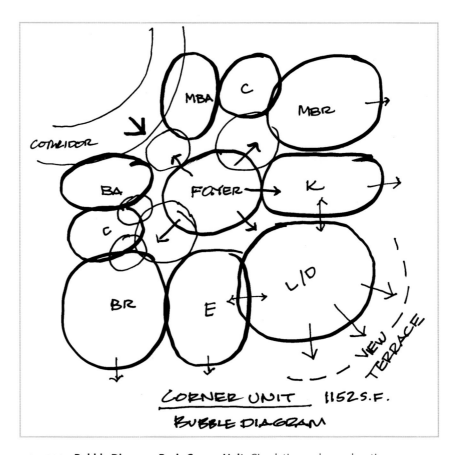

FIGURE 8.7A **Bubble Diagram: Basic Corner Unit.** Circulation and room locations.

pay. They will of course have the final say as to whether or not it's worth the additional cost to choose a standard bay apartment.

Standard Corner Unit

The corner unit based on the standard grid will also have a more generous area (1,620 square feet) compared to the basic corner unit (1,152 square feet). The additional space can be used for true bonus rooms, such as a library or an eat-in kitchen. Additional closet or storage space, a broom

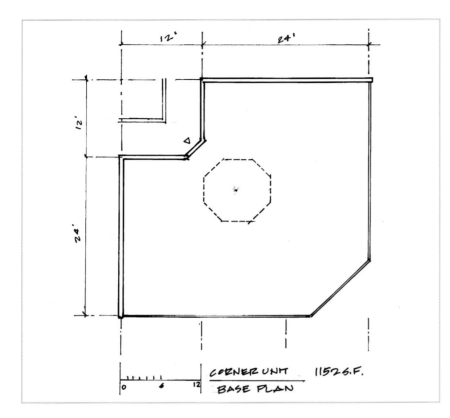

FIGURE 8.7B **Base Plan: Basic Corner Unit.**

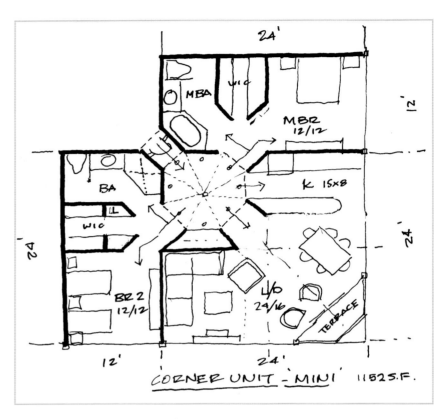

FIGURE 8.7C **Space and Furniture Plan: Basic Corner Unit.**

closet, pantry, and utility room are always welcome additions, and they actually fit in this generously sized two-bedroom unit.

The standard structural grid is adapted to turn the corner in this unit. **Figure 8.9a** shows the overall grid as it might appear on an entire building floor. It also includes detail of how that grid turns the corner for the end units. The relationship of site planning and this structural grid will be demonstrated in Chapter 10.

It is important to remember that when the bubble diagram (**Figure 8.9b**) is imposed on the grid, the column spaces for this unit must work at the parking garage level as well. Sometimes the corner unit becomes

the entry to the building and the elevator lobby. The resulting base plan (**Figure 8.9c**) forms the perimeter of the apartment layout. A space plan (**Figure 8.9d**) shows one possible placement of rooms and how to fit in some bonus spaces.

Client Profile

A couple with two young children of the same gender. They require a separate room for quiet activities. It can be used for study or, when the children are asleep, as a reading room for the adults. It is also possible to use this bonus room as an occasional guest room.

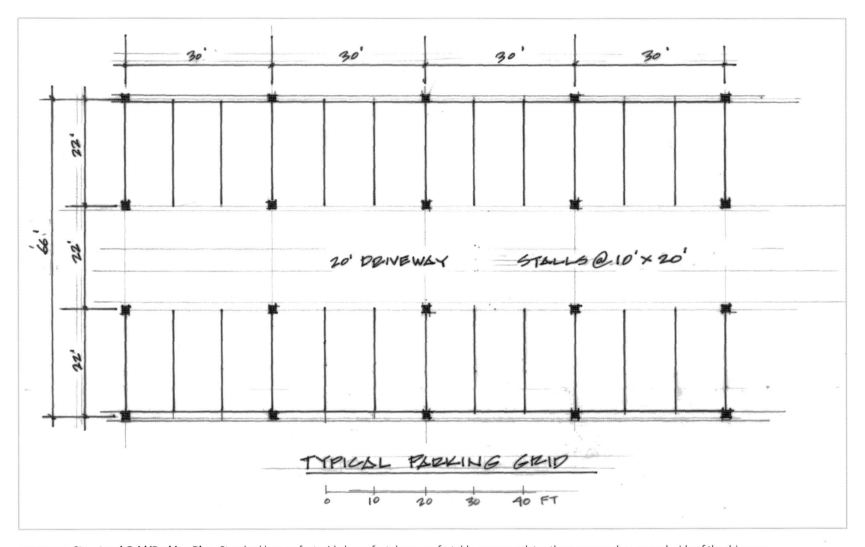

30'   30'   30'   30'

22'

66'

22'

20' DRIVEWAY   STALLS @ 10' x 20'

22'

TYPICAL PARKING GRID

0   10   20   30   40 FT

FIGURE 8.8A **Structural Grid/Parking Plan.** Standard bay, 30 feet wide by 22 feet deep comfortably accommodates three cars per bay on each side of the driveway.

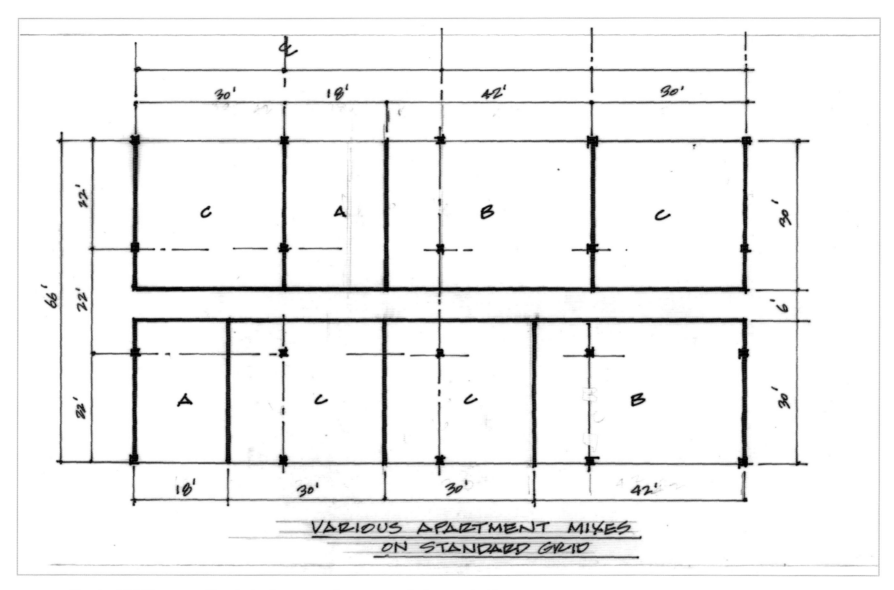

FIGURE 8.8B **Structural Grid/Apartment Plan.** A mix of apartments shown on a standard structural grid.

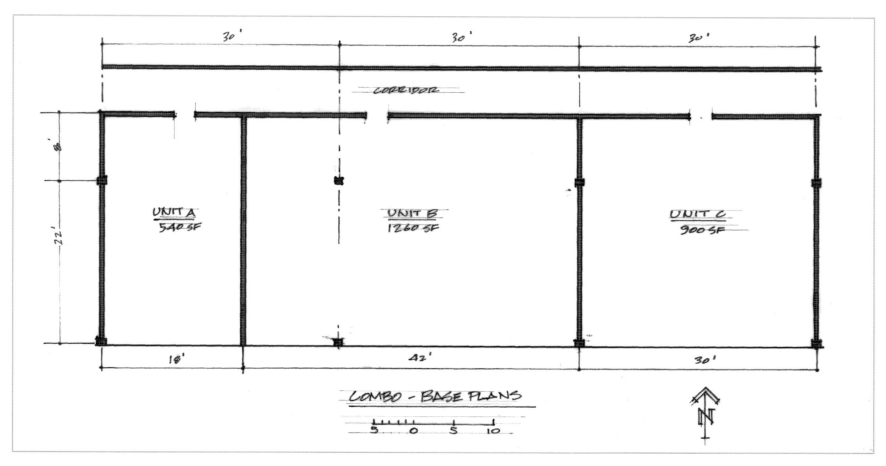

FIGURE 8.8C **Standard Base Plans.** Three units on same bay size. Unit A is a studio of 540 square feet, Unit B is a two-bedroom apartment of 1,260 square feet, and Unit C is a one-bedroom apartment of 900 square feet.

Program
- Large formal entry with adequate coat space for family and guests
- Great room
- Separate breakfast space in kitchen
- Formal dining area, with or without walls
- Library or study
- Master bedroom with bathroom
- Children's bedroom with bathroom

Exercises
1. Use the base plan to design the space and furniture layout.
2. Convert the library or study room to an occasional guest room. Consider the effects of this option on furniture selection and layout.

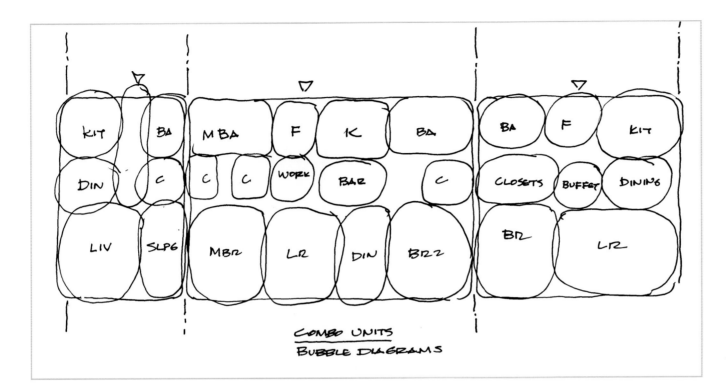

FIGURE 8.8D **Standard Bubble Diagrams.** *Left to right*: Studio, two-bedroom, and one-bedroom units.

3. Design a formal dining room with walls separating it from the kitchen and living areas. Compare it to an open plan with no dividing walls.

Luxury Corner Unit

The standard corner unit (**Figures 8.9a–d**) is adequate for two bedrooms, but when three or four bedrooms are necessary the base plan can be expanded, using the same structural grid.

Client Profile

Four adult professionals with high incomes have purchased a four-bedroom apartment on Telegraph Hill in San Francisco with exquisite views of the city. They each want an independent space for privacy and sleeping with a private bathroom, while sharing the common areas of kitchen/living/dining. They also may need to occasionally work at home, so adaptability for office space is necessary. There should also be a space for public meetings, which must be kept separate from the living space.

General Requirements

- Total area required: approximately 2,400 square feet (600 square feet per resident). The clients feel that they would prefer to share a large luxury unit rather than four small, separate studios.
- Privacy must be maintained, though there will be shared use of kitchen, living, and dining areas.
- A large outdoor terrace is important. The weather in San Francisco is great, so outdoor space is usable living space.
- Bicycle storage must be provided in the building.

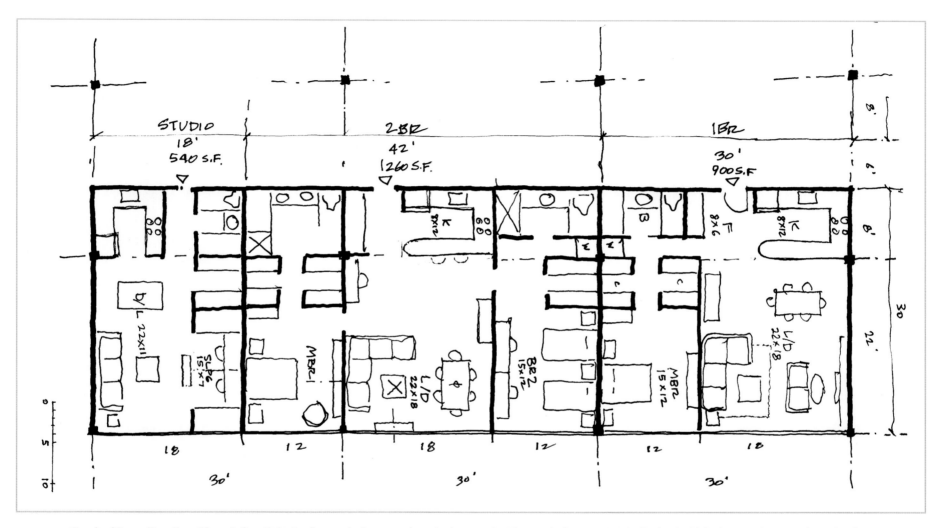

FIGURE 8.8E **Standard Space/Furniture Plans.** *Left to Right:* Studio, two-bedroom, and one-bedroom units. The two-bedroom unit is "split plan," with bedroom suites on either side of a great room. This is a particularly useful unit for shared apartments.

CASE STUDY 8.4

Porte d'Asnieres, Paris

Jean-Paul Viguier, S.A. d'Architecture

Specifications recommended by the City of Paris dictated, for the most part, the construction of medium-height buildings surrounding an internal garden. Two of the buildings contain 29 apartments each and are separated by a ten-meter-wide space that opens up to the Opéra Comique. Transparent entrance halls on either side of this void offer residents a long vista toward Porte d'Asnières. For the facades facing the boulevard, there is a need for acoustic protection. There are sliding-glass screens enclosing the 1.5-meter-deep loggias. The other facades are in brick, for unity with the other buildings of the neighborhood. At ground level, private terraces give way to landscaped areas. Commercial spaces at ground level enliven the square.

facade

mixture

streetscape

facade, tree

facade

balconies

exterior detail

continued from the previous page

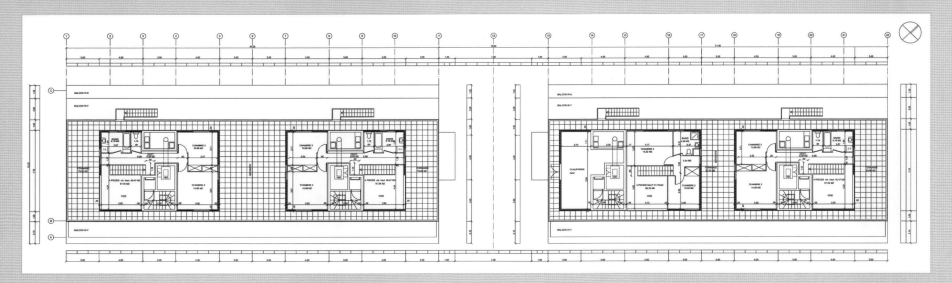

floor plans

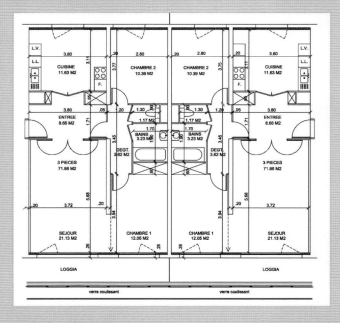

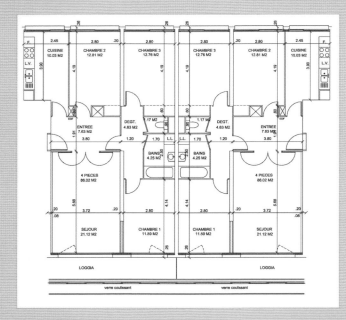

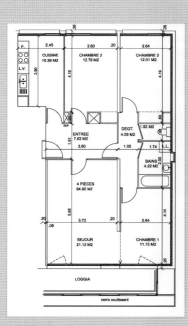

two bedrooms

three bedrooms

corner

aerial view

facade trees

lobby

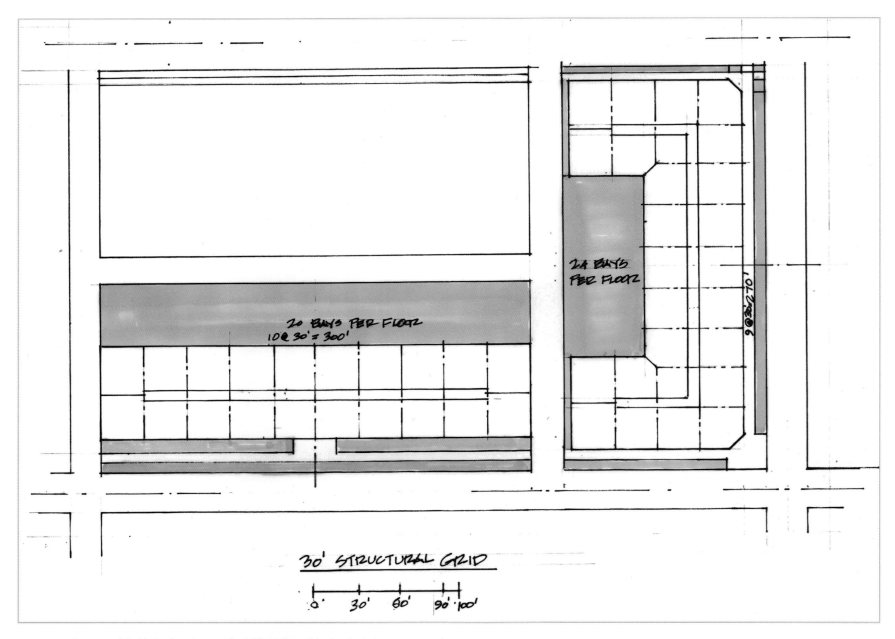

FIGURE 8.9A **Structural Grid Conforming to Block/Site Plan.** This plan includes a corner unit.

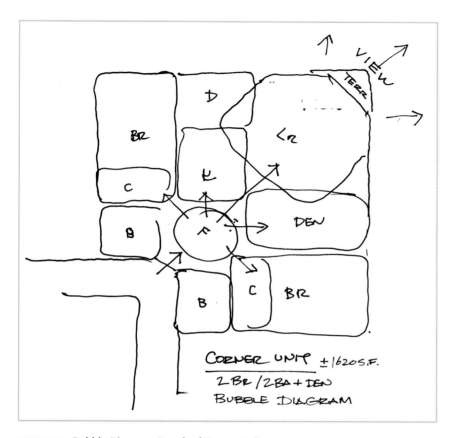

FIGURE 8.9B **Bubble Diagram: Standard Corner Unit.**

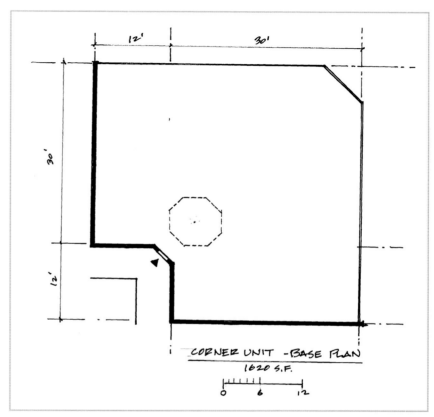

FIGURE 8.9C **Base Plan: Standard Corner Unit.**

Special Requirements

- Each person requires a generous private room and bathroom, which must accommodate sleeping, closet and study, and possibly entertainment, including TV and stereo. Each person cooks individually, though they may occasionally share a meal. The common kitchen must be efficient, with separate storage for individuals and a nearby dining table.
- A corner sofa and coffee table with several lounge chairs are needed in the living room for entertaining guests. Small parties are antici-

pated. Business conferences may also be accommodated in the living/dining space.

Region/Climate

- San Francisco. Though rarely freezing, it can be fairly cool much of the year.
- Heating is required. Individual controls in each room are desirable so that heat can be greatly reduced when people are away.
- Energy efficiency is a necessity.

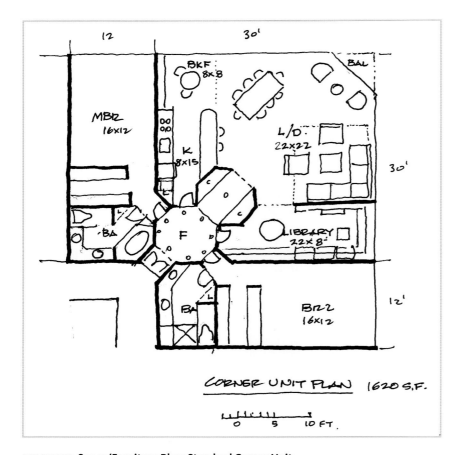

FIGURE 8.9D **Space/Furniture Plan: Standard Corner Unit.**

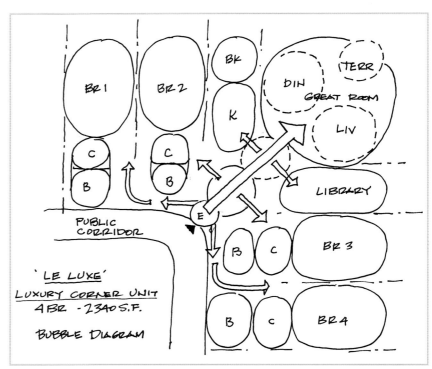

FIGURE 8.10A **Bubble Diagram: Luxury Corner Unit with Four Bedrooms.**

- There is a bicycle path in a nearby park.

Site
- Apartment with separate parking garage in rear.

Furnishings
- Traditional wood and marble with classic nineteenth-century designs.
- Bookcases are required in each room to the full extent possible.
- It is desirable to allow adequate wall space to exhibit artwork in common areas.
- Wood floors exist. Area rugs are required.

- Availability of solar energy will be greatly increased in San Francisco in the next few years.

Community
- San Francisco, Telegraph Hill
- Mixed-use zoning
- Daily shopping and entertainment are within walking distance.
- Public transportation is available within walking distance as well.

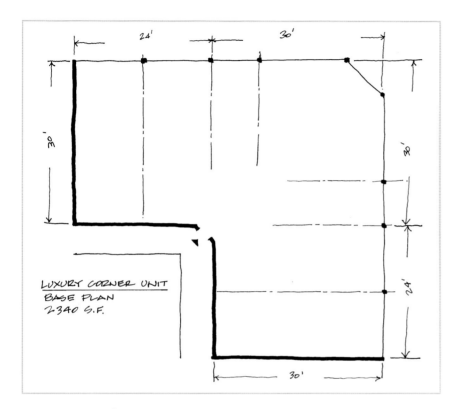

FIGURE 8.10B **Base Plan: Luxury Corner Unit.**

- Window covering to be shades or venetian blinds. Curtains are also needed to create a softer interior feeling. Designer to determine type and color.
- Wood moldings, baseboard, and trim to be used throughout.

Program
- Generous entry, with adequate guest and resident coat storage.
- Kitchen/breakfast room/pantry
- Library/reading room

- Four-bedroom suites, 360 square feet each, including private bathroom and walk-in closets. There should be adequate space for a desk or small table in each room.

Budget (interior furnishings, fixtures, casework)
It is assumed that the space is relatively well laid out as a "standard" apartment, with walls for the four bedrooms and four adjoining bathrooms, as well as a kitchen, dining room, and living room. There is a generous budget of $125,000 per person, or $500,000 total for all appliances, furniture, and finishing materials.

Exercises
1. This program is designed for four independent people. How is this type of client different from a family of related individuals? Identify the design considerations necessary to ensure privacy. Make freehand sketches showing these concepts.
2. Design a plan that would use the great room as an open space. Then show how it would work with partitions for a library, offices, or studio space. This could become a live/work space. Flexibility is important.
3. Try incorporating a small cooking/refrigerator/sink into the bedroom, not for large meals but for tea and small snacks.
4. Prepare interior materials and furnishing boards. Provide photos of furniture, swatches of floor and window covering materials, paint colors, molding and trim, kitchen and bathroom cabinets and fixtures and hardware.

Point Towers
A **point tower (Figure 8.11a, b)** is a compact high-rise building, constructed around a central core. This design minimizes corridor space. The core includes elevators and emergency stairways. This type of structure can be tall and thin, with dramatic views. Half of the units can be corner exposures, which are more valuable. However, operating and maintaining the elevators, particularly in very tall buildings, is expensive in energy consumption. It also raises the question as to what happens in the event of power blackouts. It could be difficult to enter and exit the unit, and

provide basic services like water and ventilation. This must be balanced against the cost of the land and the desirability of dramatic high views.

Program

Each unit is 900 square feet. The floor plans should be designed for combination units so that larger units of 1,800 and 2,700 square feet or even a whole floor are possible. A 7,200-square-foot penthouse would be nice. Some apartments can be left empty to accommodate generous outdoor spaces and rooftop gardens. A modernized, and more generous version of this prototype is shown in Case Study 8.5, Museum Place.

Exercises

1. Imagine what type of client would want a space like this and how the space could be used. For example, a combined live/work space or room for an extended family. Write programs for these, and make bubble diagrams or space plans
2. If families with children live in tall buildings, what kinds of spaces should be included within the building to accommodate them? Consider day care or after-school programs.

Chapter Summary

This chapter explored almost every type of apartment and apartment building. It began with historical background of how apartments came into being and the evolution to modern apartment living. A brief explanation of the two structural grids, basic and standard, in the context of the apartment building, showed how they influence and are influenced by apartment layouts. Examples were given of existing urban street patterns and how apartment buildings fit into them. Bubble diagrams encouraged students to break down the units into various elements. Base plans offered a view of the perimeter of the unit so that different approaches could be tried. Exercises suggested ideas for each project, and then encouraged the student and instructor to come up with some more of their own. At the end of this design process, students should test their design solutions by presenting them to a jury of outside professionals. This critique is an

opportunity for the student to learn how a professional must cope with criticism and become flexible with the design process.

As in other chapters, examples of prototype space plans and furniture layouts were presented. These help students to work on specific approaches and, with the help of an instructor, understand the reasons for the plan. The prototypes are meant as diagrams rather than as finished products. There may be differences of opinion as to the approach to be

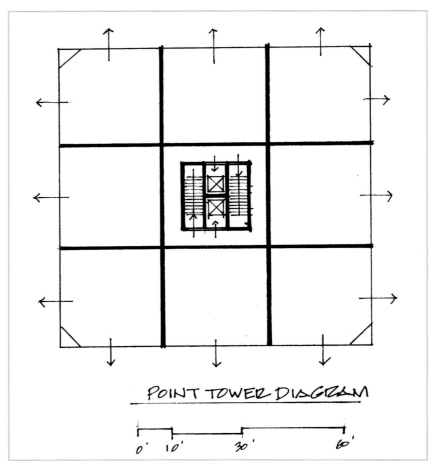

FIGURE 8.11A **Base Plan Diagram: Point Tower.**

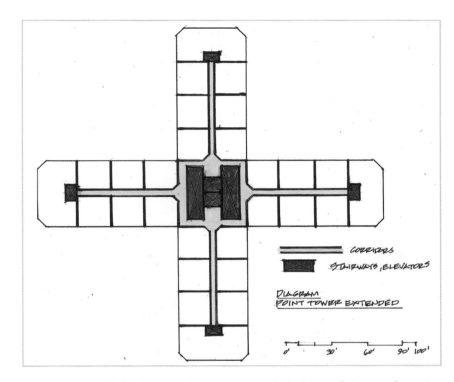

FIGURE 8.11B **Extended Point Tower Diagram.** Due to the high cost of elevators, fire stairs, mechanical ventilation, and vertical plumbing stacks, point towers are often "extended" off of the central core. Three or four additional "wings" are added so that the additional units can share the cost of the vertical shafts. There is also the opportunity for a grand panorama for the end units, with views in three directions.

taken in solving design problems. These are living, breathing projects, with real clients. Instructors may change the client profiles or direct students to do so.

Finally, the case studies illustrated some of the best examples of current residential design. These were accompanied by statements of the architect's or designer's approach. Completing this chapter should make students familiar with the many different types of apartments and apartment buildings, their advantages and disadvantages, and the design opportunities they present. Since attached apartments make up the majority of housing stock, this is indeed essential information.

FIGURE 8.12 **Lake Point Tower, Chicago.** Completed in 1968, this was an early prototype of the Point Tower prototype. Designed with three wings attached to the central core, it affords spectacular views of Chicago's lakefront and downtown parks (architect: Schipporeit/Heinrich).

CASE STUDY 8.5

One Museum Park East

Pappageorge/Haymes Ltd., Architects
Chicago, Illinois

Uniquely positioned on the prominent southeast corner of Grant Park in downtown Chicago, One Museum Park East is the second tallest all-residential tower in the United States. The multi-colored blue and silver glass façade gestures towards the reflective waters of Lake Michigan. The graceful, amorphous massing allows every unit to capture primary views of both the lakefront and Grant Park. A series of stepped, curved terraces rise up the flanks of the tower, slowly receding to reveal the building's core which soars 720 feet, gracing Chicago's skyline with its illuminated silver elliptical peak.

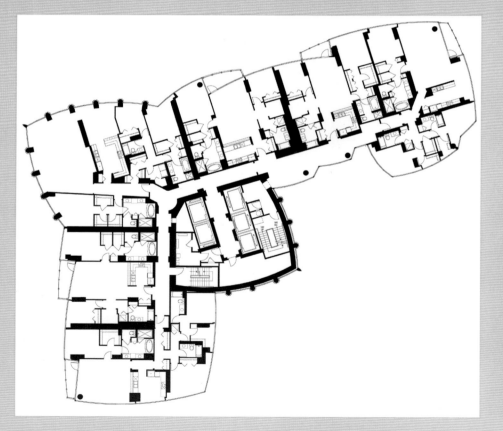

site plan

tower from park

tower close up

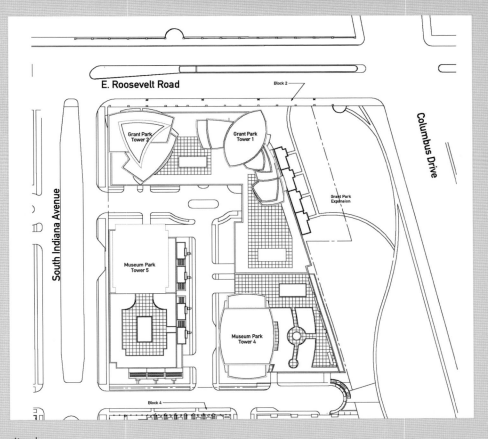

site plan

KEY TERMS

Basic units: Compact units based on a minimal room size, about 12 feet wide by 24 feet deep, which can be practical for starter units, for students, and for retirees on modest budgets.

Boardinghouses: Houses designed to accommodate "respectable" single people in the nineteenth century. Usually divided by gender. Hot meals were provided with the rent.

Condominium: Form of collective ownership with individual title to the unit owner, and a responsibility for a share of the common elements.

Cooperative: Form of collective ownership where the title is held by, and governed by, a board of directors. Individuals own shares in the co-op, rather than title to their own units.

Entry sequence: The series of steps and activities one must take when entering a building. In apartment buildings, this includes the walk from the public space or parking, the front hallway, a possible anteroom, an elevator or stairway, and the corridor to the private apartment.

French flat: Used to describe residential hotels similar to the Parisian style of the late nineteenth century

Mansard roofs: In Parisian apartments circa 1900, a roof that created a room with slanted walls, usually of zinc, commonly found on the top floor.

Point tower: A compact high-rise building, constructed around a compact core that contains elevators and emergency stairways

Residential hotel: Residential apartment buildings with luxurious common entries and amenities

Structural bay: The horizontal distance between the columns in a building

Structural grid: The layout of structural bays on the floor plate of the building. The column spacing forms the grid and other vertical elements, such as mechanical systems, are related to it.

Tenements: A derogatory term for apartment buildings. First used in the nineteenth century to describe a ramshackle ensemble of shacks that were typical housing for workers in rapidly industrializing cities.

Split unit: A unit that is laid out to separate the two bedroom/bathroom suites, with the living/dining/kitchen space at the center. This affords more privacy for the individuals using the two bedrooms.

Standard units: More generous in size than basic units and, of course, more expensive. The bay size is larger and creates rooms 8 and 12 feet wide within the 30-foot column spacing. This corresponds to the structure of a parking garage below.

ENDNOTES

1. Andrew Alpern, *Luxury Apartment Houses of Manhattan* (Mineola, NY: Dover Publications, 1992), 10–15.
2. Perry R. Duis, *Challenging Chicago* (Chicago: University of Illinois Press, 1998), 84.
3. George Orwell, *The Road to Wigan Pier* (New York: Harcourt Brace, 1958), 51–74.
4. Gwendolyn Wright, *Building the Dream* (Cambridge, Mass.: MIT Press, 1981), 66–72.
5. Perry R. Duis, *Challenging Chicago*, 84–85.
6. Andrew Alpern, *Luxury Apartment Houses of Manhattan*, 17.

PART V

Mixing It Up

CHAPTER 9

Mixed-Use Buildings

Chapter Purpose

This chapter focuses on the very important mixed-use type of residential units that are found above commercial spaces. Mixed-use buildings benefit everyone involved. The commerce serves the residential community and the residential dwellers serve as a ready market for the stores. This configuration is common in Europe and was also prevalent in U.S. cities until the early twentieth century. Many U.S. cities such as New York, Boston, and Chicago still have many mixed-use strips. Newer cities, such as Portland, Oregon, are consciously developing them. There are many advantages and opportunities for designers in this specialty, which is gaining in importance due to concerns about the environment and transportation costs.

Mixed-use developments often occur along transportation arteries and this can be both an advantage and a disadvantage. The advantage is that transportation and shopping are very convenient for the residential inhabitants and shoppers from other neighborhoods. A disadvantage is that apartment dwellers don't have private yards. Balconies and terraces on the apartments help to solve this problem. Container gardens and green roofs also help the environment. The other disadvantages of noise and crowds can be ameliorated with wide sidewalks, street landscaping, and rear courtyards and gardens. It is very important for the design com-munity to participate in civic life and help to bring forth ideas to improve the community as a whole.

Advantages of Mixed-Use Buildings

From medieval times until the twentieth century, most cities developed as strings of mixed-use buildings, along a "Main Street." People lived above their shops and rented extra space to relatives or other tenants. This was successful both economically and socially. People lived near their work and could shop for daily needs nearby. They knew their merchants personally and there was a strong sense of community among them. However, in the twentieth century, the United States enacted federal laws and financing regulations that prohibited loans for buildings that were more than 25 percent commercial. In the 1920s, the U.S. Department of Commerce drew up a "model zoning enabling act". Herbert Hoover, who was then Commerce Secretary, promoted the act and urged adoption throughout the country to adopt it, and thousands of localities did. This in turn influenced financing by the Federal Housing Authority (FHA) (see Chapter 1).

FHA financing was intended for single-family detached housing. Today, the Federal National Mortgage Association, known as Fannie Mae, buys mortgages on multifamily units, but only 25 percent of projected rent can come from nonresidential sources. In his book *The Wealth of Cities,* John Norquist, president of the Congress for New Urbanism, explains that, per FHA regulations, any building with retail at grade and two stories of residential space above cannot be financed by the FHA.[1] "This basically makes Main Street illegal."[2] With all the present discussion of "Helping Main Street as well as Wall Street," it's time to look into the advantages of mixed-use residential development.

According to a recent study led by Reid Ewing of the National Center for Smart Growth Research and Education at the University of Maryland[3] mixed-use, walkable development greatly alleviates traffic by cutting down on the use of automobiles. Trips starting and ending within the same compact development, referred to as the **internal capture rate**, are substantially increased in mixed-use developments. In Houston, Texas, which is not known for its walking or transit, the internal capture rate was an astounding 28.3 percent for mixed-use developments. Sacramento, Seattle, and Portland, Oregon, also had relatively large recapture rates, ranging from 11.2 to 15.1 percent for mixed-use developments. The study concluded that "mixed-use developments with a diverse array of activities, capture a large share of trips internally, reducing traffic."[4]

Another recent study, by Norman Garrick and Wesley Marshall of the University of Connecticut, concluded that 24 percent fewer parking spaces are needed when uses are mixed. The study included six centers—three mixed-use and three conventional suburban centers.[5] There are obvious environmental advantages to mixed-use developments, but how about living in them? Is it desirable to live above a store? The answer is different for different people. In European cities, which were not segregated by zoning prohibitions, residential apartments as high as six stories are very attractive and in demand. They would be even more desirable if automobile traffic could be made cleaner and quiet electric trams or trolleys were built. American cities such as Portland, Oregon, are following this model. For many people, it is a great advantage to walk no more than five minutes for all their daily needs. It's not necessary for everyone to live in a dense mixed-use development, but their development can have a positive effect on the environment as well as the economy.

Modern residential designers should consider how they can help to create mixed-use space for a modern city or even for a suburb. They should investigate the local market, , what types of businesses are required in the area, and what kind of demand exists for them.

Mixed-Use Prototypes
Transportation Grid for Mixed Use
Mixed-use residential/retail development is often based on a grid that includes walking as a means of transportation. The one-mile grid provides a structure for a ten-minute walk from the neighborhood core to the commercial street. For discussion purposes, the transportation grid is based on a hierarchy of main streets approximately one mile apart. Some of these streets have higher volumes of traffic and are more ideally suited to commercial development. They probably include some form of public transportation as well, such as bus, trolley, or subway. Recent developments also include transit buses, such as those in Curitaba, Brazil, which are made up of multiple cars. They require little infrastructure and are therefore more economical to provide. One drawback is that they rely on petroleum.

At each major intersection, there is a "prime corner," which benefits from the volume of traffic. To walk from the center of the one-mile grid to the edge would take approximately ten minutes. That means that each person can walk to transportation and shopping within that amount of time. The center of the one-mile grid is a desirable place for parks, schools, or community centers.

Mixed-Use Boulevard
This prototype describes a six-story residential building on top of a ground-level retail development. **Figures 9.2a and b** show the site plan and section view, respectively.

The roof includes penthouse units and roof gardens. The street right-of-way, which is the overall public legal easement including sidewalks, is 100 feet wide. There is a 12-foot landscaped median strip in the center, which becomes a turning lane at the end of the block. This median strip

CASE STUDY 9.1

Broadway

San Francisco, California
Solomon E.T.C.-WRT, Architecture and Urban Design

This mixed-use building is located on Broadway Avenue in San Francisco, with stunning views of the Bay. It consists of seven residential stories above ground-level retail. There is a private lobby for the residential portion.

streetscape

lobby

continued on the next page

continued from the previous page

plaza

walkway

streetscape

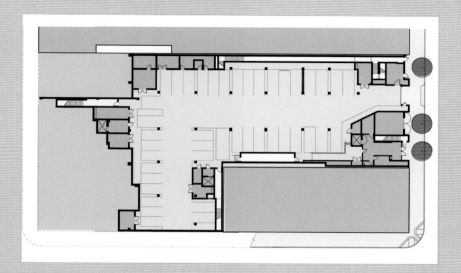

garage level plan

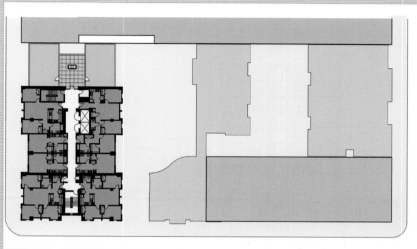

seventh level plan

podium level plan

upper level plan

continued on the next page

continued from the previous page

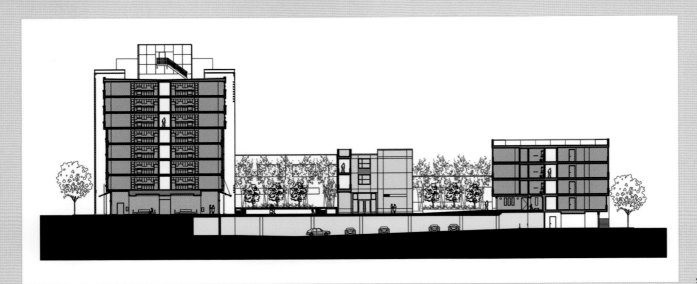

section

foyer

interior

view

display

lobby

CASE STUDY 9.2

Fine Arts

Berkeley, California
Solomon E.T.C.-WRT, Architecture and Urban Design

This project, designed for students at the University of California at Berkeley, is located in downtown Berkeley. The five-story building consists of four levels of residential accommodation above a tall ground floor containing the 200-seat Fine Arts movie theater, retail, and parking, as well as the building entrance lobby. The upper floors are arranged around a landscaped south-facing courtyard. There are several different unit types responding to site conditions and the special needs of student tenants. The basic unit type, located on the perimeter of the building, contains two bedrooms and a living/ dining area, kitchen, and bathroom. The two bedrooms interlock in such a way as to create an articulated building facade with deep recesses, breaking down the scale of the elevation. The use of parking lifts reduces the space devoted to parking. (64 cars are parked in 24 stalls, 195 square feet per car in contrast to the typical 350 sq ft per car.)

The architectural design reinterprets the Art Deco tradition as found in other buildings in Downtown Berkeley with the use of horizontally proportioned corner windows, sun-shading elements and other details.

courtyard

streetscape

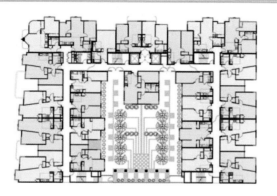

SECOND - FLOOR PLAN

Nested Bedrooms

Bedrooms interlock to create an articulated building facade with deep recesses and reduces the perimeter per unit ratio.

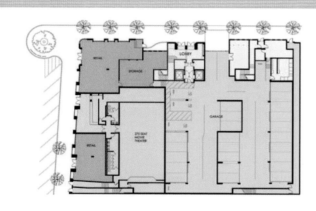

GROUND - FLOOR PLAN

Walkable Streets

The project reduces the footprint needed for parking, and minimizes the competition for ground floor space between pedestrian oriented uses along the street frontage and parking.

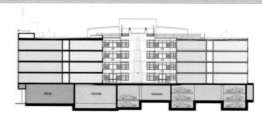

EAST - WEST BUILDING SECTION

Parking Lifts

The parking stalls are housed in mechanical parking lifts corresponding in height to the retail and theater floor, and reduces the floor area per car by half.

plan sections

continued on the next page

continued from the previous page

Specifications

NUMBER OF UNITS: 100 (280 beds)

UNIT CONFIGURATIONS: One and Two Bedroom

PARKING RATIO AND TYPE: 0.25 spaces/0.64 cars using parking lifts

ACCESS TO UNITS: Elevator and Corridor

SQUARE FOOTAGE: 100,000 GSF

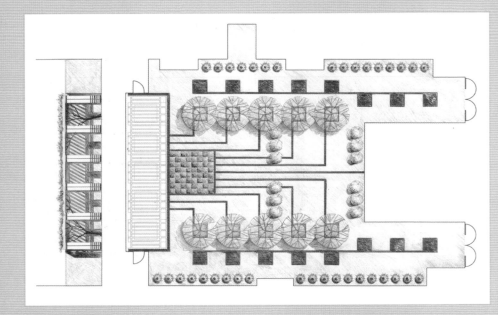

courtyard plan

facade

interior

interior

balconies

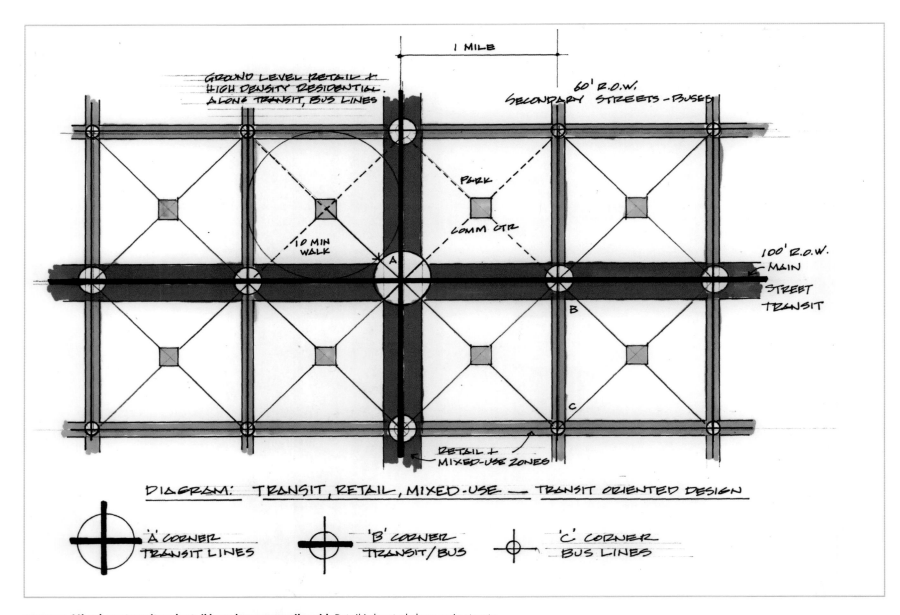

1 MILE

GROUND LEVEL RETAIL +
HIGH DENSITY RESIDENTIAL.
ALONG TRANSIT, BUS LINES

60' R.O.W.
SECONDARY STREETS - BUSES

PARK

COMM CTR

10 MIN
WALK

A

100' R.O.W.
MAIN
STREET
TRANSIT

B

C

RETAIL +
MIXED-USE ZONES

DIAGRAM: TRANSIT, RETAIL, MIXED-USE — TRANSIT ORIENTED DESIGN

'A' CORNER
TRANSIT LINES

'B' CORNER
TRANSIT/BUS

'C' CORNER
BUS LINES

FIGURE 9.1 **Mixed-use transit and retail based on a one-mile grid.** Retail is located along main streets.

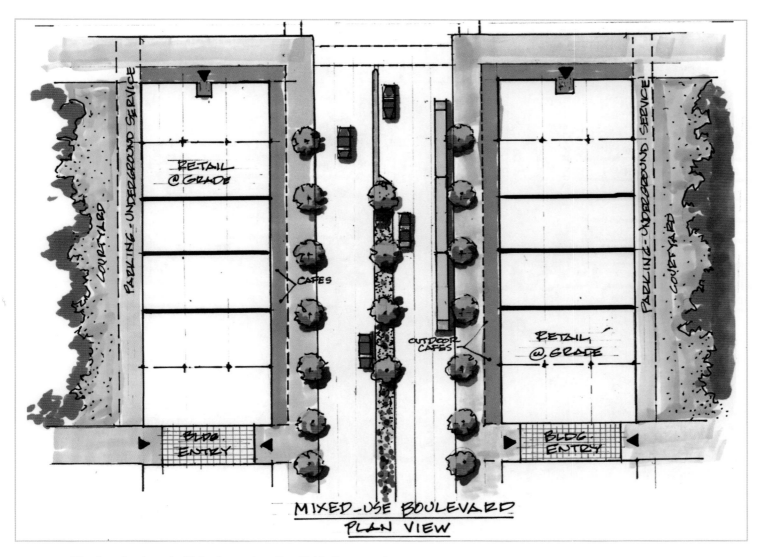

FIGURE 9.2A **Mixed-use boulevard with landscaped median.** Right-of-way = 100'.

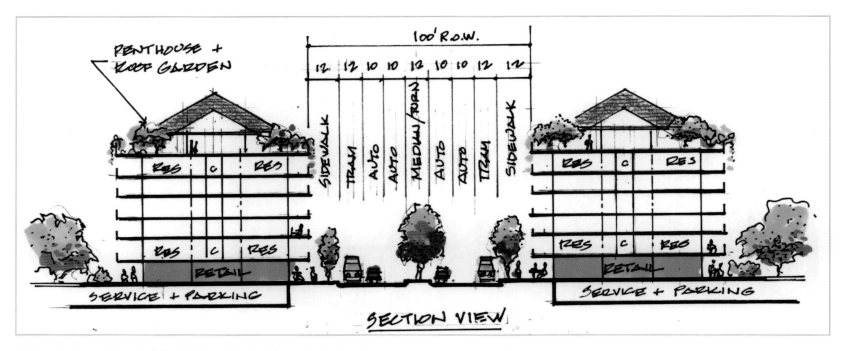

FIGURE 9.2B **Ground-Floor Retail with Six Residential Floors Above.** Includes a penthouse and green roof.

helps to calm traffic and creates a leafy boulevard atmosphere. It places apartments and terraces in the treetops. These terraces are an extremely important part of mixed-use residential planning and should be generously planted. Apartment dwellers desire green space as much as home dwellers, but it is rarely available to them. When it is available, it's in the form of a hang-on balcony that is not very inviting. Instead, consider inserting terraces into the building structure, so it is sheltered from rain and summer sun (**see Figure 9.2b**). It's a great pleasure to leave the patio doors open on a hot, humid, summer day, even during a rainfall. The smells of the plants and trees are invigorating at this time. In summer, the angle of the sun is high. The overhang keeps the sun from warming the apartment. This takes some of the load off the air conditioning to cool the interior. In the winter, when the sun angle is lower, the sunlight can clear the overhang and warm the apartment.

This street is wide enough to accommodate a trolley along the curb. The trolley lane is dedicated solely for transit, so there is no need to turn into different lanes to stop. Pedestrians can board and dismount without stepping into traffic. The sidewalks are 12 feet wide with additional space under the building's balconies for sidewalk cafes, farmers markets, and other outdoor activities. This is a very desirable walking environment and is conducive to shopping. Besides the sidewalk width, it's much more interesting to walk at night along brightly lit and varied storefronts. The walking distances seem much shorter than when walking alongside parking garages or vacant spaces. The retail spaces are in bays 30 feet wide, which can be combined into as much space as a retailer needs. Since these bays are based on the residential structure above and the parking structure below (see Chapter 8) they are open and free between columns and completely flexible for retailers.

CASE STUDY 9.3

Lakeview Development

Chicago, Illinois
Pappageorge/Haymes Ltd., Architects

This mixed-use development consists of three residential stories above a ground-floor retail level. The residential units have an open-plan living/dining/kitchen area. There are inset balconies for comfortable outdoor use. The broad, full-height windows show a distinctive view of urban living in Chicago, including the famous "El" train. The streetscape shows a welcoming presence to the retail shops.

Specifications

5 stories

33 units

6,500 square feet of commercial space

corner view

streetscapes

continued on the next page

continued from the previous page

first floor plan

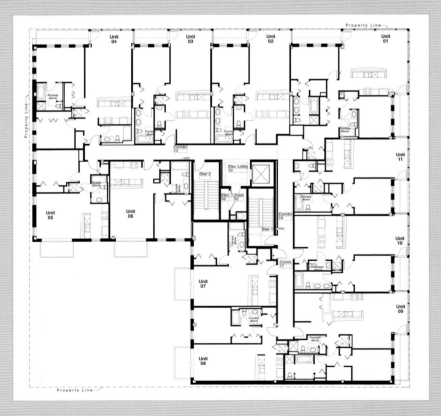

fourth floor

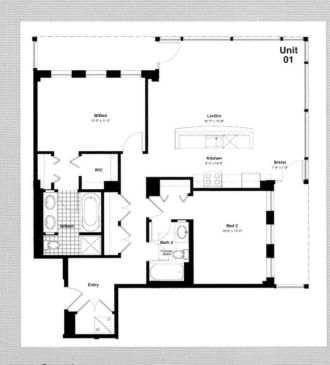

unit floor plan

interior

balconies

interior

There is a private entrance to the residential building, which accommodates fire stairways and elevators. These occur every 150 to 200 feet, depending on local codes and conditions. Parking and servicing are underground, leaving the rear courtyard available for landscaped gardens and recreation. The importance of a landscaped courtyard behind the buildings cannot be overstated. Without it, the build-up of heat caused by asphalt and concrete that covers urban areas contributes greatly to global warming. Planting trees and using green roofs wherever possible can substantially attenuate this heat build-up. This space is much too valuable to waste on open parking lots. Not only is it a great asset to the residential dwellers, it can provide a substantial tree canopy to combat the **urban heat island**. The apartment dweller can have the impression of looking out into a forest preserve, while having the convenience of all the urban amenities nearby.

Mixed-Use Building on Conventional Street

Mixed-use developments can also function very well on conventional streets with a 60-foot-wide right-of-way (**see Figure 9.3a for site plan**). In this example, there is street parking on both sides and a clearly marked mid-block crossing at the building entry vestibule. There are also emergency exits at the ends of the buildings and **bump-outs** at the corners to make it easier and safer for pedestrians to cross, without restricting traffic flow. Again, the retail spaces are based on the columnar structure of the residential building, with each commercial space measuring 30 by 66 feet. They can be combined as desired. (See Chapter 8 for column grid spacing.)

There should be a plumbing stub for an employee washroom in each space. For restaurants, additional sinks and toilets are necessary, as well as dishwashing and cooking facilities and vents. There are many options for street layout for a 60-foot right-of-way, as shown in **Figure 9.3b**. In all of the sections shown, the designer should give the same considerations for sheltered balconies and terraces as discussed in the previous example. A well-designed terrace can add substantial living space to an apartment, as well as greatly enhance the pleasure of living in it.

Chapter Summary

This chapter showed how apartments can be combined with flexible retail spaces at ground level. Ways in which the designer can plan residences to include improvements in the environment, creating a sustainable neighborhood, were discussed. It also explained how mixed-use developments follow the transportation grid and respect reasonable walking distances. Prototype examples of residential units above commercial spaces were provided. (The residential units are similar to the apartments in Chapter 8.)

A variety of streetscapes for mixed-use developments and suggestions for keeping street noise down were discussed, including the incorporation of sidewalk cafes, parking and bike lanes, landscaped medians, and public transportation. The chapter presented ideas for creating a residential atmosphere for apartment dwellers that included generous balconies and terraces. Solutions provided include wide sidewalks, street landscaping, and rear courtyards and gardens.

KEY TERMS

Bump-outs: Widening of the sidewalks at corners to facilitate pedestrian crossing. This is a common traffic-calming device that cuts down on the amount of roadway while increasing sidewalk space.

Internal capture rate: Trips starting and ending within the same development

Street right-of-way: The overall public legal easement. Includes sidewalks, planting, traffic lanes, medians, and public transportation.

Urban heat island: The build-up of heat caused by asphalt and concrete in urban areas, which contributes greatly to global warming. This can be attenuated by planting trees and using green roofs wherever possible.

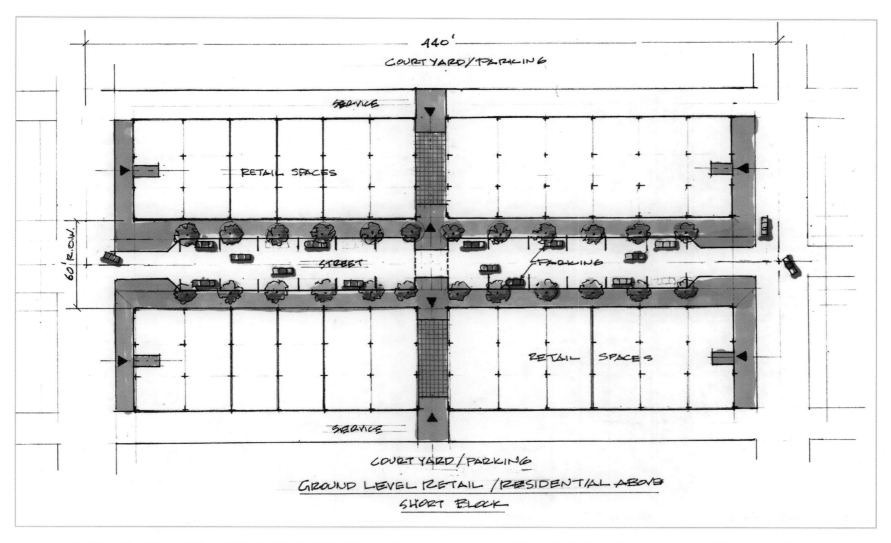

FIGURE 9.3A **Site Plan: Mixed-Use Building with 60-foot right-of-Way**. Showing alternate street and sidewalk uses for 60-foot right-of-way: transit, parking, and bicycles.

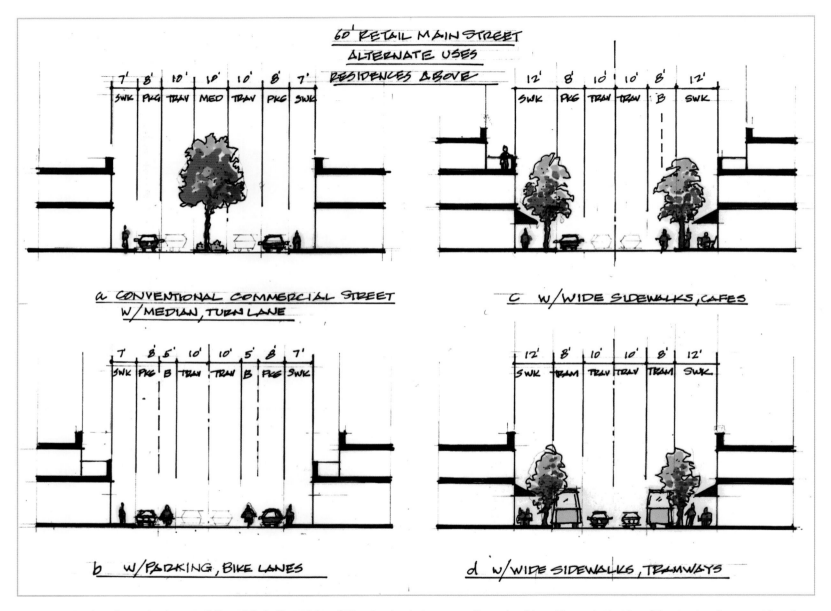

FIGURE 9.3B Options for a Mixed-Use Building with 60-foot Right-of-Way. Section A shows a median strip with parking on both sides of the street and narrow sidewalks. Section B shows parking on both sides of the street with two bike lanes instead of a median. Section C shows landscaped sidewalks 12 feet wide with parking on one side and a bike lane on the other. Section D shows wide sidewalks with trolley or bus lanes adjoining and automobile traffic in the center.

CASE STUDY 9.4

Armitage and Leavitt Streets

Chicago, Illinois
Pappageorge/Haymes Ltd., Architects

This small mixed-use building on Chicago's north side consists of three residential stories above ground-level retail. There is a private lobby for the residences and the retail shops are accessed from the sidewalk. There are four corner units per floor. Parking is underground. This is an ideal in-fill project.

front view

detail view

continued on the next page

continued from the previous page

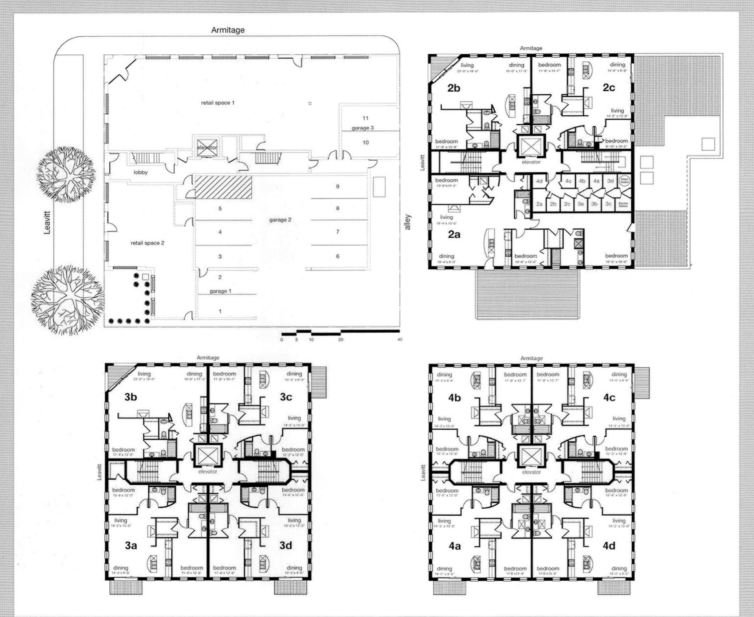

floor plans

corner retail

lobby

EXERCISES

1. Take a series of walks in different types of safe locations. Some should have complexes of stores and cafes and others can be located along vacant areas, even parks and parking garages, as well as purely residential communities. Time the walks and guess the distances traveled. After the walks, consult a map to see what distances were actually covered. How do these compare with your guesses? Which distances *seemed* shorter, the retail walks or the others?

2. Visit multipurpose complexes in the community that include the workspaces of artists and artisans, such as ceramists, cabinetmakers, and tailors, who make and sell their own products. These people often work irregular hours and find it convenient to live above or even inside their shops. Lay out some live/work spaces on the ground floor, based on the 30-foot-by-66-foot bay, or multiples thereof. Try a duplex arrangement, with living on the floor above connected by an internal stairway. Write a brief description of the impact of the type of space on the community.

ENDNOTES

1. George W. Liebmann, *Modernization of Zoning, A Means to Reform* (An unbound article in the Cato Review of Business and Government, 1996.)
2. John Norquist, *The Wealth of Cities,* (New York: Basic Books, 1998).
3. As cited by Philip Langdon in his article "Studies: Mixed-use Walkable Development Alleviates Traffic," *New Urban News* 2008 (September), 1, 7.
4. Ibid.
5. Norman Garrick and Wesley Marshall, University of Connecticut, 2005, as cited by Philip Langdon, "Studies," 8.

PART VI

The Big Picture

MIXED-USE ON MAIN STREET

R. GORDON 3/99

CHAPTER 10

Urban Design

The Context of Residential Planning: Putting It All Together

Chapter Purpose

This chapter gives the context for all residential planning and shows how it is fundamental to most of the decisions a designer will make with a client. There is a brief background of site surveying and planning in the United States. Working from early maps, the chapter shows the reasons for the sizes and shapes of most sites and how they relate to the residential floor plan. An example illustrates how to perform a neighborhood survey, taking into account factors that may affect the residential design.

Building heights and spacing are affected by the angles of the sun at different times of the year. Building spacing is expressed as **density**, which is the number of inhabitants or dwelling units per land measurement (e.g., people per square mile or acre or dwelling units per square mile or acre). Prototypes are provided to illustrate how different housing types can occupy the same one-block, five-acre site. Diagrams are provided to compare different densities on the same site.

Case studies illustrate four large-scale urban design projects and a comparison of four cities—New York, Chicago, and Paris. Students can get a better feeling for different housing types by studying these prototypes and they will gain an understanding of the importance of good environmental design and urban context for the changing world.

Principles of Urbanism

Principles of urbanism begin in the smallest human settlements. According to *Webster's New World Dictionary*, the word *urban* means "comprising a city as distinguished from the country . . . an incorporated or unincorporated place with at least 2,500 inhabitants." Also, residential planning and design are not based on individual buildings, but rather on their place in the community. Current concerns about the environment emphasize the need for sustainable places. What good is it to create a green or sustainable home if the resident must drive many miles to go to work, shop for food, and take children to school?

Sustainable design has been a repeated theme in this book. The walkability of the neighborhood and relationships between streets, parking, sidewalks, building entries, yards, balconies, and terraces, as well as the solar orientation of the building must all be considered by designers and their clients. All of these features are affected by the location of the home within the context of its surrounding environment.

Attention to sustainable neighborhoods has been gaining dominance in the planning and design professions. The Leadership for Energy and Environmental Design (LEED) rating system is now applied to neighborhoods in much the same way as the original LEED rating system was applied to buildings.[1] This new rating system is called LEED-Neighborhood Development (LEED-ND) . According to this system, points are given for a number of aspects of urban design, a few of which include:

- Compactness
- Diversity of housing types
- Smart location
- Transit facilities
- Reduced automobile dependence
- Bicycle network
- Proximity to water
- Proximity to jobs
- Access to surrounding vicinity (schools, shopping, public space)

Residential designers must offer choices to their clients. Large front and rear yards may be desirable for some people, but are just a nuisance for others. Interior stairways might work well for some, but are impossible for others to use. Driving may always have its place in society, especially as automobiles are built more efficiently, but it comes at a cost to home buyers. Clients should be given the option to build a garage or a studio or do neither and save the money. Owning a second car for shopping requires a substantial increase to the housing budget. An option might be to live in an area with better amenities. While this may be more expensive, the cost of a second car is saved. It is also possible for all of these housing choices to exist in the same neighborhood, town, or city. The challenge to the designer is to determine how they can all fit together.

Background

Where do dimensions of building sites come from? How is ownership described? Why do we even bother measuring sites? Lines of latitude and longitude began to appear on maps in about 300 BCE. By 150 CE, the cartographer/astronomer Ptolemy had drawn 27 maps in his first world atlas, all of them containing latitude and longitude lines.[2] (**See Figure 10.1.**)

Long before George Washington became president of the United States, he had a keen interest in land surveying. He worked as a public land surveyor and private real estate speculator before he became a Revolutionary War general. Thomas Jefferson, as his father before him, was also an accomplished surveyor. This signifies the importance of surveying to real estate speculation and political power. If you can measure

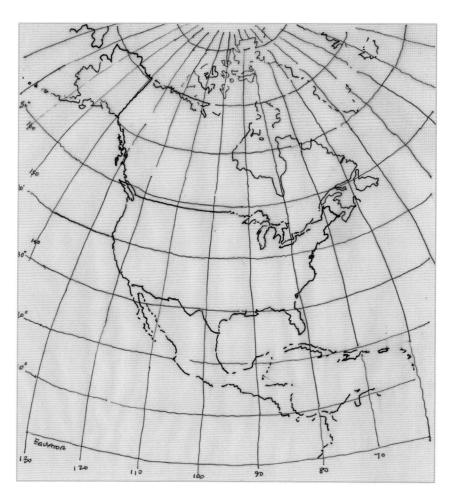

FIGURE 10.1 **The Western Hemisphere.** The earth's grid—longitudes and latitudes.

CASE STUDY 10.1

Seaside Square

Seaside Florida
Solomon E.T.C.-WRT, Architecture and Urban Design

Seaside, Florida, was the first planned development to exemplify the goals of New Urbanism. It is a living example of a community with walkable dimensions, a town center, local retail, mixed-use buildings, and residences with street parking and access.

Seaside Square is a key part of the New Urbanism plan for the community. It is a mixed-use residential and retail building. The program includes 10,000 square feet of retail space in four 20-foot-high spaces, lined with a 20-foot-high arcade as mandated by the Seaside Design Code. The retail stores surround two courtyards that open to the town square at the front and to a street called Quincy Circle at the rear. Above the retail stores are ten luxurious condominiums, ranging in size from 1,600 to 3,100 square feet. All units have outdoor terraces with views of the town square or the Gulf of Mexico. The townhouse units have terraces overlooking the civic lawn that function as box seats for events.

gateway

apartments with balconies

continued on the next page

continued from the previous page

plaza

gateway

pedestrian walkway

view between buildings

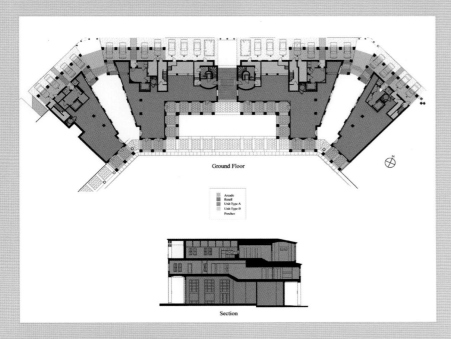

ground floor plan and section

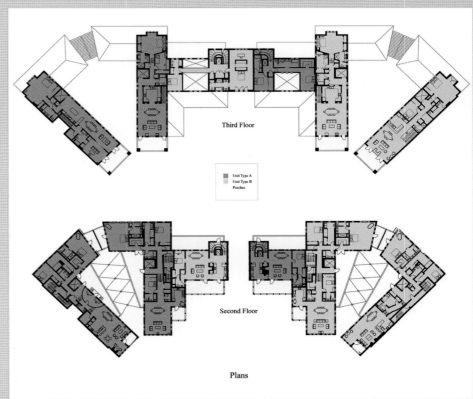

building plans, second and third floors

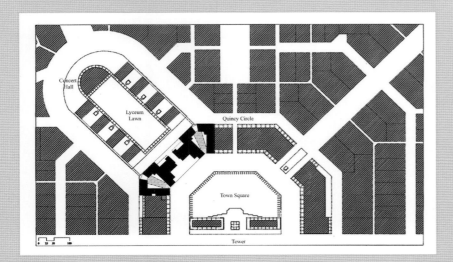

site plan

continued on the next page

continued from the previous page

interior, great room

balcony with sea view

foyer

walk-in closet

storage/room divider

bathroom

kitchen

it, you can own it. The rectangular survey system was first proposed by Thomas Jefferson and enacted into law by the Land Ordinance of 1785. It still forms the structure of U.S. land surveys.

The Public Land Survey System is a way of subdividing and describing land in the United States. All lands in the public domain are subject to subdivision by this rectangular system of surveys, which is regulated by the U.S. Department of the Interior, Bureau of Land Management.[3]

Over the last 200 years or so, almost 1.5 billion acres have been surveyed into townships, sections, and ranges marked with monuments. (**See Figure 10.2a.**) The U.S. Department of the Interior counted about 2.6 million section corners throughout the United States. They are located about one mile apart.[4]

Based on this Federal Public Land Survey System, the mile-square grid remains the basis for most urban and suburban street grids. (See **Figure 10.2b** for application of this grid in Chicago.) One mile is not just an artificially imposed measurement. It is also generally recognized as an easily walkable distance, taking about 20 minutes. Many ancient communities, even cities, measured approximately one mile by one mile. This size reinforces our ideas of neighborhood and community. It is much easier to identify with a community on foot than driving through in a car. The mile grid recognizes both the 10-minute walking radius from the center and a shorter 5-minute walking distance from the center of the half-mile quadrants. (**See Figure 10.3.**) The primary streets and roads at the perimeter support necessary daily shopping. A town square or civic center can be located in the center. A park or school can be placed in the middle of each of the smaller half-mile quadrants. The mile-square community, with its half-mile-square neighborhoods, forms the structure of a convenient pedestrian neighborhood. (**See Figure 10.4.**)

Within this one-mile grid, many different block sizes and patterns can be developed. By varying the sizes and directions of the blocks, streets can be offset. This creates more interesting walking patterns and calms local traffic. (**See Figure 10.5**) These offset blocks also create **perspec-**

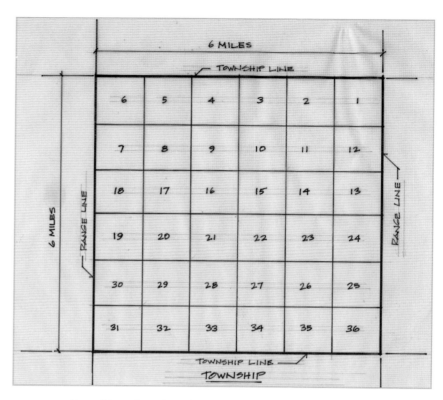

FIGURE 10.2A **Township and Sections.** (a) Land divisions based on the original U.S. Surveys of the Public Lands.

tive terminals, landmarks that tend to shorten the perceived distance of walks. A fixed, visible end to a walk makes it seem more attainable than a perspective that appears to go on forever.

Shorter blocks also offer variety and more shortcuts. This gives the impression of an easier walk. In her groundbreaking book, *The Death and Life of Great American Cities*, Jane Jacobs describes this phenomenon: "Most blocks must be short; streets and opportunities to turn corners must be frequent."[5] This has become a mantra for the current generation of urban planners and residential designers.

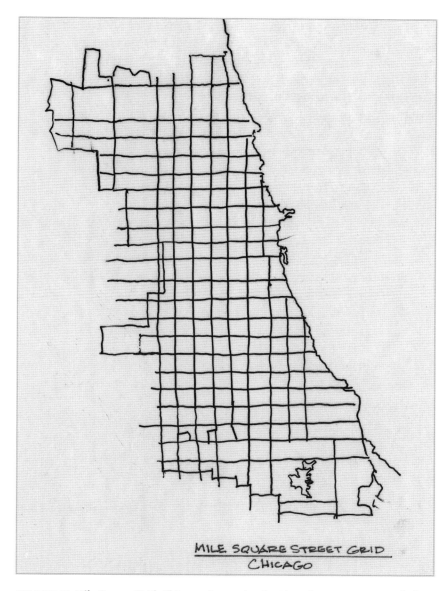

FIGURE 10.2B **Mile Square Grid, Chicago**. A map showing the mile-square street grid of Chicago.

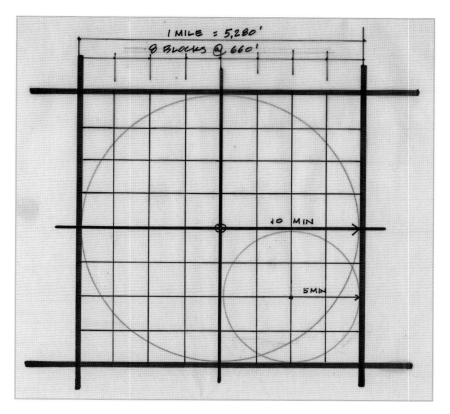

FIGURE 10.3 **The Mile Grid.** A 64-block community with a 10-minute walking radius from the center to the periphery. The walking radius for each quadrant is about five minutes.

As described in Chapter 9, planners normally designate street rights-of-way at 60 and 100 feet for the various roadways, depending on the projected traffic volumes. These rights-of-way can be arranged in a variety of ways. (**See Figures 9.2a and 9.3a.**) Local variations can include the following:

- The width of sidewalks, which can be used just for walking or as locations for cafe seating or outdoor sales areas.
- The type of **streetscaping**, lighting, and landscaping.
- Incorporation of street parking.

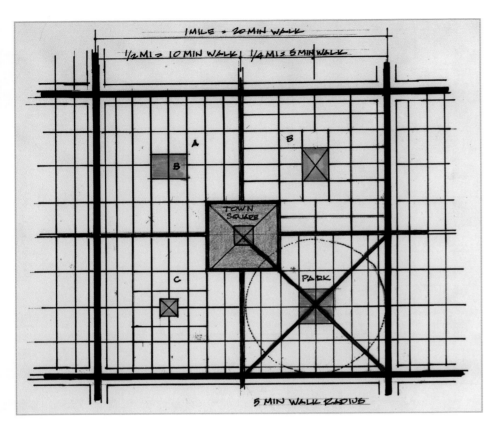

FIGURE 10.4 **Geometry of a Mile.** Mixed-use along main streets and residential units at the interior. Parks and civic centers are in central locations, accessible to the residences.

- Bicycle lanes.
- Trolley or bus lanes.

Even though suburban grids are sometimes curved or modified due to hilly terrain or for marketing purposes (**Figure 10.6**), they eventually must relate to the highway, section, and township grids as staked out by surveyors. They must also conform to the normal transportation systems and walking distances that make up most communities and neighborhoods. For example, picturesque hillside towns in Italy are built on steep slopes and sharp curving roads, while larger cities are built on flatter terrain with regular street grids. Diagonal streets often intersect the regular grids, which adds some variety (**Figure 10.7**).

Design and Planning Considerations
Existing Community Context
Before beginning a residential design, prepare a community or neighborhood context diagram. Clients appreciate this type of attention to their projects. First, walk the area thoroughly and become familiar with it. Take notes of walking time using sample itineraries. Obtain aerial photographs of the entire site/neighborhood area from Google Earth. Then, with an overlay tracing, start sketching very freely, considering the following:

- Show main street corners; main transportation routes, including transit, automobile, bicycle, and walking; interesting and functional walking itineraries; key neighborhood facilities.
- Be aware of the surrounding building heights and density. Do they vary? If there are high buildings near low buildings, how does it affect them?
- Is it desirable to create a varied streetscape, consisting of single family homes, townhouses, walkup apartments, and elevator buildings on the same block? How does it make a difference?
- Is it desirable to retain existing structures, which may have historic importance?
- Is it desirable to maintain a similarity in style to the historic buildings that remain or does the designer want a friendly mix of historic and modern?
- Show negative environmental impacts, such as garbage dumps or freeways, and design ways to minimize them.

A general community survey is shown in **Figure 10.7**. The designer should enlarge and enhance the map as more details about the community are learned. Notice that in this existing community there are many anomalies. An expressway slices through the eastern portion, dividing the neighborhood in two. Though there are parks in each half-mile

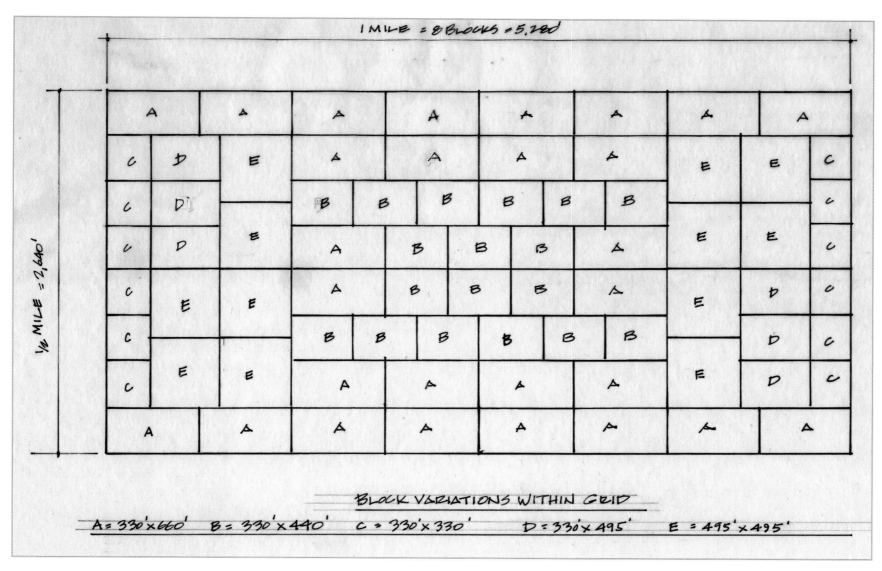

1 MILE = 8 BLOCKS = 5,280

½ MILE = 2,640'

BLOCK VARIATIONS WITHIN GRID

A = 330' x 660'   B = 330' x 440'   C = 330' x 330'   D = 330' x 495'   E = 495' x 495'

FIGURE 10.5 **Diagram Showing Block Configuration.** Different size blocks within the mile structure create offsets to the streets, which can serve to calm traffic and make walking more interesting.

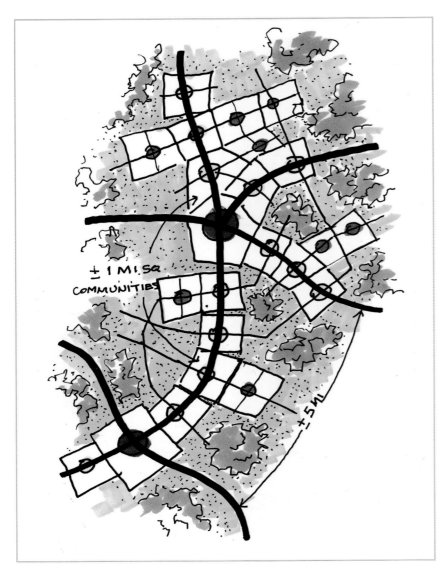

FIGURE 10.6 **Schematic City Plan.** This urban land-use diagram is based on curving transit routes in natural terrain. Main streets are also commercial streets.

quadrant, two of them are near the expressway. This makes them noisier and more polluted. A diagonal street runs through the primary street corner, creating interesting traffic circulation and pedestrian challenges at the crosswalks. There is a conveniently located Metro stop at the main corner, which serves as a community magnet and reinforces the commercial center.

The Site

The first act of planning a residence is to survey the available building site. The site creates opportunities and imposes limits on residential design. The size of the site, with associated **zoning and subdivision regulations** and restrictions, determines the size of the building. For historical surveying reasons, normal block sizes are 330 by 660 feet to the centerlines of streets, which amounts to 5 acres. **(See Figure 10.5, Block A.)** Streets are normally planned 60 to 100 feet wide. A site is usually a subdivision of the block dimension, such as 1 acre, ½ acre, and smaller. Lot sizes are often even multiples of 25, 37.5, 50, 75, and 150 feet wide. These are nice, even dimensions that are easy to draw and easy to sell.

Climate is another site characteristic that determines the orientation of a structure as well as the materials needed. In a warm, humid climate, windows should be oriented away from the sunlight and placed to encourage ventilation. In cold climates, southern orientation is important for solar gain. Access to transportation also affects residential design.

The relationship of the site to the community is equally important. A vacant lot in a dense urban area has different design constraints than a lot in the country. How valuable is the land? Is it located in a high-density area with tall buildings adjoining it or in a neighborhood of single-family homes? What are the neighborhood amenities available to the site? (These include natural amenities, such as parks and forests, and built amenities, such as shopping and schools.) Will daily shopping and children's school attendance require driving? If so, how many cars and parking spaces are required per family? If there is available shopping and transportation, it may not be necessary to include as much parking. In many urban neighborhoods, as few as 40 percent of households have cars. This greatly affects the site layout.

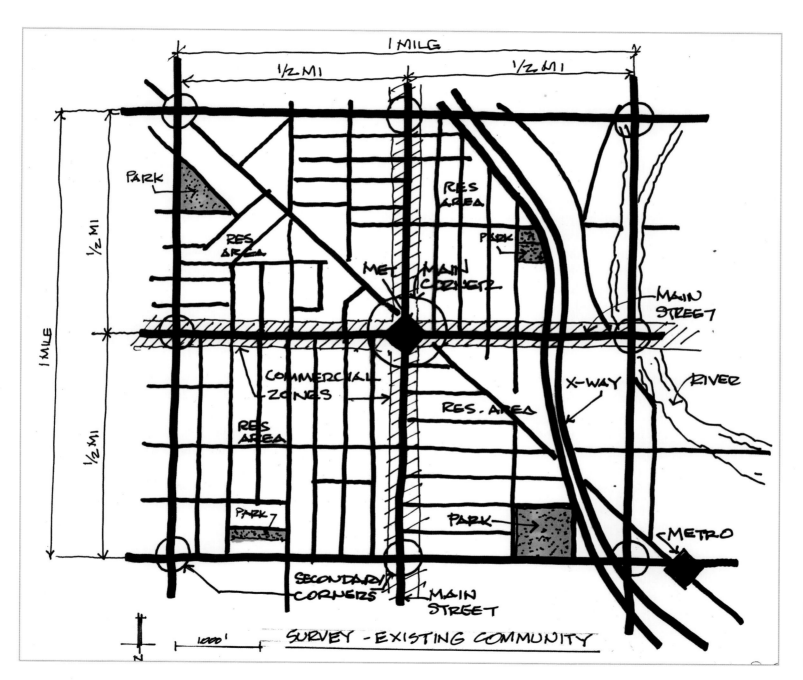

FIGURE 10.7 **Community Survey Diagram.** An existing community with transportation, shopping, and parks.

Tip: When first considering a residential design for a client, it is very important to personally visit the site. Become familiar with the uniqueness of the site and the neighbors. If possible, walk around and visit the neighborhood. Bring a sketchbook or camera and make notes. Besides impressing the client, you may also gain ideas for the project.

Ideal Community Plan

After the preliminary neighborhood and site research is complete, it's time to decide on the placement of new buildings on the site and the spacing between them. This is especially critical on large sites with multiple buildings. It is helpful to contact local planning agencies for a copy of the land-use plan in place for the community, if one exists. A general idealized plan may look like the diagram in **Figure 10.8**, which shows the main streets, major transportation routes, transit or subway stops, commercial areas, parks, schools, civic buildings, and residential areas.

Modern urban planners propose **transit-oriented design**, which seeks to locate higher density and mixed-use residential units near transit stops. This increases the possibility and convenience of using public transportation or walking for daily activities, which, in turn, is good for the environment. These high-density mixed-use transit-oriented developments are therefore located at the four main intersections of the mile streets, with attendant transit stations. The main shopping streets connect these four corners. If there is an adequate market, the secondary half-mile streets may also require mixed-use projects of low or medium density. These locations might be ideal for live/work residences.

In the center of the mile square is a town square with a civic building or, possibly, a school. In the center of each half-mile quadrant is a park or recreational facility. These can be connected by diagonal streets from the four corners.

Spacing and Placing of Residential Buildings on a Site

The number of dwelling units for a given site is determined by a **feasibility study**. Before a project is undertaken, a financial and/or real estate consultant analyzes the economic potential of the site, the building, and the client's ability to pay for it. A bank will not finance a project if the feasibility is doubtful. Cost estimates based on conceptual site plans, designs, and local construction costs are figured in. These studies should be made at the earliest stages of design so that a specific budget can be agreed upon before time is wasted. It might be difficult to achieve an "ideal" plan, especially in an existing community. Design compromises should be agreed upon, prior to committing to more detailed construction documents.

The appropriate density for the site is based on the feasibility study. Density may be calculated in several ways. The most common are inhabitants per square mile or acre, or dwelling units per square mile or acre.

For our purposes, density will be based on dwelling units per acre. Each typical block is 330 feet by 660 feet to the centerlines of the streets, which is *exactly five acres*. Population density figures are based on the gross density, taking into account the street areas. Existing population, household size, and land area can be obtained from the U.S. Census Bureau and its equivalent in foreign countries.[6] (Case studies 10.5 and 10.6 are good examples of different densities.)

It is necessary to determine the appropriate density for a given site. Residential designers may not always be involved in this determination, because a developer must make a financial decision based on the cost of land, site utilities, and the market. This is usually undertaken during the feasibility stage. Sometimes the existing zoning for the subject site will not support a proposed development, so **zoning variations** must be sought. These variations might include reducing setback lines, raising density, and increasing height limitations. The designer should assist the client in investigating the consequences of these changes and even assist the client in making the case that they are justified. Justifications might include benefits to the community or potential environmental benefits. All of these determinations must be made in collaboration with the client, the township or city, and the adjoining property owners.

In addition to other feasibility considerations, there is a standard of sunlight. Most people would like at least a few hours of sunlight in their homes during the day, especially in winter, so the angle of the sun at the site location must be determined. There are many Web sites that can help to determine solar angles in given locations for different times on different days.[7] An example is given in **Figure 10.10** for 42 degrees latitude at

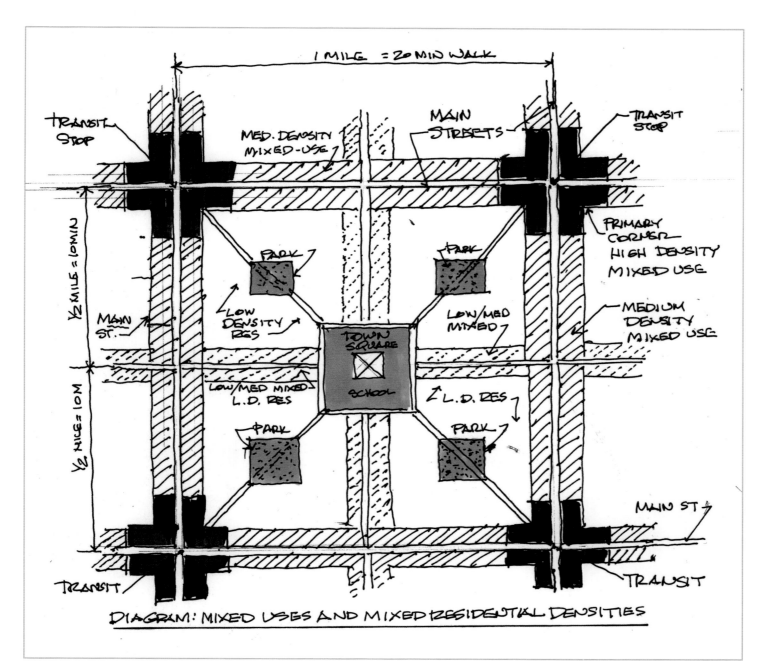

FIGURE 10.8 **Density.** Mixed-use and mixed residential densities are shown along transit routes.

CASE STUDY 10.2

The Roosevelt Collection

Chicago, Illinois
RTKL Associates/Architecture and Master Planning

An important urban-design feature of this site plan is that it connects several roads of different elevations. Roosevelt Road on the south is on a bridge, higher than Wells Street below. The planners used this elevation difference to provide grade level access to Roosevelt Road for pedestrians and auto access. The lower levels, from Wells Street up to Roosevelt Road, are used for parking. This connection repairs a tear in the urban fabric and allows the north and south portions of the community to come together.

The Roosevelt Collection is a 1-million-square-foot mixed-use development located in Chicago's rapidly expanding South Loop neighborhood. The project consists of approximately 400 residential units above 600,000 square feet of retail and entertainment space.

The plan features a grand boulevard down the center, flanked on each side by retail shops with apartments above. A 16-screen multiplex theater and a fitness club provide a 24-hour streetscape on the Roosevelt Road commercial corridor.

The boulevard culminates in a pedestrian-friendly plaza, anchored by large-scale entertainment uses and intimate restaurants.

The Roosevelt Collection contains structured parking below street level, with over 1,300 parking spaces for retail customers, as well as a dedicated space for each residential unit. Shoppers have easy access to the parking garage from the development's main entrance on Roosevelt Road, a major arterial street. Residents have separate parking as well as a separate entrance off of Wells Street.

project entry

view of urban boulevard and plaza with shops and residences above

night life

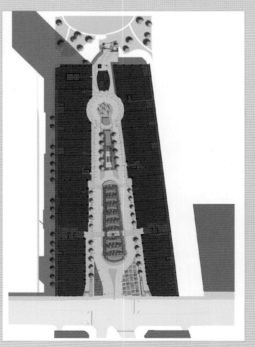

site elevation

site plan

continued on the next page

continued from the previous page

bird's-eye view of plaza and city

the time of the summer solstice (June 21) and winter solstice (December 21). This diagram shows what portion of the yard and adjoining building will be in shade at noon for three different building heights.

The same principle can be used for determining spacing between residential buildings of varying heights (i.e., buildings of three, five, ten, twenty, or even thirty stories). (**See Figure 10.11.**) Taller buildings require more space between them to avoid casting shadows on their neighbors or on landscaped yards. This type of attention to sunlight in residential planning is called **passive solar design,** which includes passive solar lighting and heating. In conjunction with the use of **sunscreens** (**Figure 10.10**)**,** passive solar heating can be used to keep out hot summer sunlight while allowing lower angled sunlight to enter in the winter.

Other factors in the placement of residential buildings on a site include the location of alleys, parking considerations, yard space, existing landscaping on the street, and public parks. **Figure 10.9b** shows a typical Chicago alley, with trash cans and garage parking in the rear. In some cities, such as New York and Paris, trash must be picked up in front when there are no alleys. Servicing and parking in the rear is more efficient, but front pickup is tolerable to achieve higher densities.

Mixed Site Plans to Accommodate Different Housing Types

In previous chapters, prototype drawings showed site plans for various housing types such as single-family homes, rowhouses, walk-up apartment buildings, elevator buildings, and mixed-use residential/commercial buildings. The approximate relative densities for these types are as follows:

- Single-family homes, wide lots: 5 to 8 units per acre.
- Rowhouses: 10 to 12 units per acre.
- Walk-up apartment buildings with single entries; three stories: 30 to 40 units per acre.
- Elevator apartment buildings with corridors, depending on building height: 50 to 150 units per acre.

FIGURE 10.9A **An Alley in Chicago.**

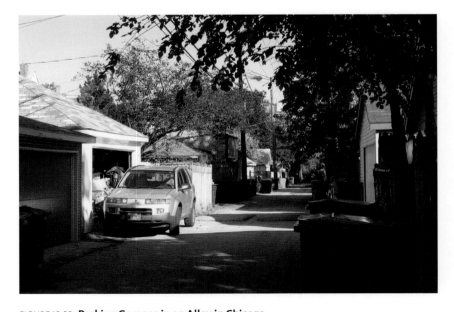

FIGURE 10.9B **Parking Garages in an Alley in Chicago.**

FIGURE 10.9C **Front Street Trash Removal, New York.**

FIGURE 10.9E **Front Street Trash Removal in Paris.**

FIGURE 10.9D **Garbage Bags on Sidewalk in New York.**

For the most part, this book has explored these housing types individually. However, in the real world, the designer is faced with the challenge of mixing housing types and land uses on certain sites. There also may be old buildings that should be preserved. The developer may want to mix single-family homes, rowhouses, and apartments on the same site. Mixed-use buildings may share site lines with single-family homes or apartments. All of these housing types are part of the urban fabric. The residents of each type of home contribute to the richness of community life and benefit from the diversity among which they live.

Mixed Residential Types on a Single Site

Figure 10.15a shows a two-block area in which each block contains five acres, from the centerline of one street to the centerline of the next. The single five-acre block will be used as the unit of comparison for the various mixtures that following, in terms of dwelling units per acre.

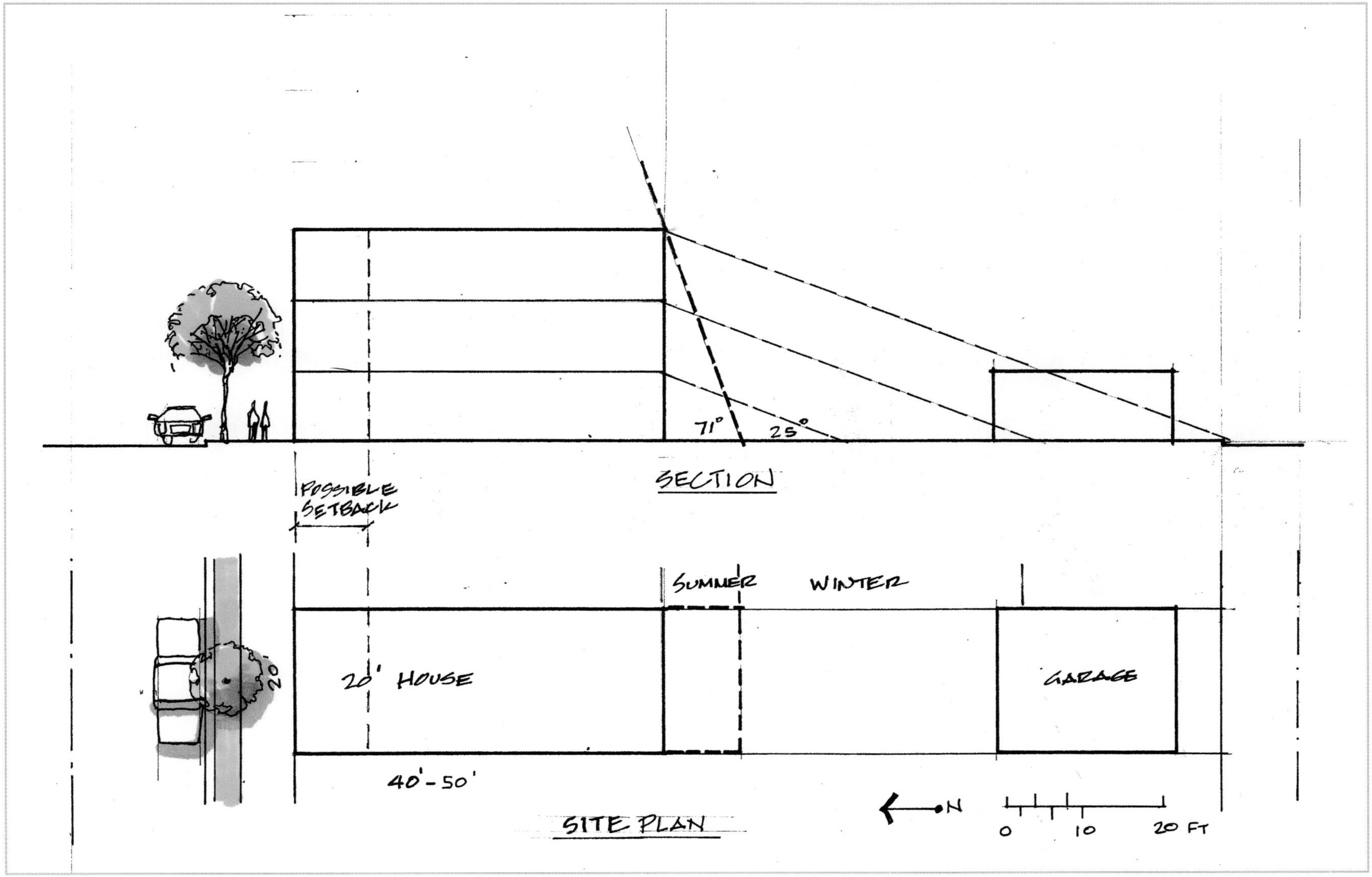
71°
25°
SECTION
POSSIBLE SETBACK
SUMMER
WINTER
20' HOUSE
20
GARAGE
40'-50'
SITE PLAN
N
0
10
20 FT

FIGURE 10.10 **Solar Diagram.** This diagram shows the shadows cast by the sun at summer and winter solstice.

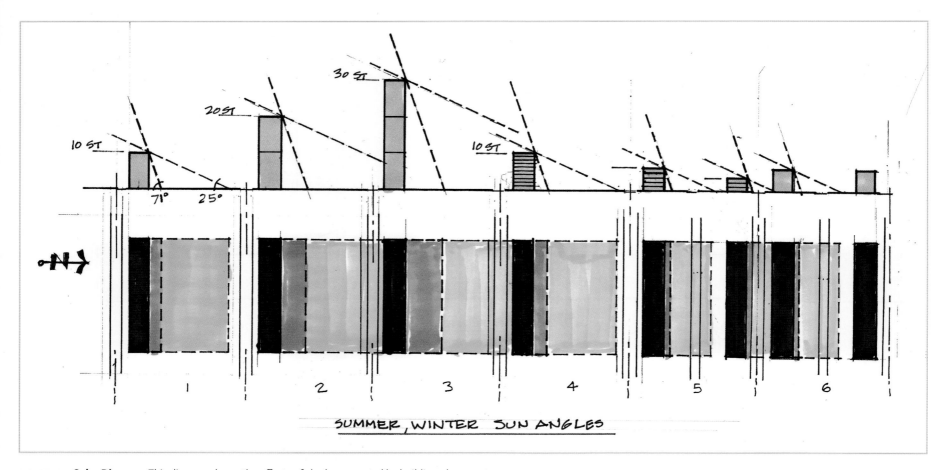

FIGURE 10.11 **Solar Diagram.** This diagram shows the effects of shadows created by building placement.

Mixed Single-Family and Rowhouses: Six Units per Acre

In **Figure 10.15b** the single-family homes are on 50-foot lots and the rowhouses are on 25-foot lots. There are 32 dwelling units on the site for a density of six units per acre.

Mixture of Single-Family, Rowhouses, and Walk-ups: 30 Units Per Acre

The one-block site consists of eight single-family detached homes, eight attached rowhouses, and four walk-up corridor-type apartment buildings comprising 132 dwelling units (**Figure 10.15c**). The apartment buildings are L-shaped and connected by a pass-through atrium entry. There is a total of 148 dwelling units on the site, or 30 units per acre.

Note that the apartment buildings are reversed in their site placement. For some sites, it might be desirable to have a courtyard garden at the front entry. For others it would be located in the backyard. If there are commercial uses on the ground floor, it would be better to have them close to the sidewalk. More choices offer a more varied streetscape.

All Walk-up Apartment Buildings: 43 Units per Acre

Figure 10.15d shows a community made entirely of walk-up apartment buildings, sometimes called **garden apartments**. Some of the buildings have single entries, as in **Figure 8.3**. Others have internal corridors, as in **Figure 8.4a and b**. This diagram of walk-up apartments shows the significant density that can be achieved without the use of elevator buildings or towers.

Twelve single-entry walk-up units totals 72 dwelling units. Four corridor-type apartment buildings of three stories each (36 apartments) totals 144 dwelling units. The total for the block is 216 dwelling units, or 43 units per acre.

FIGURE 10.12B **Chicago Walk-up with Courtyard Entry.**

FIGURE 10.12A **Modern Chicago Walk-up.**

FIGURE 10.12C **Chicago Walk-up with Bay Windows.**

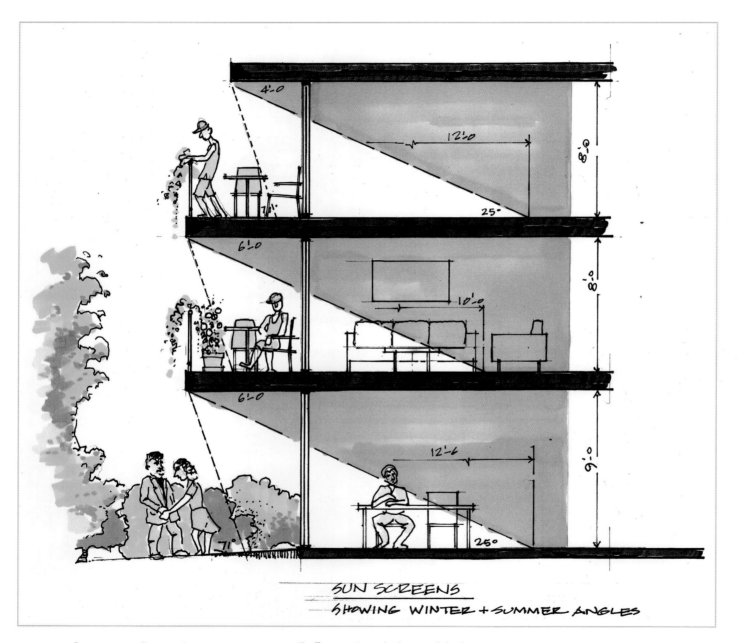

FIGURE 10.13 **Sunscreen or Canopy.** A sunscreen or canopy will affect passive solar heat and shade.

There is a glass atrium/entry connecting the two apartment buildings, making them in effect one building with a single secured entry. The option is to leave an opening between the buildings for a pass-through from front to rear. This might be practical on a site where there is a courtyard in the rear that serves as a common garden.

Since elevators use a substantial amount of energy, walk-up apartment buildings present a practical solution for saving money and the environment at the same time.

Elevator Buildings, Walk-ups, and Townhouses on One Site: 64 Units per Acre

Figure 10.15e presents a diverse mixture of housing types. This would allow a developer to market to a variety of clients: Four six-story elevator/corridor apartment buildings, each with 66 dwelling units gives 264 total units; courtyard entries are on the front of the buildings. Eight three-story walk-up apartments for total 48 apartments, and eight rowhouses provide 8 units. Total dwelling units for this plan equals 320, or 64 units per acre.

High-Density Primary Corner at Transit Stop: 100 Units per Acre

Figure 10.15f shows mixed-use commercial/residential buildings of six and ten stories. The ground floors of all the buildings house retail spaces, such as grocery stores, cafes, bookstores, pharmacies, clothing, and other high pedestrian uses. There are approximately 500 to 550 dwelling units for the block; about 100 units per acre. The streetcar, subway, or light-rail system intersects at this corner. High-density buildings should be located near main transit stops and adjacent to neighborhood shopping to cut down on automobile use. Note that residents in all four of the corner buildings, a total of more than 700 units, have direct access from their buildings to the transit and commercial spaces.

Due to the high density, underground parking is feasible with a park/plaza deck above to be shared by residents and shoppers. The roofs and terraces are green, with walk-out roof gardens. All of the residential buildings have common-area party room/exercise spaces, and possibilities for swimming pools and roof gardens.

FIGURE 10.14A **Apartment Terrace.**

FIGURE 10.14B **Terrace Courtyard.**

CASE STUDY 10.3

Othello Station

Seattle, Washington
Solomon E.T.C.-WRT, Architecture and Urban Design

In this development the streets have been replanned for the whole neighborhood, creating an orderly circulation pattern in place of the existing hodge-podge. There is on-street parking, with additional spaces behind the units. A green space is built in the center of the development. The residential buildings consist of mixture of new townhouses over accessible flats, combined with single-family homes. This creates a density and diversity of housing types while still maintaining the residential feel of the community.

streetscape

common yard

Holly Park, a project funded under the Hope VI HUD program, replaces existing public housing built during the 1940s with a new, dense neighborhood consisting of mixed uses for residents of diverse incomes. The master plan extends the existing street grid into the 36-acre site and is organized around a spine of public parks, providing a pedestrian connection between residences and neighborhood shopping and transit. The approximately 400 new housing units will vary in type and density; from rowhouses on the interior of the site to apartments-over-retail along the perimeter streets. This master plan includes planning of the future light-rail station area on an additional 11-acre site, which builds upon the vitality of the existing Asian neighborhood shopping district. By introducing structured parking and civic facilities, and by refocusing existing retail, including a grocery store on the main street, a future senior housing campus will be connected to the neighborhood shopping district and the new residential neighborhood.

aerial view

continued on the next page

continued from the previous page

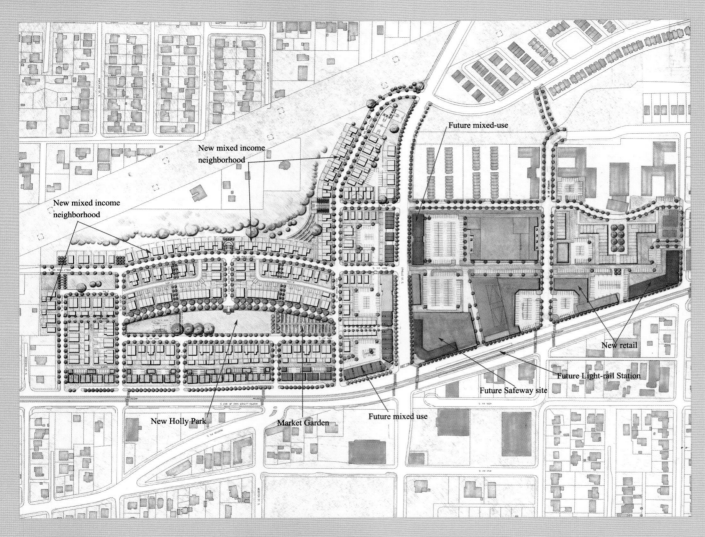

Future mixed-use

New mixed income
neighborhood

New mixed income
neighborhood

New retail

Future Light-rail Station

Future Safeway site

New Holly Park

Market Garden

Future mixed use

neighborhood plan

elevations

houses facing park

Residences Surrounding a Park or Civic Space

The plan illustrated in **Figure 10.15g** may be conducive to higher density solutions as well, since there are open landscaped views and recreation opportunities to ameliorate the crowding.

Existing Cities

Existing cities have developed over centuries, and have proven to be useful to their residents. While there are differences between them, there are also a number of similarities. They are diverse and dense. They offer mixed low and high-rise dwellings. There are various patterns of street layout, not just one. They have residential and commercial mixed-uses, often in the same building. And they are enjoyable to walk around in. They front on dramatic natural features, like rivers, lakes, and oceans. They offer numerous cultural amenities within a very compact radius. Much more can be said about cities, and certainly they don't suit everybody. By studying the way these cities are planned, or spontaneously developed, we can hope to understand what has worked best in residential development around the world.

In the following figures and photographs, there is a comparison between New York City, Chicago, and Paris. Note that the density variation is sometimes surprising, with a relatively high density for the five and six-story buildings of Paris. A mile square in Manhattan, with all its towers, can contain a population of about 84,372 people, but the equivalent area in Paris, with only five-six story buildings can contain 52,590 inhabitants. Even Chicago, with its large area of 227.2 square miles and neighborhoods of single-family dwellings manages a density of 12,470 people per square mile.[8]

The corresponding ground coverage diagrams (sometimes called **figure/ground diagrams**), and photographs help to illustrate how these conditions feel on the ground in these cities. These visual comparisons help each residential client and designer determine what they feel is the optimum size for planned residential buildings in the future. Combined with the necessary commercial services and transportation, these cities provide a living human context for all residential design.

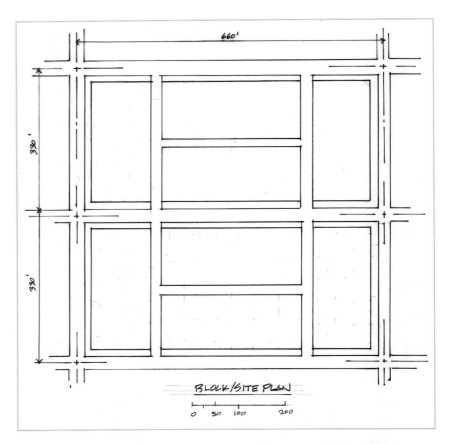

FIGURE 10.15A–G **Site Views**. Two blocks, consisting of five acres each (a), provide the basis for density analysis. Mixed residences (b), single-family and rowhouses, illustrate 32 dwelling units (d.u.), or 6 d.u. per acre. Mixed single-family, rowhouses, and walk-up apartments (c) provide 150 d.u., or 30 d.u. per acre. A block with all walk-up apartment buildings (d) provides 204 d.u. (40 d.u./acre). View shows the corridor and single entry. This is a good configuration for a possible live/work space. A block with rowhouses, walk-ups, and elevator apartment buildings (e) can accommodate 320 d.u. (64 d.u./acre). A view of a primary corner (f) with a transit station (500–550 d.u.; 100 d.u./acre). Residences surround a park in this view (g).

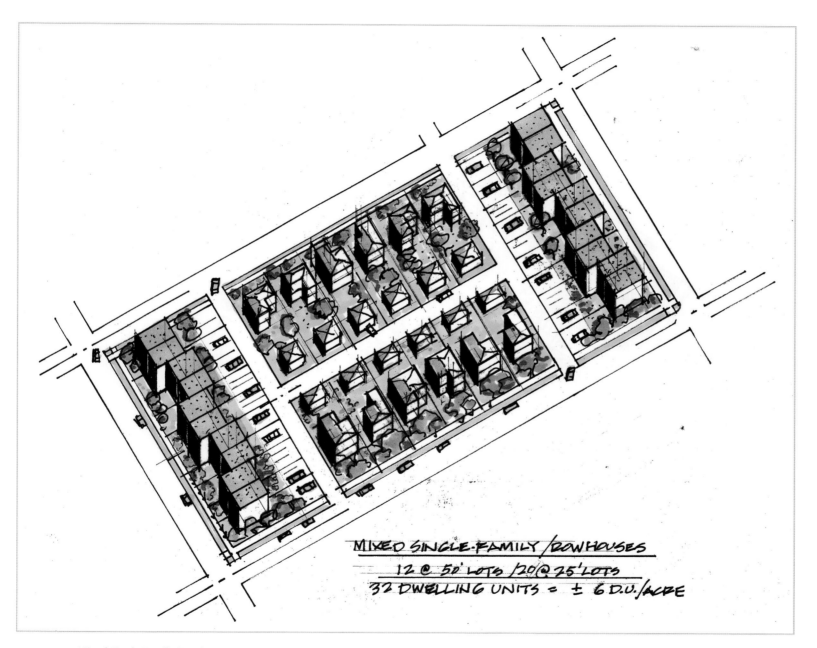

MIXED SINGLE-FAMILY / ROWHOUSES
12 @ 50' LOTS / 20 @ 25' LOTS
32 DWELLING UNITS = ± 6 D.U./ACRE

FIGURE 10.15B **Mixed Single Family/Rowhouses.**

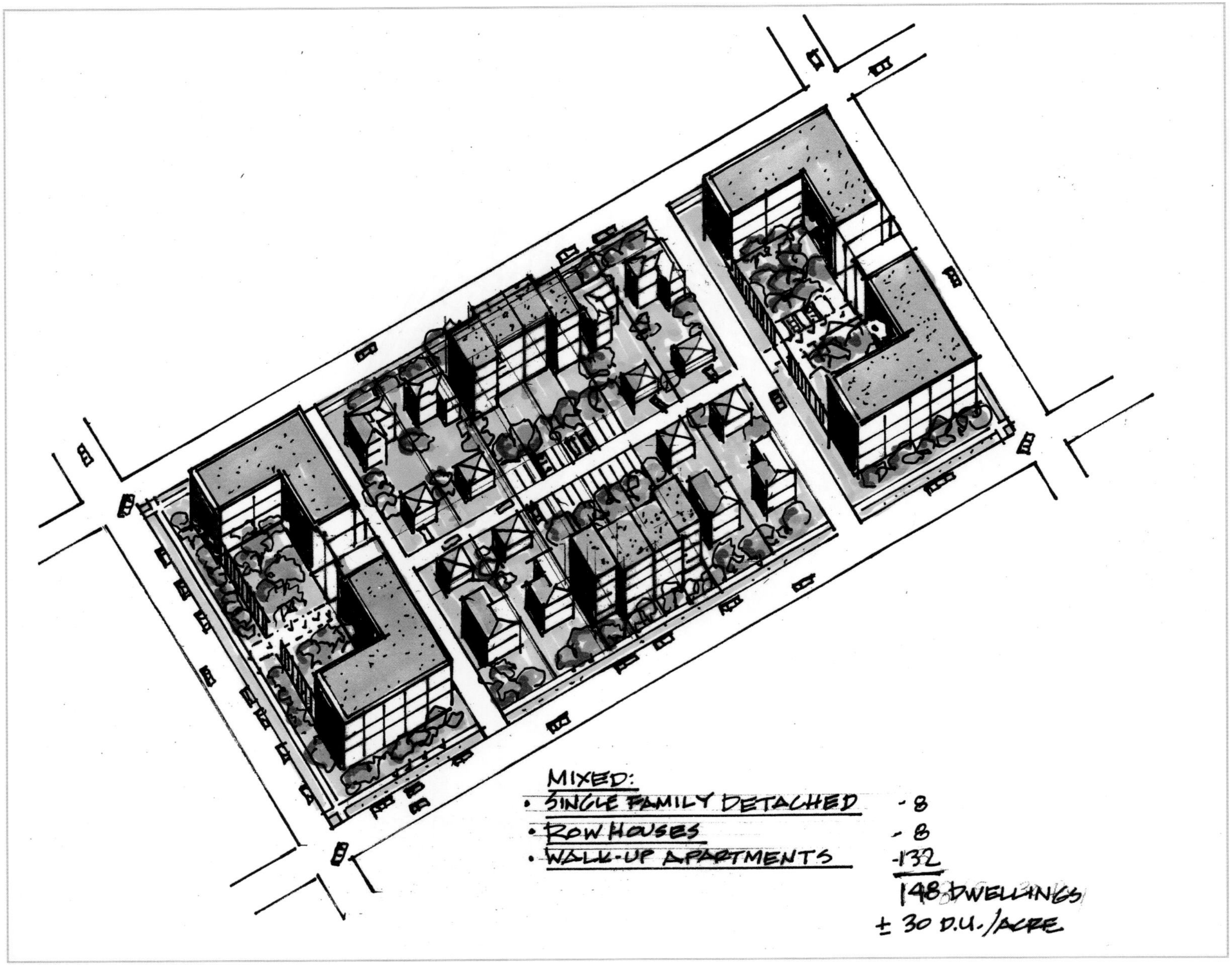

MIXED:
- SINGLE FAMILY DETACHED   - 8
- ROW HOUSES   - 8
- WALK-UP APARTMENTS   -132

148 DWELLINGS
± 30 D.U. /ACRE

FIGURE 10.15C **Mixed Housing Types.**

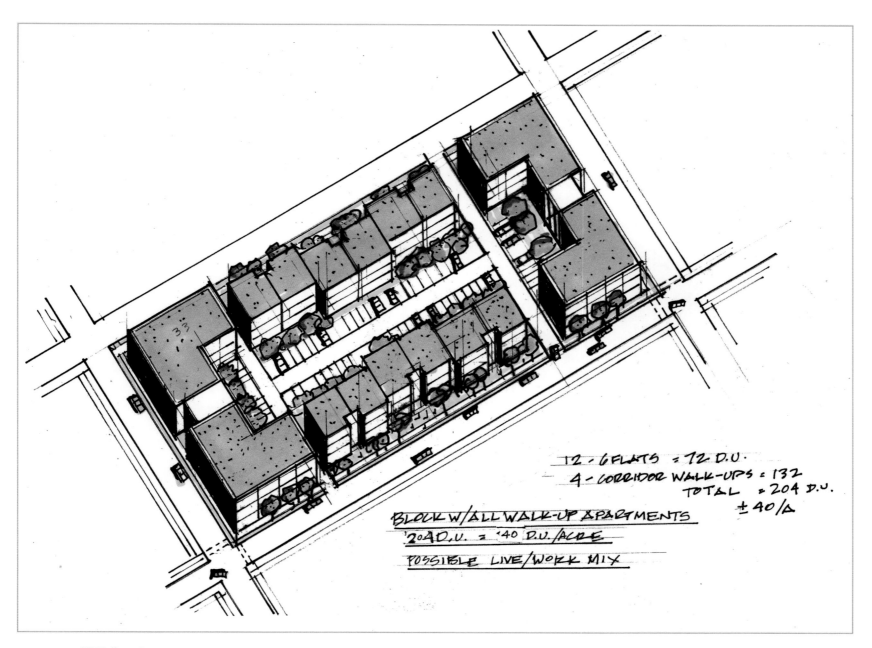

T2 - 6 FLATS = 72 D.U.
4 - CORRIDOR WALK-UPS = 132
TOTAL = 204 D.U.
± 40/A

BLOCK W/ ALL WALK-UP APARTMENTS
204 D.U. = ±40 D.U./ACRE
POSSIBLE LIVE/WORK MIX

FIGURE 10.15D **All Walk-up Apartments.**

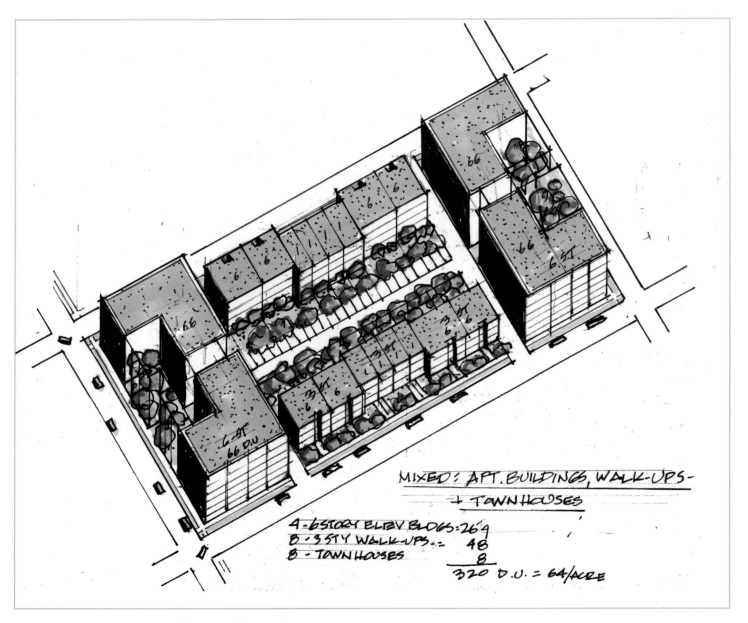

FIGURE 10.15E **Mixed Apartment Buildings, Walk-ups, and Townhouses.**

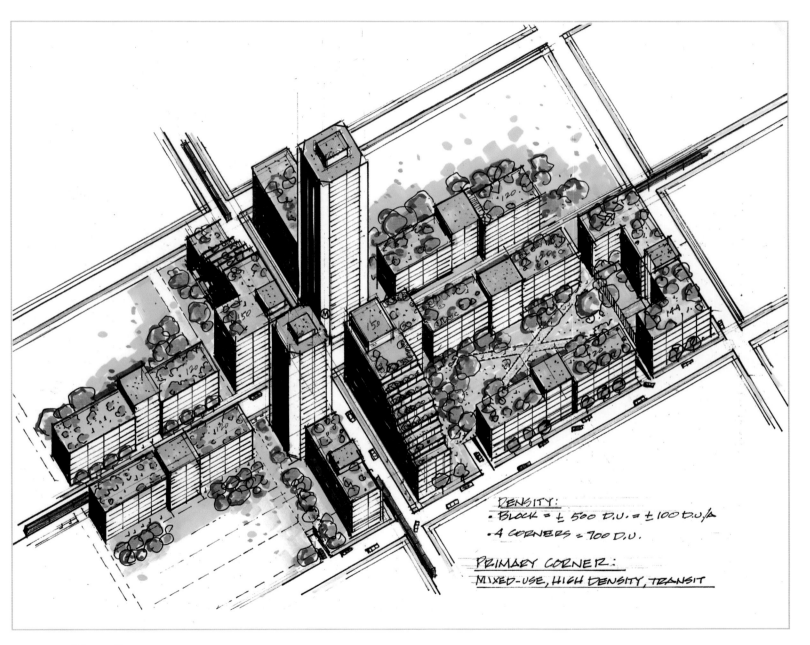

DENSITY:
- BLOCK = ± 500 D.U. = ± 100 D.U./A
- 4 CORNERS = 700 D.U.

PRIMARY CORNER:
MIXED-USE, HIGH DENSITY, TRANSIT

FIGURE 10.15F **Primary Corner.**

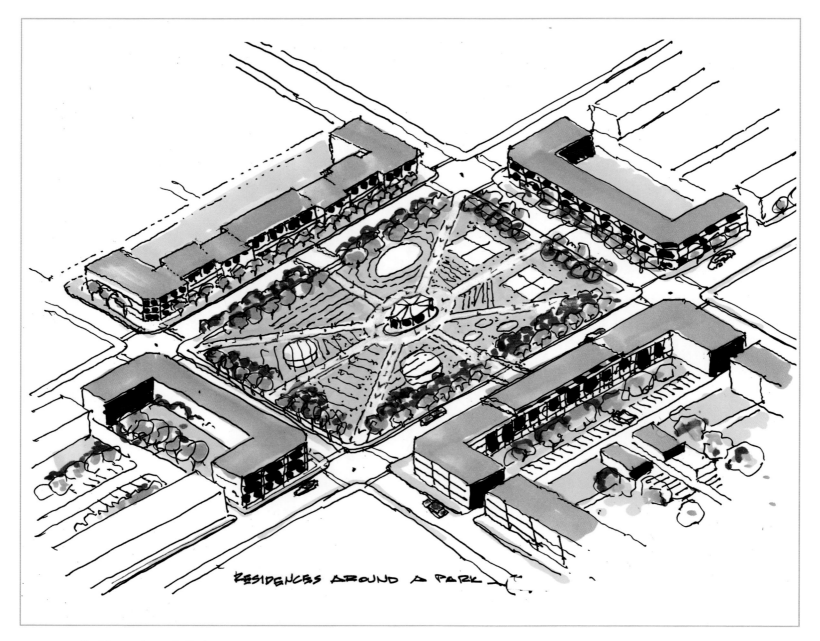

FIGURE 10.15G **Residences Around a Park.**

Chapter Summary

This chapter described the importance of site context in designing a residential space, including the interior. It traced the history of surveying and land subdivision, which served as a background for community and neighborhood planning. Subdivision of townships and sections are the bases for standard lot sizes. The impact of transportation systems and location of retail shopping on residential planning and how this planning can substantially affect the orientation and floor plans of the residential spaces was described.

Key factors involved in spacing and placement of individual residential buildings within large sites were discussed, including feasibility, density, sunlight and passive solar heating, green space, and alleys and servicing.

A variety of site plans for different mixtures of housing types, including single-family homes, rowhouses, walk-up apartment buildings, and high-rise towers were provided. Case studies illustrated a comparison of the densities in New York, Paris, and Chicago, and the ratio of building footprint to land coverage. Most importantly, this chapter sought to

address the *specific effects of different site contexts on the floor plans of the residential spaces*. Even if a client comes to the designer with an idea for a residence, the designer may be asked to help locate an appropriate site for it and help to determine whether or not the project is feasible. Site context is an essential ingredient of residential design.

Unlike the cookie-cutter Levittowns of the postwar era, new residential development is taking place in compact communities large and small, with clear centers. Some are located in large central cities with a mixed housing stock of new and old, low, medium and tall structures, and others are located in smaller cities and towns. These new developments provide efficient and economical home layouts with multifunctional spaces for all types of dwellings, regardless of the type. And there is a growing use of sustainable materials and solar and wind power to cut down the cost of construction and energy use. These elements are all related by context. The author hopes that this chapter has shown an integrated approach to urban design and the many different types of housing the designer may be asked to produce within the context of a variety of different communities.

CASE STUDY 10.4

101 San Fernando

San Jose, California
Solomon E.T.C.-WRT, Architecture and Urban Design

101 San Fernando is a mixed-use project located in the heart of newly revitalized downtown San Jose. The building consists of 322 rental units (with 1.75 cars per unit) and 10,00 square feet of commercial space organized around a series of midblock pedestrian lanes, which are accessed through large portals in the street wall as well as from secured parking areas. Streets and mid-blocks are animated by stoop-served walk-up units with elevator-served units above.

street view

corner units above store

aerial view

continued on the next page

continued from the previous page

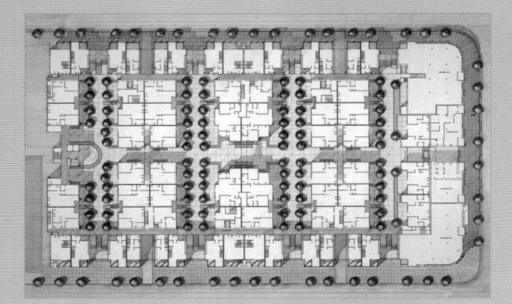

building site plan

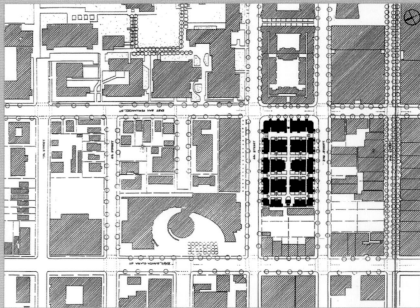

neighborhood plan

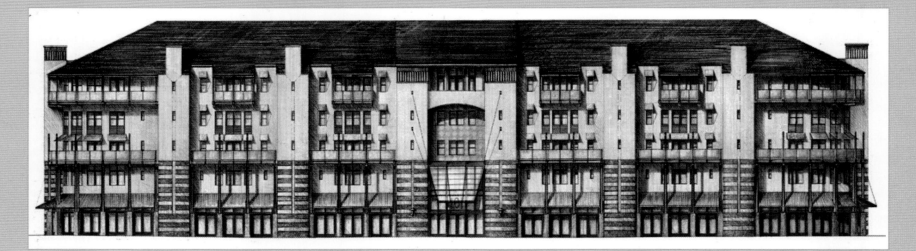

elevation toward street

courtyard

Conclusion

Many different types of residential designs, including single-family, town-house, walk-up apartment buildings, high-rise towers, and mixed-use buildings, are all part of the neighborhood, community, and city fabric. Regardless of the size and type of community, no individual residence stands alone. It affects, and is affected by, the neighborhood in which it exists.

All housing types are valid for specific clients, and this book attempts to show a wide range of client possibilities, both traditional and nontraditional, for which the designer may work. Designers in a new and changing world must become adept at recognizing this new clientele, as well as the context in which they work. In the future, designers will have to become better at planning smaller homes in compact communities that reduce automobile dependence. They also must take great care to learn about and improve the environment in the cities and towns where they live and work. It is up to design professionals to take on leadership roles and responsibility for making residential design part of constantly changing and sustainable world.

KEY TERMS

Density: The number of inhabitants or dwelling units per land measurement, for example, inhabitants per square mile or acre or dwelling units per square mile or acre

Feasibility study: Financial and real estate consultants are invited to determine the feasibility of the site. Whether it is for a developer or an individual owner, bankers want to have objective standards for measuring the value of the project. Residential designers are part of the team that determines feasibility. Cost estimates are based on conceptual designs and local construction costs. These studies should be made at the earliest stages of design so that a specific budget can be agreed upon before time is wasted.

Figure/Ground diagrams: A method of rendering buildings in solid black to contrast against the white background of the site. This type of rendering provides a clear image of actual building coverage on a site.

Passive solar heating: The use of building placement and orientation toward the sun to add to heat gain into the interior of a residence in winter and to protect it from the sun in the summer.

Perspective terminal: An urban marker at the end of a perspective, such as a building at the end of an offset street. These markers not only contribute to the form of a city, they contribute to its walkability. A fixed end to a walk makes it seem more attainable than a perspective that seems to go on forever.

Streetscape: The design of the street adjoining the site (usually public); specifically includes the curb, landscaping, street lighting, sidewalk, fences, bollards, and the ground level land use of the property.

Sunscreen: An overhang or canopy over a window on the south side of a building that shields out high angled summer sunlight but allows winter sunlight and warmth to enter.

Transit-oriented design: Planning the location of higher density and mixed-use residential units to be built near transit stops. This increases the possibility and convenience of using public transportation or walking for daily activities, which in turn is good for the environment.

Urban: Comprising a city as distinguished from the country. The U.S. Census Bureau defines it as, "an incorporated or unincorporated place with at least 2,500 inhabitants."

Zoning/subdivision regulations: The local laws that regulate the land use, size, height, setbacks, and other restrictions to building.

Zoning variation: When existing zoning regulation is in conflict with the client or community interest, the designer and/or developer may ask for a variance. This can include changing setback lines, density, and height limitations.

CASE STUDY 10.5A–C

Comparative mile-square grids in New York, Paris, and Chicago, showing respective densities of 84,372 people per square mile, 52,590 people per square mile, and 12,470 people per square mile, respectively.

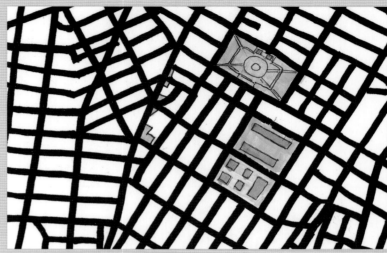

New York

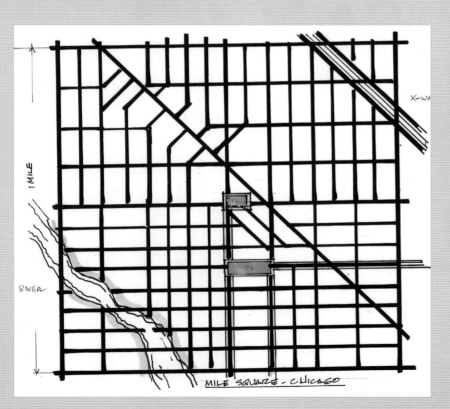

Chicago

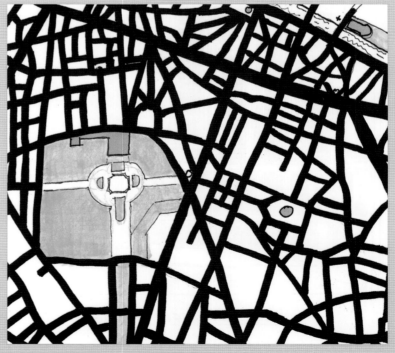

Paris

CASE STUDY 10.6A–C

Building coverage/density diagrams for New York, Chicago, and Paris. Sometimes called **figure/ground diagrams**, these show the different percentages of ground covered by buildings and streets and how the buildings are accessed.

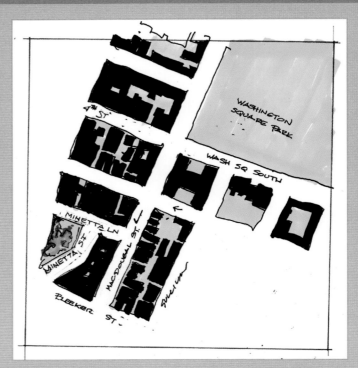

New York

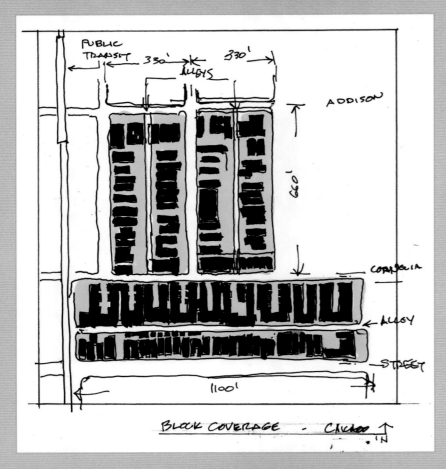

Chicago

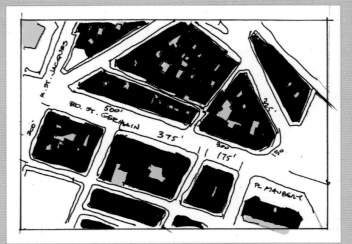

Paris

EXERCISES

1. Walk around a chosen community. Measure distances and times and take photographs or sketch the important community features, particularly daily shopping and access to transportation, schools, and parks. Mark the important daily facilities the client may need, such as grocery store, library, cinema, school, employment, and hardware store. How far are they from the proposed home site? Are they within a 5- or 10-minute walk?

2. What is the density in the selected community? How many people live in how many square miles? Obtain population figures from the U.S. Census Bureau (www.census.gov) and area dimensions from Google Maps.

3. What are the heights of existing nearby buildings? Will they cast shadows on the proposed site? Will the proposed residence cast shadows on neighbors' homes?

4. Keep a notebook of residential projects that includes photographs, maps, transportation, shopping, walking distances, population densities, and land coverage.

5. Calculate the site area for a planned residential site and estimate the number of planned units for that site. Practice comparing the planned densities to real-world densities in order to get a feeling for how the site will function.

ENDNOTES

1. Leadership for Energy and Environmental Design (LEED) is a rating system developed through a partnership of the Congress for New Urbanism, the Natural Resources Defense Council and the U.S. Green Building Council. Similarly, LEED-ND gives points for the different elements of neighborhood design and development that help to make a development sustainable.

2. Dava Sobel, *Longitude* (New York: Penguin Books, 1995), 2–3.

3. See the National Atlas of the United States website at www.nationalatlas.gov/articles/boundaries/a_plss.html.

4. See the U.S. Department of the Interior, Bureau of Land Management website at www.blm.gov/wo/st/en/prog/more/cadastralsurvey/cadastral_history.html.

5. Jane Jacobs, *The Death and Life of Great American Cities* (New York: Vintage Books, 1961), 178–186.

6. See the U.S. Census Department State and County QuickFacts for Chicago 2005 at (quickfacts.census.gov/qfd/states/17/1714000.html); for New York City at quickfacts.census.gov/qfd/states/36/3651000.html; and the French Land Registry at www.cadastre.gouv.fr/scpc/accueil.do.

7. See solar diagrams from London Metropolitan University, available at www.learn.londonmet.ac.uk/packages/clear/thermal/climate/sun/sunpath_diagrams.html.

8. Density statistics for New York, Paris, and Chicago, were taken from the official government agency websites of the respective cities:
   - Official website of the Manhattan Borough President
   - French Land Register, 2005
   - Website: egov.cityofchicago.org 2006–2007

Alpern, Andrew. *Luxury Apartment Houses of Manhattan.* Mineola, NY: Dover Publications, 1992.

Bai, Matt. "Home-Office Politics, Why Americans Who Work for Themselves Deserve a New Deal." *New York Times Magazine,* 11/04/07. Statistics on the increasing use of the home office.

Baker, Kermit. "Architecture Firms Design a Quarter of Single-Family Homes." *AIArchitect*, Volume 8, September 2001, pp. 1 and 2.

Brookings Institution's Urban Markets Initiative and the Center for Neighborhood Technology. *The Affordability Index: A New Tool for Measuring the True Affordability of a Housing Choice.* January, 2006. Available at: www.brookings.edu/reports/2006/01_affordability_index.aspx. Analysis of the relationship between transportation and housing costs.

Bush, Akiko. *Geography of Home.* Princeton, NJ: Princeton Architectural Press, 1999. Ms. Bush gives many good examples of the historical and emotional reasoning that affects our concept of what kinds of rooms we would like in our homes.

Cranz, Galen. *The Chair: Rethinking Culture, Body, and Design.* New York: W.W. Norton & Company, 1998.

Cusato, Marianne, and Ben Pentreath. *Get Your House Right.* New York: Sterling, 2008. For those who are interested in traditional and classical style, this is an excellent and beautifully diagrammed book.

Dickens, Charles. *Hard Times.* New York: Bantam, 1981. Provides vivid descriptions of peoples' lives during the industrial revolution in England, including the narrow streets and rowhouses of the nineteenth century.

Duany, Andres, Elizabeth Plater-Zyberk, and Jeff Speck. *Suburban Nation: The Rise of Sprawl and the Decline of the American Dream.* New York: North Point Press, 2000. In this book, a footnote reference is also given to: Kenneth Jackson, *Crabgrass Frontier* (see separate source listing). The connection of the dwelling space to shopping, work, and other necessities, as well as the design of the roadway, must all be taken into account when considering residential design. These authors have been very influential in explaining the values of compact development based on pedestrian orientation and town centers. They have convinced many homebuilders that this is what the public wants, and sales figures have proven them right.

Duis, Perry R. *Challenging Chicago.* Chicago: University of Illinois Press, 1998. Includes an excellent discussion of housing strategies, the development of different types of housing in Chicago from the late nineteenth to the early twentieth century.

Fletcher, Sir Banister. *A History of Architecture on the Comparative Method.* New York: Charles Scribner's Sons, 1958. Still a classic, but later editions give much better detail and a broader scope of world architecture.

Holtz Kay, Jane. *Asphalt Nation*. New York: Random House, 1997. A thorough explanation of the real cost of automobile-oriented life.

Hunter, Christine. *Ranches, Rowhouses and Railroad Flats*. New York: W.W. Norton and Company, 1999. A beautifully illustrated book on the different housing types, their origins, and their characteristics.

Institute of Transportation Engineers. *Context-Sensitive Solutions in Designing Major Urban Thoroughfares for Walkable Communities*. Washington, DC: Institute of Transportation Engineers, 2006. Made with the cooperation of the Federal Highway Administration and Environmental Protection Agency, this important document sets new standards for streets and boulevards. In many ways, these streetscapes determine the basic character of the adjoining residential buildings. Participating organizations included the Congress for the New Urbanism and the Bicycle Federation of America.

Jackson, Kenneth. *Crabgrass Frontier: The Suburbanization of the United States*. New York: Oxford University Press, 1985.

Jacobs, Jane. *The Death and Life of Great American Cities*. New York: Vintage Books, 1961. Jane Jacobs was the first to recognize the destructive aspects of urban renewal in the 1960s. Specific problems of the functions of urban neighborhoods are given, along with a sharp criticism of high-rise communities, expressways, and urban discontinuity. Her book demonstrates the advantages of "living above the store." It is the gold standard for all urban planners today.

Kira, Alexander. *The Bathroom*. New York: Viking, 1976. As much information about the functions of this popular room as one would ever like to have.

Kunstler, James Howard. *The Long Emergency*. New York: Grove Press, 2005. In this book, Kunstler lays out the growing cost of petroleum use. He believes that we may already have reached "Peak Oil," and that further exploration will be significantly more expensive. Not only does Kunstler consider the use of the private automobile in today's urban design, but also the cost of petroleum used to bring food to our tables. Having a corner grocery store, or local farmers markets, has a great affect on home design. If one must drive to a supermarket, provision must be made for giant-sized refrigerators, freezers, and storage pantries, which affects the kitchen design. Having an automobile available to transport food, as well as haul kids to school and parents to work, might require a three-car garage. Living in a dense community, where shopping is nearby, children walk to school, and parents walk to work, there might not even be a need for a car. At the present time, these are personal choices, but if Kunstler's premise is right, we may have already reached the limit of cheap oil and our personal choices may be a lot more expensive in the future.

McAlester, Virginia, and Lee McAlester. *A Field Guide To American Houses*. New York: Alfred A. Knopf, 1990. An overview of the many historical styles used in U.S. domestic architecture. Contains photographs, drawings, and construction details, but no floor plans.

McFadden, Christine. *The Essential Kitchen*. New York: Rizzoli, 2000. Planning a good kitchen requires a thorough understanding of the tools the client will be using, and how they will be stored when not in use.

McIlwain, John, and Melissa Floca. "Multifamily Trends." Washington DC: Urban Land Institute, May/June 2006. Article regarding the trend toward smaller homes.

National Association of Homebuilders. *Facts, Figures, and Trends*. March 2006. Available at www.nahb.org/publications_details.aspx?publicationID=2028. An ongoing look at the trends, consumer demands, costs, and design issues facing the homebuilding industry.

National Kitchen and Bath Association. http://www.nkba.org/guidelines/default.aspx. Up-to-date standards for kitchen and bath planning. Hard copy available as well through the website.

Norquist, John. *The Wealth of Cities*. New York: Basic Books, 1998. Mr. Norquist was for many years the mayor of Milwaukee, Wisconsin. His insight into the effects of urban planning on housing have the authenticity of a person who has been in the trenches with the developers, politicians, businesspeople, and homeowners. Particularly interesting is his description of the attempts by homebuilders to obtain subsidies from the city to build there. Mr. Norquist explains how the value of the city itself is enough, and that homebuilders would profit from building there. He was proven right, as the value of many neighborhoods in Milwaukee increased without the use of subsidies. His experiences are invaluable to anyone who wants to understand the relationship of housing to its urban context. John Norquist is currently the president of the Congress for the New Urbanism.

Orwell, George. *The Road to Wigan Pier.* New York: Harcourt Brace, 1958.

Pollan, Michael. *The Omnivore's Dilemma.* New York: Penguin, 2006. Pollan makes a strong case for a local agriculture, from a culinary and health point of view. This also affects location of future human settlement.

Chapman, Wid, and Jeffrey P. Rosenfeld. *Home Design in an Aging World.* New York: Fairchild, 2008. Many good ideas in the evolving requirements of housing programs and designs as a growing number of people age in their own homes.

Rybcznski, Witold. *Home: A Short History of an Idea.* New York: Penguin, 1986. Mr. Rybcznski gives a thorough history of the considerations that go into current home design. He is particularly interested in the subject of public vs. private spaces in a home.

The Green Guide, Paris. Michelin Travel Publications, 2003.

Trachtenberg, Marvin, and Isabelle Hyman. *Architecture from Prehistory to Postmodernity.* 4th ed. New York: Harry N. Abrams, 2002.

Wright, Gwendolyn. *Moralism and the Model Home.* Chicago: The University of Chicago Press, 1980. Gwendolyn Wright has demonstrated how the social setting of a period in time greatly affects residential design. Design of the model home in Chicago from the late nineteenth to the early twentieth centuries documents her thesis in great detail.

U.S. Census Bureau. American Community Survey. American FactFinder, Units in Structure: Housing Units. U.S. Census Bureau, 2006. Basic information on the makeup of the American housing inventory. Includes single-family detached dwellings and the various types of multifamily dwellings. Updated frequently.

Wikipedia. World City Population Densities. Available at http:// en.wikipedia.org/wiki/Image:World_population_density_map. PNG. The sources behind the data are often the websites of the cities in question.

Wright, Frank Lloyd. *The Natural House.* New York: Bramhall House, 1954. Mr. Wright was the most influential residential architect of the twentieth century. His houses were often controversial. Wright suggested that one should live as far away from the city as possible, so his homes were often rural or suburban designs. He was perfectly suited for his time, which witnessed the suburbanization of most American cities in the post-World War II era.

Wright, Gwendolyn. *Building the Dream.* Boston: MIT Press, 1981.

Page numbers in italics refer to figures.

Distances

English	Metric
1 inch	2.54 centimeters
1 foot	0.3048 meter / 30.38 centimeters
1 yard	0.9144 meter

Metric	English
1 centimeter	0.3937 inch
1 meter	3.280 feet

Weights

English	Metric
1 ounce	28.35 grams
1 pound	0.45 kilogram

Metric	English
1 gram	0.035 ounce
1 kilogram	2.2 pounds

General formula for converting:

Number of Units × Conversion Number = New Number of Units

To convert inches to centimeters:
[number of inches] × 2.54 = [number of centimeters]

To convert centimeters to inches:
[number of centimeters] × 0.3937 = [number of inches]

To convert feet to meters:
[number of feet] × 0.3048 = [number of meters]

To convert meters to feet:
[number of meters] × 3.280 = [number of feet]

To convert yards to meters:
[number of yards] × 0.9144 = [number of meters]

To convert ounces to grams:
[number of ounces] × 28.35 = [number of grams]

To convert grams to ounces:
[number of grams] × 0.035 = [number of ounces]

To convert pounds to kilograms:
[number of pounds] × 0.45 = [number of kilograms]

To convert kilograms to pounds:
[number of kilograms] × 2.2 = [number of pounds]